American Christian Support for Israel

American Christian Support for Israel

Standing with the Chosen People, 1948–1975

Eric R. Crouse

LEXINGTON BOOKS
Lanham • Boulder • New York • London

Published by Lexington Books
An imprint of The Rowman & Littlefield Publishing Group, Inc.
4501 Forbes Boulevard, Suite 200, Lanham, Maryland 20706
www.rowman.com

Unit A, Whitacre Mews, 26-34 Stannary Street, London SE11 4AB, United Kingdom

British Library Cataloguing in Publication Information Available

Library of Congress Cataloging-in-Publication Data

Crouse, Eric Robert, 1960-
American Christian support for Israel : standing with the Chosen People, 1948-1975 / Eric R. Crouse.
pages cm.
Includes bibliographical references and index.
ISBN 978-0-7391-9718-9 (cloth : alk. paper) -- ISBN 978-0-7391-9719-6 (electronic)
1. Christian Zionism--United States--History. 2. United States--Relations--Israel. 3. Israel--Relations-
-United States. I. Title.
DS150.5.C76 2014
327.7305694--dc23
                                    2014031639

Printed in the United States of America

Contents

Preface

My academic interest in Israel began years ago before I started teaching my Tyndale University College third-year course "The United States and the Middle East since 1945." In the summer of 2008, I presented: "Under the Radar: Bible Prophecy, U.S. Foreign Policy, and the Arab-Israeli Conflict, 1948–1967" at the Society for Historians of American Foreign Relations Conference, Ohio State University, Columbus. Since that conference, I read books, gathered research, and made plans to write a book manuscript on the American Christian reaction to Israel and its first five wars. My plan was to take scholarship of Israeli national security, American Christian Zionism, and some U.S. foreign policy history and offer a synthesis that introduces key themes in an introductory format for readers not having specialized knowledge of each of those three fields. I provide details and context of the Arab-Israeli wars without losing sight of the role of American Christian Zionism and its primarily uplifting message about Israel.

It was fascinating to learn that evangelicals and other conservative Christians were stalwart supporters of Israel despite the often cool reactions from the American Jewish community and some Israelis.

A group of Israeli academics referred to as the "new historians" are very critical of Israeli policy and they add important perspective. Statements by new historian Avi Shlaim, in a 2009 interview, shed some light on new historian thinking: "Security for Israel is a non-issue. Israelis keep banging on about security, but it's a red herring." Shlaim also claims that "Iran needs nuclear weapons for deterrence, to deter Israel from attacking them."

I differ in that I find traditional interpretations sympathetic to the national security concerns of Israel more convincing. I place emphasis on the importance of religion and culture in understanding the Arab-Israeli conflict. Although I tried to be fair-minded, most of my accounts of war and conflict covered what the Israelis faced. To say more about Arabs (Muslims and Christians) would require a much larger study. I do recognize that the ongoing conflict resulted in heart-breaking grief and injustice for innocent Palestinians. Books such as Izzeldin Abuelaish's *I Shall Not Hate: A Gaza's Doctor's Journey* (2010) remind me of the horrible crimes that ordinary people experienced on both sides of the conflict.

Perhaps my religious faith explains why I am sensitive to the influence of religious ideas whether voiced by Christian Zionists or devout

Muslims. What I offer is a combination of American Christian Zionism and Israeli military and national security history. I am hopeful that readers will find it a good introduction to the complicated history of the Arab-Israeli conflict and the important role that Christian Zionist writers played in explaining events to many in their communities and beyond. My goal is to present the voice of conservative Christians typically missing in history books on the Arab-Israeli conflict and American foreign relations.

I am delighted to once again work with Lexington Books. I am thankful for the editorial direction of Erin Walpole; I have benefited greatly from her professionalism and helpfulness with this book and my earlier, *The Cross and Reaganomics*. I am thankful for the Tyndale University College Faculty Research Fund that assisted me with my research. In this day when the presence of conservatives in academia is shrinking, I count my blessings that I am in a position to take part in the exchange of ideas on how history unfolded.

Introduction

The dominant political theme of the State of Israel is the perpetual quest for security. Since the rebirth of Israel in 1948, Israeli politicians have understood that guaranteeing Israel's physical existence ultimately overrides all other concerns. In its first twenty-five years, Israel experienced five wars with Arab states. Consistent with the position of other Israeli leaders, Shimon Peres (future prime minister) wrote in 1970 that the "Arab purpose is all-absorptive—the destruction of Israel and the annihilation or banishment of her inhabitants." Many others understood that wars and terrorism have "left their mark on Israel's national consciousness."[1] When referring to the Arabs one cannot speak of a political monolith, but most Muslims in the Middle East shared a degree of hostility toward the existence of Israel or, at least, found Israeli policy inequitable.

As Israel faced war and persistent threats to its security one group of Americans consistently supported it—conservative Christians. This conservative support for the Jewish community was not new; it stretched back in history many decades before 1948.[2] By the mid-1970s, the difference on how liberal and conservative Christians viewed Israel was evident to those who looked carefully. Others outside of church circles missed this development mainly because conservative Christians did not take part in any organized political lobbying for American backing of Israel. Under the radar of most policymakers, the conservative Christian stand for Israel was nonetheless a potent one in grassroots evangelical circles.[3] There was one key verse from the Bible behind much of conservative Christian support for Israel, but Israel's embodiment of western ideals and its economic development also gave conservative Christians good reasons to favor the Jewish state in a troubled Middle East.[4]

The Middle East conflict is a "subject of incomprehensible fascination." While the term "Arab-Israeli conflict" is not satisfactory for some, it makes sense with an examination of 1948 to 1975 when the military and political actions of the Egyptians, Syrians, Jordanians, Lebanese, and to a lesser extent the Iraqis and Saudis played a prominent role in the conflict. In fact, for many years after World War II most western literature used the general term "Arabs" when referring to the Palestinians. Before 1948, there were "Palestinian Arabs" and "Palestinian Jews," after 1948 there were "Arabs" and "Israelis" (of course, there were also Arab Israelis). U.S. government documents for the next twenty years made reference to the "Arab refugees" and thus in policymaking circles the Palestinians were missing.[5] The virtual nonexistence of the term "Palestinian" in the mid-twentieth century is one more fact adding fuel to a contentious history.

There is no shortage of politics in the competing histories of this region. A fierce debate over the history of the Arab-Israeli conflict continues to rage as "historians elegantly maul each other's version of events."[6] Writings of a very pro-Arab nature see the creation of the State of Israel as a terrible mistake and injustice. The historians who dismiss any Jewish historic tie to the land echo the ideas of Arabs, such as mid-twentieth-century lawyer Henry Catton, who defended Arab arguments opposing Jewish nationhood. In a book published years later, Catton wrote that the Jews from the first century to the twentieth century "had almost ceased to exist in Palestine." Even the Jews of biblical times represented only "an episode" in the long history of Palestine. According to Catton, most modern Jews "can hardly claim to be descendants of the ancient Hebrew." And thus for Catton it was the Arabs who, as early as the late nineteenth century, sought "a purely Arab state independent of the Turkish Empire."[7] The argument goes that due to Zionist control of media operations in many countries, this Arab perspective remained mostly hidden in the West. "The Zionist propaganda machine," Catton declared, represented "a danger to the world."[8]

One group composed mostly of Israeli Jews calling themselves "new historians" are sympathetic to various Arab interpretations to the point of viewing Israel as primarily the guilty party of the Arab-Israeli conflict.[9] They are critical of the so-called "popular-heroic-moralistic" interpretation of the War of Independence that sees the struggle as a Jewish David against an Arab Goliath. For example, Avi Shlaim argues that it was the Jews who enjoyed a numerical superiority of soldiers in the first Arab-Israeli conflict and that in subsequent years Israel was the most "intransigent" not the Arab states.[10] He claims that Israelis' talk of "security" is a "red herring," a distraction from "real" issues such as Israel's "territorial expansionism."[11] These historians, writes one critic, gave "the Palestinian argument its intellectual firepower."[12]

At odds with the "new historians" is traditional historiography, which is less disparaging of former Israeli leaders and more appreciative of the importance of religion. Even though it is generally sympathetic to the struggle of the Jewish people, this history is closer to the truth, argue scholars such as Michael Oren, who claims that the traditional historians "examine historical events on their own merits, free of contemporary influences."[13] One thing is clear. In books supportive of Israel, there is greater attention paid to the security issues that ordinary Israelis face year after year with the Arabs who take Islam seriously.

With their focus on modernity many academics are reluctant to pay much attention to religious beliefs, but scholarship on religion offers important insights in understanding the conflict between Arabs and Jews.

Bernard Lewis writes of the "discontents of the Middle East not as a conflict between states or nations, but as a clash between civilizations." Islamic leaders became infuriated that capitalism and western democracy offered "an authentic and attractive alternative to traditional ways of thought and life." Many were angry over the subordination of their culture to the West. A "feeling of humiliation" was due to "a growing awareness, among the heirs of an old, proud, and long dominant civilization, of having been overtaken, overborne, and overwhelmed by those whom they regarded as their inferiors."[14] Arabs admired and hated western productivity that supplied their everyday material needs. What modern daily items from telephones to automobiles were of Arab manufacturing? Even pro-Arab westerners living in the Middle East in the first half of the twentieth century wrote of Arab countries "becoming increasingly poisoned with hatred and distrust for the West."[15]

The focus on Muslim resentment of the West resulted in compelling explanations of Middle East conflict. In the mid-twentieth century, American religious studies scholar Wilfrid Cantrell Smith wrote of the Muslim "spiritual crisis" as followers of Islam struggled with the task of reconciling modernism with traditionalism.[16] Since the Six-Day War, American Christian leftists sympathetic to the economic plight of Arabs increasingly took aim at the capitalist success of Israel.[17] Political scientist Efrain Inbar argues that Islamic and Marxist interpretations converged. Many Muslims saw Israel as "an alien extension of the West" and "lackey of Western imperialism" and, thus, a corrupting cultural and economic force to the Islamic way of life.[18]

But beyond the issues of land, population, and wealth, Israel's main offense to Muslims had to do with theology. Muslims could not accord full equality to the Jews or any others who did not practice Islam. In the eyes of many Arab militants, Jews are "the brothers of apes, the killers of prophets, bloodsuckers, the descendants of treachery and deceit, who spread corruption in the land of Islam."[19] Historian Paul Charles Merkley maintains that Muslims refuse to live at peace with Israel because it is the only non-Muslim sovereign state in the Middle East. By turning part of the Muslim world into non-Muslim, Israel achieved something Muslims believe is theologically impossible. In the Quran (Sura II: 61; Sura III: 112) there is a judgment against the Jews for refusing to heed the prophet Muhammad: "The creation of the State of Israel is an ostensible reversal of this judgment, an assault on the credibility of Islam that cannot be permitted to stand."[20]

In 1948, the Muslim Brotherhood, an Islamic political-religious group, declared: "Jews are the historic enemies of Muslims and carry the greatest hatred for the nation of Muhammad."[21] Months earlier in Egypt, a fatwa (theological decree) warned Muslims against doing business with Jews; an offender "is a sinner and criminal . . . who will be regarded as an apostate to Islam, he will be separated from his spouse. It is prohibited to be in contact with him."[22] Given that such interpretations were common in the Muslim world, the violent rhetoric and actions of Arabs against Israel were no surprise to conservative Christians. To his credit, Benny Morris of the "new historian" school argues that it is a mistake when historians ignore or dismiss the jihadi rhetoric of the Arab world. Championing the righteousness of a holy war, Muslims fought to protect and free sacred Islamic territory violated by infidels.[23] American evangelicals were aware of the political power of Islam. In the early first century much of Paul's missionary efforts covered the area in what became Turkey. As was the case in Arab nations, churches disappeared in this area and *Christianity Today* estimated fewer than 150 Protestants in Turkey in 1957. Five years later, American fundamentalist Wilbur M. Smith found it amazing that in the Ankara library, housing 450,000 volumes, there was not one Arabic Bible.[24]

Some scholars vigorously argued against what they saw as simplistic characterizations of the Arab world. Influential was the work of Palestinian Edward Said, professor of English and comparative literature, who analyzed how many westerners accepted "orientalist" stereotypes that viewed Arabs as inferior, violent, and culturally "backward."[25] In *Orientalism* (1979), Said took aim at westerners who professed to "know" the Arabs, calling out scholars such as Bernard Lewis for their "political propaganda" as they purported to be fair and objective. According to Said, Lewis was guilty of not mentioning "such a thing as a Zionist invasion and colonization of Palestine," for seeing Islam as something that "never changes," and for "getting nearly everything wrong."[26] Said found the prominence of "unverifiable fictions and vast generalizations" in the West frustrating, but some of his responses were weak:

> There has been so massive and calculatedly aggressive an attack on the contemporary societies of the Arab and Muslim for their backwardness, lack of democracy, and abrogation of women's rights that we simply forget that such notions as modernity, enlightenment, and democracy are by no means simple and agreed-upon concepts that one either does or does not find, like Easter eggs in the living room.[27]

Interestingly, Said faced problems getting his work published in Arabic. Although an Israeli publisher published his book *The Question of Palestine* in Hebrew, all Arabic publishers showing an interest in the book wanted him "to change or delete those sections that were openly critical of one or another Arab regime (including the PLO)."[28] In the end, Said refused to comply.

In the mid-1920s, British military officer John Bagot Glubb resigned his commission in the British army to live among the Arabs. His devotion to the Arab people won him the admiration of the Jordanians, who in 1939 asked him to assume command of the Arab Legion (Transjordan's army). He "loved" the Arabs, speaking highly of their charm and generous hospitality, but he also wrote that they were "hot-headed, hasty and volatile . . . [and] proud and touchy, ready to suspect an insult and hasty to avenge it. To hate their enemies is to them not only a natural emotion but a duty. Should any man claim to forgive an enemy, they find it difficult to believe in his sincerity and suspect a trap."[29] Although Glubb's stereotyping does not do justice to the diversity of the Arab people, his observation was not uncommon.

Glubb also acknowledged the bitterness between different Arab groups in the region. In the mid-1940s, a number of Arabs loyal to the Mufti (Muslim judge) of Jerusalem declared that the Arab Legion was a greater danger than the Jews. Neither Egyptian nor Saudi leaders were happy that the Arab Legion won more glory than any other Arab army in 1948.[30] More discouraging was Glubb's conclusion concerning Arab democracy. Accustomed to autocratic rule over the centuries, the Arabs were prone to "anarchy and mob rule, scarcely even pausing at the intermediate stage of democracy."[31]

Walter Livingston Wright, Jr., historian of the Near East, told a study group in 1948 that "Islam is not a religion, as religion is conceived in the West. It is a totalitarian religion; it tells its followers what to believe, how to think, what to do. It is a complete way of life, a complete culture."[32] The contrast of the Islamic world and Israel was stark on a number of important issues. In the 1950s there was considerable discussion on why slavery was legal in Saudi Arabia. The slave trade was especially vibrant in Islam's holy city of Mecca, where public slave markets existed and where "unfortunates" on their pilgrimage found themselves forcibly enslaved. With slave girls selling for $560 to $1,120, the business was lucrative for some.[33]

Arab leaders found Israel a convenient topic to divert their people from problems within Arab communities. Militant Arab rhetoric put Israel on guard and the perceived inevitability of war led Israeli leaders to speak of conflicts as "no choice wars."[34] In contrast to the rhetoric of Arab political and religious leaders, Israeli prime ministers or foreign ministers had no wish (and Israel had no capability) to destroy its Arab enemies, who numbered in the tens of millions.[35] But with the reality of wars, terrorism, and other acts of violence, Israel acted forcefully, actions that generated worldwide criticism.

Finding loyal friends in the Arab world in general was almost impossible, but after 1967 Israel also experienced difficulty in gaining reliable support from European leaders. For decades, various European leaders argued that Israel was a mistake. In his memoirs of his life among the Arabs, published in 1957, John Glubb pondered the future of the "Zionists." Will the Israelis "be able, twenty, fifty or a hundred years hence, to maintain themselves as a foreign element on a beach-head on the shores of Asia?" Glubb acknowledged there were those who saw the Jews' return to Palestine as a fulfillment of prophecy, but they were wrong. There was "evil" behind the creation of Israel: "To drive a million Arabs from their homes and country cannot be justified by any consideration."[36]

Given such strong anti-Israel interpretations, the State of Israel needed American friends. Passionate were the differences expressed in the United States between Christians supportive of Israel (more recently identified as Christian Zionists) and other Christians critical of Israel's treatment of Arab Israelis and its relations with Arab nations. Various Christian groups presented contrasting interpretations of the Arab-Israeli wars. There are always exceptions and nuances, but in the broad categories of conservative Christians and liberal Christians (nonevangelical) there were distinct visions on what Israel means in history and the world.[37] Each group adopted peculiar language to clarify its own narrative of what was and was not important.

Embracing both spiritual and ideological themes, conservatives observing the Arab-Israeli conflict saw oppositional spiritual forces in play and, also, viewed Israel as representing western values of personal and economic freedom.[38] For them, the existence of the State of Israel in the Middle East gave compelling evidence of the "Sovereignty of the Lord of History." Was not God's promise to Abraham of a "great nation," written in the Old Testament, realized?[39] Liberals said little about conflicting spiritual forces and showed, at best, modest enthusiasm for Israel as a vanguard of western ideals. With their rejection of a literal interpretation of the Bible, liberals were more open to the idea of seeing the State of Israel as a mistake. A number of liberals took an additional step toward the ideas of the secular Left and pointed to a flawed western civilization (democracy and capitalism) rather than Islamic teaching as the root of problems in the Middle East.[40]

Conservative Christians were champions of the "blessings of liberty" evident in the West and especially so in the United States.[41] In a theological sense, conservative Christians generally included fundamentalists, Pentecostals, and other Christian groups adhering to orthodox doctrine. However, the majority of conservative Christians are evangelicals. Recent historians define evangelicalism as a movement with four major defining features: the Bible understood as the ultimate religious authority, the importance of a born-again experience, "an energetic, individualistic approach to religious duties and social involvement," and "a focus on Christ's redeeming work as the heart of essential Christianity."[42] As a subset of evangelicalism, Protestant fundamentalism upholds these characteristics, but it also has an intense focus on evangelism, the "fresh infilling of the Holy Spirit after conversion," "the imminent, premillennial second coming of Christ," and tends to be more reactionary and separatist than evangelicalism. The term fundamentalism took root in 1920, coined from *The Fundamentals: A Testimony to the Truth*, a collection of essays written by conservative Christian scholars defending the fundamentals of orthodox doctrine shortly before World War I.[43] In 1970, historian Ernest R. Sandeen wrote that the "Fundamentalist movement . . . calling itself Evangelicalism" showed "an expected vitality and appeal" over the previous twenty years.[44]

Pentecostalism shares much with evangelicalism and fundamentalism, but is normally set apart as a result of its charismatic displays of the baptism of the Holy Spirit, speaking in tongues, and faith healings. These groups do share the belief that the Bible told of things yet to come—the literal fulfillment of biblical prophecies.[45] In this study, conservative Christians within Roman Catholic circles receive less attention mainly because of their weaker or ambiguous ties to Christian Zionism. While this book relies heavily on the broader term "conservative Christian," it also uses evangelical, fundamentalist or another term whenever additional information allows more precise labelling of an individual or group embracing Christian Zionism.

The understanding of the end times of the world accepted by a significant number of conservative Christians was that the millennium, or 1,000 years of peace and righteousness, would only begin with the physical second return of Christ. This premillennialism was the opposite of post-millennialism, which predicted the return of Christ after 1,000 years of peace on earth. It is important to note that no respectable Christian claims to know the date of this return. Followers of Christ on earth are to be caught up to meet the Lord Jesus in the sky, an event referred to as the Rapture. Next is a seven-year period called the Tribulation followed by a 1,000 year Kingdom of God on earth and final victory over Satan.[46] For premillennialists, a key prerequisite for this unfolding of world history was the Jews' return and reestablishment of a Jewish state in the Holy Land identified in the Bible.[47]

Many Christians marveled at how God used Israel to make "known His plans for the world." Paul Erb writes: "Almost all of the writers of the Bible were Jews. Three-fourths of the Bible is Old Testament, and 95 percent of the Old Testament is about Israel. The Messiah was God incarnate in Jewish flesh. Israel is the instrument through whom God has revealed and carried out His saving purpose." As conservative Christians understood it, Israel would continue to play a vital role in God's plans: "He has not told us that He has no further use for that instrument"[48]

A small minority of evangelicals believe in premillennial dispensationalism, a doctrine dividing human history in dispensations (or eras). Not peculiar to a specific denomination, dispensationalists commit to a literal interpretation of the Bible and reject "replacement theory in which Israel has been done away with in God's plan for history and thus superseded by the Church."[49] They have an admirable record of supporting evangelism and missionary work throughout the world. In the first half of the twentieth century, dispensationalism was popular in various fundamentalist circles, evident from the success of the Scofield Reference Bible published by Oxford University Press. With almost 3 million copies

sold since 1909, the Scofield Bible provided readers with detailed interpretation of the prophetic Scriptures—a feature vigorously defended by a
number of conservative Bible scholars.[50]

Some connection to Bible prophecy is a key feature of Christian Zionism. The better known secular notion of Zionism gained significant attention in Jewish and other circles at the turn of the twentieth century. Its
founder was Theodore Herzl (1860–1904), a secular Jew born in Budapest
and educated as a lawyer. In *The Jewish State* (1896), he argued that a
separate Jewish national state was the answer for Jews seeking security in
a hostile anti-Semitic world. The general idea of Christian Zionism had
existed for centuries with roots in sixteenth century Protestant theology
(Christian Restorationism). Herzl used the term "Christian Zionist" when
he referred to Christians supportive of the idea of the Promised Land.
However, the term Christian Zionism only received wider usage in the
late twentieth century.[51] Since Herzl's day almost all the major political
players in Palestine who advanced the idea of a Jewish state in the Middle East were secular Jews.

In the second half of the twentieth century, conservative Christian
supporters of Israel received considerable criticism from a small but vocal
group of Christian leaders repulsed by the biblical claims of Christian
Zionists. In recent years, this criticism became intense among anti-Zionist
Christians. Seeing Christian Zionism as a serious threat to Middle East
peace, critics such as the Rev. Naim Ateek characterizes Christian Zionists as those Christians who falsely interpret the Bible as supporting "the
ingathering of all Jews to Israel" and the denying of Palestinian rights.
Ateek argues that Christian Zionism is a Christian heresy that promotes
"a violent theology of the End of History," particularly the "massacre of
millions." A full-time director of the Sabeel Liberation Theology Centre,
Jerusalem, Ateek warns of those not "living Christ's love and justice today."[52] Simply put, he and other Christian leftists equate Christian Zionism "with the ideology of empire, colonialism, and militarism."[53]

Opponents of Christian Zionism typically concentrate their attacks on
dispensationalism and the issue of Bible prophecy. The Rev. Donald
Wagner defines Christian Zionism as "a movement within Protestant
fundamentalism that understands the modern state of Israel as the fulfillment of Biblical prophecy and thus deserving of political, financial, and
religious support." This in turn means support for "Israel's sovereignty
over the entirety of historic Palestine including Jerusalem."[54] However,
such a definition of Christian Zionism leaves out a much larger number
of Israel supporters who do not fit the fundamentalist label.

In his recent book *Evangelicals and Israel*, Stephen Spector finds the
dispensationalism focus of most Christian anti-Zionist leaders too nar-
row since many Christian allies of Israel are not fundamentalists. In fact,
many evangelical supporters of Israel do not necessarily base their convictions on a comprehensive study of biblical prophecy.[55] Often lost in

many discussions of Christian Zionism is that there are many Christian Zionists who do not adopt a premillennial approach or pay much attention to the end-times interpretative framework of dispensational-premillennialim. Actually, the details of dispensationalism are unknown to most Christian Zionists.[56] And as for genuine dispensationalists, there is little evidence of them having a great interest in politics.[57]

Christian anti-Zionists are guilty of sloppy analysis when they discuss some of the finer points of dispensationalism. Despite the claims of Christian anti-Zionists, for example, many Christian Zionists pay no attention to the idea of rebuilding the Temple in Jerusalem where Israel's two temples once stood and, indeed, there are key dispensationalist leaders who believe the rebuilding will happen *after* Christ returns.[58] Christian Zionists are not counting down the hours or, in other words, attempting to hasten Armageddon.[59] Anti-Zionist Christians often reveal their faulty understanding of dispensationalism and its acceptance of a "pre-tribulational rapture of the Church." Dispensationalist Michael Stallard makes two important points: "war is not a necessary pre-condition for the rapture of the Church to take place" and "to say one is *expecting* war is not the same thing as affirming that one *wants* war." Affirming the truth of Bible passages predicting war "does not turn the interpreter into a warmonger." It is more accurate to view dispensationalists as promoting Israel's security rather than desiring war.[60]

So why do Christian Zionists who are not dispensationalists favor Israel? Virtually all conservative Christians affirm the link between the Israelites of the Bible and modern Jews and their support is actually quite straightforward. Most conservative Christians simply support Israel because "God promised to bless those who bless the Jews (Genesis 12:3)."[61] Although this is Bible prophecy, a major focus on only one verse is distinct from the far-reaching Bible prophecy approach of dispensationalists. In keeping with Spector's observations, helpful is a broader definition of Christian Zionism as representing "Christians whose faith, often in concert with other convictions, emotions, and experiences, leads them to support the modern state of Israel as the Jewish homeland."[62] That Israel supported western values only added to its attractiveness for conservative Christians in the United States.[63]

Conservative Christians generally did not sidestep the issue of Arab hostility toward Israelis as was often the case with liberal Protestants who often upheld ethical imperatives above all else. The focus of many liberals was on the social misfortunes of Palestinian Muslims and Christians. Taking an opposing position, many conservative Christians recognized that Israel embodied freedoms rooted in western civilization; they expected economic and other freedoms in Israel would lead to prosperity beneficial to both Jews and Arabs. Conservatives rejected a zero-sum interpretation embraced by those liberals who saw Israel's advance coming at the expense of the Arabs.[64] Well-represented by the magazine

Christian Century, mainline Protestant leaders focused on their liberal understanding of justice that often lacked appreciation of Israel's genuine national security concerns. If Christian Zionists were guilty of not fully comprehending the suffering of Palestinian Arabs or not reaching out adequately to Palestinian Christians experiencing grim economic conditions, liberal Christians were often naïve on issues relating to Israel's life and death struggle to survive as a nation.[65] The socialist spell of "Third World Theologies" captivated those favoring the Palestinian struggle against the "neo-imperialism" of Zionists.[66] Others argued that Christian Zionists spoke too critically of secular Palestinian leaders and Islamic teaching, even to the point of demonizing Islam. There is the suggestion in liberal circles that Arab leaders such as Yasser Arafat deserved more credit than they received.[67]

Conservative Christians believed that their arguments shared some common ground with those Jews who argued for the righteousness of their cause. In the early twentieth century, a notable Jewish nationalist was Vladimir (Ze'ev) Jabotinsky (1880–1940) who founded Revisionist Zionism, representing the right wing of Zionism. Having impressive writing skills, Jabotinsky wrote two important articles in 1923 outlining "The Iron Wall" theory of Revisionism. One historian identifies the following as Jabotinsky's policy in a nutshell:

> We cannot promise any reward either to the Arabs of Palestine or to the Arabs outside of Palestine. A voluntary agreement is unattainable. And so those who regard an accord with the Arabs as an indispensable condition of Zionism must admit to themselves today that this condition cannot be attained and hence that we must give up Zionism. We must either suspend our settlement efforts or continue them without paying attention to the mood of the natives. Settlement can thus develop under the protection of a force that is not dependent on the local population, behind an iron wall which they will be powerless to break down.[68]

Jabotinsky saw no chance of the Arabs agreeing to Jewish statehood, thus Jews had to rely on military force to establish Jewish settlement in Palestine. Critics viewed this as immoral, but Jabotinsky countered: "A sacred truth, whose realization requires the use of force, does not cease thereby to be a sacred truth. This is the basis of our stand toward Arab resistance; and we shall talk of settlement only when they are ready to discuss it."[69] Jabotinsky's notion of Jewish military power as key to Jewish success in the Middle East was influential on the "Zionist movement as a whole."[70] Religion for Jabotinsky was a private matter, but his understanding of Jewish territory made sense to dispensationalists.[71] After the rebirth of Israel, Christian Zionists persisted to see Jewish statehood by way of military power as moral, even in the face of the hostility of Arabs angered over Israel's "iron wall."

With the creation of the State of Israel, a number of conservative Christians wrote enthusiastically on biblical prophecy and the Middle East. The literalist teachings of fundamentalism contrasted sharply with the language of liberal Protestants and Washington policymakers. But for many Christian Zionists what mattered most was God's promise of blessing those who supported Israel. Fundamentalists and other conservative Christians imposed biblical meaning on Middle East events in a manner that promoted a distinct pro-Israel position. In light of the revelations of the horror of the Holocaust and the deaths of 6 million Jews (70 percent of European Jews), liberal Protestant leaders in the United States had voiced their sympathy for Jewish people in the immediate post-World War period. But these leaders had reservations about Zionist political goals that they viewed as oppressive. Believing that Israeli policies were the problem, some liberals argued that once the economic conditions of the Palestinians improved, Arabs would be more welcoming of the Jews. Protestant and secular liberals believed the best chance for peace was when the Arabs received their fair share of the rewards from a type of "global New Deal."[72]

Conservative Christians gave Israeli leaders the benefit of the doubt on many issues relating to Israel's national security. One historian of Christian Zionism notes three important realities that Christian Zionists recognize. First, Arab leaders in November 1947 gave potential peace with the Jews a pass when they rejected the United Nations' two-state solution for Jews and Arabs. Second, Israel's Arab neighbors did not stop their hostility toward Israel, opting for wars and sponsoring ongoing terrorist activities against the Israelis. Third, Arab leaders continued to deny the legality of Israel's existence. All parties paid a high price when the Arabs refused "to try to live at peace with Israel." In the Middle East, the Arab treatment of Jews was no secret to Christian Zionists. Whereas Israeli citizenship is open to Arabs and the Knesset includes elected Arab Israeli members, Jews since 1948 experienced significant persecution and banishment from areas that had been part of the Palestine Mandate. Even in the "moderate" Kingdom of Jordan, the law does not permit Jews to have "the right of permanent residency."[73]

Christian Zionists asked if it was reasonable for Christian anti-Zionists to place most of the blame for Arab-Israeli conflict at the feet of the Israelis. Conservative Christians were aware of wrongdoing on both sides of the conflict, that both the Israelis and Arabs committed grievous errors that caused great suffering. In 1970, one who was not a Christian Zionist brought it back to "original sin." Zwi Werblowsky, professor of comparative religion at Hebrew University in Jerusalem, explained: "Since the Fall, no activity is perfectly righteous and just. In whatever one does, there is an element of injustice, an element of sin." It was simplistic for Arab leaders to see Israel as "the very incarnation of brutal injustice." For Jews, it was "an existentially tragic struggle between two kinds of justice," attempting to realize "which we think to be the maximum of justifiable justice and combining with it a minimum of unavoidable injustice." Pointing out how Christians saw this balancing much differently than Muslims, Werblowsky stated: "The Christian community carries with it a sense of God's saving acts in history. The Moslem does not possess this tradition."[74]

Attentive that there were tradeoffs with all important political decisions, conservatives understood that Israeli leaders were far from faultless with their relations with Arabs.[75] However, God's promises to the Jews in the Bible and the reality of Israel's existence gave conservative Christians confidence that their overall support for Israel was the correct position. In 1948, Lewis Sperry Chafer wrote that "Jehovah may chasten His people and even use the nations to that end, but invariably judgment falls on those who afflict Israel."[76] Put another way, it was "a requirement of faith to prefer the blessing of Israel above all passing things." As Christian Zionists saw it, favoring Israel was compatible "with the will of God."[77] In addition, the creation and success of the Jewish state reassured many Christians that God continued to act in history.

When the leadership of Yishuv (Jewish community) proclaimed the State of Israel, most conservative Christians were clear on how they should respond to the intense hostility that broke out between the newborn Israelis and neighboring Arabs. Over the span of Israel's first twenty-five years, when the Israelis fought five wars, conservative Christian notions of Israeli statehood and national security and its understanding and explanation of Arab anger hardly varied. Although their characterization of Arab people was often simplistic, they recognized violence and they knew what side to support. For those paying attention it was clear that conservative Christians were serious and genuine supporters of Israel when other Christians in the United States became more critical.

NOTES

1. Shimon Peres, *David's Sling* (New York: Random House, 1970), 9. Martin Sicker, *Israel's Quest for Security* (New York: Praeger, 1989), 1. Bernard Reich, "Israeli National Security Policy: Issues and Actors," in *Israeli National Security Policy: Political Actors and Perspectives*, eds. Bernard Reich and Gershon R. Kieval (New York: Greenwood Press, 1988), 1. Also, Bernard Reich, "Themes in the History of the State of Israel," *American Historical Review* 96, no. 5 (December 1991), 1472, 1476. Nadav Safran, *Israel: The Embattled Ally* (Cambridge, MA: Harvard University Press, 1981), 165, 222. From an early age, Israelis learned from school textbooks of the possible destruction of Israel at the hands of the Arabs. See Elie Podeh, "History and Memory in the Israeli Educational System," *History and Memory* 12, no. 1 (Spring/Summer 2000), 75.

2. In 2003, Daniel Pipes notes that the media appeared to view Christian Right support for Israel as "something new." See Daniel Pipes, "[Christian Zionism:] Israel's Best Weapon?" *New York Post*, July 15, 2003. http://danielpipes.org/pf.php?id=1148 (accessed 9/8/2007). Perhaps one other part of the equation was that for centuries Christians viewed Islam as a major *competitor* since both were "aggressively evangelis-

tic." See Thomas S. Kidd, *American Christians and Islam: Evangelical Culture and Muslims from the Colonial Period to the Age of Terrorism* (Princeton, NJ: Princeton University Press, 2009), xii.

3. On fundamentalists' lack of political lobbying, see Caitlin Carenen, *The Fervent Embrace: Liberal Protestants, Evangelicals, and Israel* (New York: New York University Press, 2012), 83, 120.

4. One statement in an advertisement in an evangelical magazine explains it well: "The Abrahamic covenant is still valid, and God will bless him who brings blessing to the Jews." See "Did You Ever Weep Over Jerusalem?" *Christianity Today*, December 21, 1959, 33. "I will bless them that bless thee, and curse him that curseth thee" was a verse commonly heard in evangelical circles. See "Protesting Anti-Semitism in the Soviet Union," *Christianity Today*, October 8, 1965, 35.

5. "Palestinians" had no distinctive name; in documents, they were "Arab refugees." Kathleen Christison, "Bound by a Frame of Reference, Part II: U.S. Policy and the Palestinians, 1948–88," *Journal of Palestine Studies* 27, no. 3 (Spring 1998), 21.

6. Colin Shindler, *A History of Modern Israel* (Cambridge: Cambridge University Press, 2008), 9. The designation "Palestinian-Israeli conflict" is only appropriate when the focus is solely on the confrontations between the Israeli government and Palestinian Arabs living inside Israel, the West Bank, and the Gaza Strip. For additional discussion, see Ian J. Bickerson and Carla L. Klausner, *A History of the Arab-Israeli Conflict*, 6th ed. (New York: Prentice Hall, 2010), 2.

7. Henry Catton, *Palestine, the Arabs and Israel: The Search for Justice* (London: Longman Group Limited, 1969), 6, 9, 11.

8. Catton, *Palestine, the Arabs and Israel*, 136.

9. Michael B. Oren, *Six Days of War: June 1967 and the Making of the Modern Middle East* (New York: Presido Press, 2003), 333. Oren writes of the new historians' "distinctly leftist or Marxist orientation." For an early list of new historians, see Avi Shlaim, *The Iron Wall: Israel and the Arab World* (London: The Penguin Press, 2000), ix, and Jerome Slater, "Lost Opportunities for Peace in the Arab-Israeli Conflict: Israel and Syria, 1948–2001," *International Security* 27, no. 1 (Summer 2002), 81n3. Also, Benny Morris, ed., *Making Israel* (Ann Arbor, MI: The University of Michigan Press, 2007), 3–7. However, the "new historians" are not critical enough of Israel for some like Norman Finkelstein and Noam Chomsky. See Norman Finkelstein, "Myths, Old and New," *Journal of Palestine Studies* 21, no. 1 (Autumn 1991): 66–89.

10. Shlaim, *The Iron Wall*, 34–35, 49.

11. "Interview: Israeli New Historian Avi Shlaim," *Middle East Policy* XVI, no. 3 (Fall 2009), 97. Also, see Avi Shlaim, "The War of the Israeli Historians," *Annales* 59, no. 1 (January—February 2004): 161–67.

12. See Efriam Karsh, "Rewriting Israel's History," *The Middle East Quarterly* (June 1996): 19–29. http://meforum.org/302/rewriting-israels-history (accessed 11/20/2013).

13. Oren, *Six Days of War*, 333.

14. Bernard Lewis, *The Middle East and the West* (Bloomington: Indiana University Press, 1964), 135; Bernard Lewis, "The Roots of Muslim Rage," *The Atlantic Monthly* (September 1990), 56, 59–60. See Samuel P. Huntington, *The Clash of Civilizations and the Remaking of World Order* (New York: Simon and Schuster, 2003), 212–14. Also, Benny Morris, *1948: A History of the First Arab–Israeli War* (New Haven, CT: Yale University Press, 2008), 394. For a critique of the clash of civilizations framework, see Ervand Abrahamian, "The US Media, Huntington and September 11," *Third World Quarterly* 24, no. 3 (June 2003): 529–44.

15. John Bagot Glubb, *A Soldier with the Arabs* (London: Hodder and Stoughton, 1957), 6.

16. Matthew F. Jacobs, "The Perils and Promise of Islam: The United States and the Muslim Middle East in the Early Cold War," *Diplomatic History* 30, no. 4 (September 2006), 714.

17. The rise of Christian Left magazines such as *Sojourners* provides evidence of this as early as the 1970s.

18. Efraim Inbar, *Israel's National Security: Issues and Challenges Since the Yom Kippur War* (New York: Routledge 2008), 131.

19. Inbar, *Israel's National Security*, 130. These words are from a Hamas leaflet, putting on paper for distribution what had been delared over the years.

20. Paul Charles Merkley, *Those That Bless You, I Will Bless: Christian Zionism in Historical Perspective* (Brantford, ON: Mantua Books, 2011), 221.

21. Quoted in Morris, *1948*, 393.

22. Quoted in Morris, *1948*, 394.

23. Morris, *1948*, 394-95.

24. *Christianity Today*, November 11, 1957, 22. Also, see Ben J. Marais, "Cross or Crescent in Africa?" *Christianity Today*, May 26, 1958, 8–9. Concerning the city of Ankara (700,000), Wilbur Smith wrote: "I found in 1962 not a single Christian church of any type or persuasion." Wilbur M. Smith, *Before I Forget* (Chicago: Moody Press, 1971), 270.

25. Edward W. Said, *Orientalism*, Twenty-Fifth Anniversary ed. (New York: Vintage Books, 2004). On the pervasiveness of orientalist views in American popular culture, see Little, *American Orientalism*. Viewing Arabs as decadent, alien, and inferior justified British imperialist ventures. The British could improve the people. Little suggests Americans did the same in a later period (10). Also, Jacobs, "The Perils and Promise of Islam," 705-39.

26. Said, *Orientalism*, 307, 316–19, 342.

27. He wrote these words in 2003. See Said, *Orientalism*, xix–xx.

28. Said, *Orientalism*, 338.

29. Glubb, *A Soldier with the Arabs*, 5, 37.

30. Glubb, *A Soldier with the Arabs*, 49, 147.

31. Glubb, *A Soldier with the Arabs*, 401.

32. Quoted in Matthew F. Jacobs, "The Perils and Promise of Islam," 711.

33. *Christian Century*, August 22, 1956, 964.

34. Inbar, *Israel's National Security*, 57.

35. Sicker writes: "Israel doe not pretend to make its survival dependent on the destruction of the Arab states." Sicker, *Israel's Quest for Security*, 3–4.

36. John Babot Glubb wrote: "I believe that the creation and maintenance of the State of Israel by armed force was a mistake." See Glubb, *A Soldier with the Arabs*, 7, 31–32.

37. History can be messy. There were liberal Christians supportive of Israel, at least in the earlier period of Israel's statehood. And there were a small number of conservative Christians critical of Israel. Carenen, *The Fervent Embrace*, 59, 120.

38. Numerous commentators inside and outside church circles wrote of Israel's modern accomplishments. For example, Peres wrote of Israel establishing "a scientific, technological and industrial foundation to speed her advance towards self-sufficiency." See Peres, *David's Sling*, 18.

39. For further discussion, see Merkley, *Those That Bless You, I Will Bless*, 235.

40. However, there was significant disagreement among leftists on the issue of the Arab-Israeli conflict. In the early 1970s, leftist Noam Chomsky argued that there was "no identifiable 'New Left doctrine' on the Middle East." See Noam Chomsky, *Peace in the Middle East? Reflections on Justice and Nationhood* (New York: Vintage Books, 1974), 153.

41. For a specific discussion of American exceptionalism, see Frank Costigliola and Thomas G. Paterson, "Defining and Doing the History of the United States Foreign Relations: A Primer" in *Explaining the History of American Foreign Relations*, 2nd ed, eds. Michael J. Hogan and Tomas G. Paterson (Cambridge: Cambridge University Press, 2004), 11–13.

42. Mark Noll et al, eds. *Evangelicalism: Comparative Studies of Popular Protestantism in North America, the British Isles, and Beyond 1700–1900* (New York: Oxford University Press, 1994), 6.

43. For an excellent discussion on defining fundamentalism, see Joel A. Carpenter, *Revive Us Again: The Reawakening of American Fundamentalism* (New York: Oxford University Press, 1997): 4–11. Also, see Robert D. Woodberry and Christian S. Smith, "Fundamentalism et al: Conservative Protestants in America," *Annual Review of Sociology* 24 (1998), 25–27; George Marsden, *Fundamentalism and American Culture: The Shaping of Twentieth-Century Evangelicalism, 1870–1925* (New York: Oxford University Press 1980, 4; and David Harrington Watt, "The Private Hopes of American Fundamentalists and Evangelical, 1925–1975," *Religion and American Culture* 1, no. 2 (Summer 1991): 155–75.

44. Ernest R. Sandeen, *The Roots of Fundamentalism: British and American Millenarianism 1800–1930* (Chicago: The University of Chicago Press, 1970), ix.

45. For example, see Paul Erb, *Bible Prophecy: Questions and Answers* (Scottdale, PA: Herald Press, 1978), 33–34.

46. Wilbur M. Smith, "The Greatest Prophetic Discourse of Our Lord," *His: Student Magazine of the Inter-Varsity Christian Fellowship* 8, no. 5 (May 1948), 16. Also, see Arthur B. Whiting, "The Rapture of the Church," *Bibliotheca Sacra* 102, no. 408 (July–September, 1945): 490–99; John F. Walvoord, "Premillennialism and the Tribulation," *Bibliotheca Sacra*, 113, no. 451 (July, 1956): 193–99; Kenneth S. Wuest, "The Rapture–Precisely When?" *Bibliotheca Sacra*, 114, no. 453 (January, 1957): 60–69. A better known premillennialist is Billy Graham. See Graham, *World Aflame* (Montreal: Pocket Books, 1966). Dispensationalist premillennialists especially focus on Israel. Dispensationalist theology divides history into a number of dispensations or periods of time that point "toward a final golden age, when a messianic kingdom would come to earth." Carpenter, *Revive Us Again*, 248–49. For a discussion on dispensational eschatology, see Charles Caldwell Ryrie, *Dispensationalism Today* (Chicago: Moody Press, 1965), 156–76. Dean of Dallas Theological Seminary, Ryrie earned his PhD at Edinburgh. On Ryrie, see "Israel: Things to Come," *Christianity Today*, December 22, 1967, 35.

47. Timothy P. Weber, *On the Road to Armageddon: How Evangelicals Became Israel's Best Friend* (Grand Rapids, MI: Baker Academic, 2004), 13. As Weber put it, "everything was riding on the Jews." Premillennialist John F. Walvoord wrote that "Israel as the chosen people is destined to a prominent place in future world affairs, but not before enduring much hardship and persecution." See John F. Walvoord, *The Nations in Prophecy* (Grand Rapids, MI: Zondervan Publishing House, 1967), 17.

48. Erb, *Bible Prophecy*, 126.

49. Michael Stallard, "Is Dispensationalism Hurting American Political Policies in the Middle East?" in *Dispensationalism Tomorrow and Beyond: A Theological Collection in Honor of Charles C. Ryrie*, ed. Christopher Cone (Fort Worth, TX: Tyndale Seminary Press, 2008), 463. One dispensationalist scholar wrote: "The theological liberal quite naturally opposes dispensationalism, for he finds completely unpalatable its plain interpretation. . . . Whatever else dispensationalists are, they are conservative in their view of the fundamental doctrines of the Bible, an approach unsavory to the liberal." See Ryrie, *Dispensationalism Today*, 10. Also, John F. Walvoord, *Blessed Hope: The Autobiography of John F. Walvoord* (Chattanooga, TN: AMG Publishers, 2001), 79.

50. For example, see E. Schuyler English, "'Blessed Is He That Readeth . . .': A Defense of the Scofield Reference Bible," *Moody Monthly*, November 1951, 153–55. For Wilbur M. Smith's defense of dispensationalism, see "Books in Review," *Christianity Today*, June 20, 1960, 34.

51. Eitan Bar-Yosef, "Christian Zionism and Victorian Culture," *Israel Studies* 8, no. 2 (Summer 2003): 18–44. Shalom Goldman, *Zeal for Zion: Christians, Jews, and the Idea of The Promised Land* (Chapel Hill: University of North Carolina Press, 2010), 2. Various scholars refer to the Christian Restorationism of the sixteenth century and later years, when Protestants wrote of the eventual restoration of Jews to their land. Merkley, *Those That Bless You, I Will Bless*, 131–32, 159.

52. Naim Ateek, "Introduction: Challenging Christian Zionism," in *Challenging Christian Zionism: Theology, Politics and the Israel-Palestine Conflict*, eds. Naime Ateek et al. (London: Melisende 2005), 13, 18.

53. Merkley, *Those That Bless You, I Will Bless*, 190.

54. Donald Wagner, "A Zionist Primer (Part 11) Defining Christian Zionism," *Cornerstone* 31 (Winter 2003), 12.

55. Stephen Spector, *Evangelicals and Israel: The Story of American Christian Zionism* (Oxford: Oxford University Press, 2009), 2–3. Also, see Ronald R. Stockton, "Christian Zionism: Prophecy and Public Opinion," *Middle East Journal* 41, no. 2 (Spring 1987), 251. Stockton writes: "While Christian Zionism is disproportionately associated with the evangelical Christian base from which it historically sprang, the survey data indicate that it transcends these origins and has support in all religious, ideological, and political strata."

56. Paul Merkley writes that "it is nowhere near the truth, to portray Christian Zionism as the fruit of Dispensationalism." See Merkley, *Those That Bless You, I Will Bless*, 230. For additional discussion on dispensationalism, see George Marsden, *Understanding Fundamentalism and Evangelicalism* (Grand Rapids, MI: William B. Eerdmans, 1991), 39–41, 77. One recent study argues that evangelicals over a period of time put less emphasis "on end-of-times eschatology to focus more on the command to bless Israel in order to garner blessings for the United States." See Carenen, *The Fervent Embrace*, 210–11. Of course, it is also plausible that most evangelicals had always put greater emphasis on "blessings" than on complex end times eschatology.

57. In a 1963 letter to Yona Malachy, John Walvoord wrote: "I do not know that dispensationalists are actively engaged in support of the Zionist. . . . I have not observed in the United States of America any clear relationship between dispensationalism and political Zionism as such." Yona Malachy, *American Fundamentalism and Israel: The Relation of Fundamentalist Churches to Zionism and the State of Israel* (Jerusalem: Institute of Contemporary Jewry, The Hebrew University of Jerusalem, 1978), 159.

58. Many Bible-believing Christians took the position that the building of the Third Temple would only occur after Israel's repentance and Christ's return. For example, see "In the Wake of War," *Christianity Today*, August 18, 1967, 24.

59. For more on the claims by Christian anti-Zionists, see Stephen Sizer, *Christian Zionism: Road-map to Armageddon* (Leicester, UK: Inter-Varsity Press, 2004), 21, 183. Similar arguments are made by non-Christian liberals such as Victoria Clark, a self-proclaimed "secular humanist relativist liberal." Victoria Clark, *Allies for Armageddon: The Rise of Christian Zionism* (New Haven, CT: Yale University Press, 2007), 3, 21. A good number of dispensationalist writers believe that only God can settle the matter of the Arabs. For example, see Arthur E. Bloomfield, *Before the Last Battle Armageddon* (Minneapolis, MN: Bethany Fellowship, Inc., 1971), 64.

60. Stallard, "Is Dispensationalism Hurting American Political Policies in the Middle East?" 473–75. A rare example of a Christian Zionist using the term "hasten" when speaking of the future kingdom is Louis S. Bauman, "Israel Lives Again!" *The King's Business*, September 1950, 7. But it was not any human political activity that would hasten the day. Bauman desired that the "Lord God of hosts, [would] hasten that day!"

61. Spector, *Evangelicals and Israel*, 3. Similarly, fundamentalists believed that supporting Israel represented an act of faithfulness to God's plan in history. People and nations would be judged by God on how they treated Israel. See Carenen, *The Fervent Embrace*, 80–1, 119.

62. Spector, *Evangelicals and Israel*, 3.

63. The theme of Israel representing the front line of western values got more attention in the twenty-first century. In 2005, one Christian Zionist spoke of Islamic extremism and the diminishing of Western values in Europe. See Spector, *Evangelicals and Israel*, 2.

64. On Israel's prosperity, see Walvoord, *The Nations in Prophecy*, 111–12. On the zero-sum game of Christian anti-Zionists, see Merkley, *Those That Bless You, I Will Bless*, 235–36.

65. Critics claim that Christian Zionists have forgotten Christian Palestinians. For example, Stephen Sizer makes his point by writing of his meeting "a real-life Palestinian." He also links Christian Zionism and the threatened "extinction" of Palestinians. Like many other Christian critics of Israel, Sizer's writing on Christian Zionism provides no information about or analysis of Israel's security problems. See Sizer, *Christian Zionism*, 10, 13.

66. Malachy, *American Fundamentalism and Israel*, vii.

67. Sizer, *Christian Zionism*, 240, 247.

68. Quoted in Shlaim, *The Iron Wall*, 13.

69. Quoted in Shlaim, *The Iron Wall*, 15.

70. Shlaim, *The Iron Wall*, 16.

71. Colin Shindler, "Likud and the Christian Dispensationalists: A Symbiotic Relationship," *Israel Studies* 5, no. 1 (Spring 2000), 161.

72. The designation "global New Deal" is from David Schoenbaum, *The United States and the State of Israel* (New York: Oxford University Press, 1993), 80. Interestingly, Eleanor Roosevelt linked Israeli development with New Deal liberalism, arguing that the "democratic socialism of the labor-Zionists might indeed become the model state that would promote an international New Deal." Quoted in Michelle Mart, "Eleanor Roosevelt, Liberalism, and Israel," *Shofar* 24, no. 3 (Spring 2006), 78.

73. Merkley, *Those That Bless You, I Will Bless*, 206–207.

74. F. Dean Lueking, "Hopeful Voices from Israel," *Christian Century*, February 1970, 140.

75. Conservative Christians also wrote of corruption in Israel's government. One example is Wilbur M. Smith, *Egypt and Israel: Coming Together?* (Wheaton, IL: Tyndale House Publishers, Inc., 1957), vii.

76. Quoted in Paul Boyer, *When Time Shall Be No More: Prophecy Belief in Modern American Culture* (Cambridge, MA: Harvard University Press, 1992), 216.

77. Merkley, *Those That Bless You, I Will Bless*, 234.

ONE

The Road to War and Independence

After the United Nations voted in favor of separate Arab and Jewish states in Palestine, one female Arab organizer declared, "The UN decision has united all Arabs, as they have never been united before. . . . [A Jewish state] has no chance to survive now that the 'holy war' has been declared. All the Jews will eventually be massacred."[1] Entering into 1948, the number of Palestinian Jews was half the number of Palestinian Arabs. The main goal of Yishuv (the Jewish community in Palestine) was simple—to survive. More worrisome was that Yishuv's population of 650,000 was miniscule compared to the 40,000,000 Arabs in the surrounding states. Given the circumstances, May 14, 1948, was a glorious, historic day for the Jews as David Ben-Gurion announced the new State of Israel. Seeing the journey as a long one that reached far back in evangelical history, American Christian Zionists were also joyous, a fact realized by few Jews in Israel and the United States.

Palestine was a "region" within a larger geographical area that included Syria and Lebanon. Never governed "as a distinct unity," it was not even a province of the Ottoman Empire. The concept of nationalism was meaningless for late-nineteenth-century Arab inhabitants; certainly, there was no hint of "a separate Palestinian Arab nationalism."[2] The less than half a million Arabs living there were mostly poor, illiterate farmers with a short life expectancy.[3] Avoiding the pogroms and religious discrimination of late-nineteenth-century Europe, thousands of Jews began to flock to Palestine in the 1880s, adding to the small population of Sephardic Jews whose families had lived there for centuries (surviving assaults by the Romans, Christian crusaders, and Muslims). Initially from the Arab Peninsula, some of the Palestinian Jews were survivors of Muhammad's command: "Never do two religions exist in Arabia."[4] Given this strong Muslim position, it seemed an impossible dream to expect that the Arabs would allow the rise of a thriving Jewish presence in Palestine.

Scholars point out that when European Jews—generally known as Ashkenazim Jews—began to settle in Palestine there was no displacement of local Arabs by conquest; the Jews lawfully purchased land from Arab landowners, often at "exorbitant prices." Mark Twain's 1867 description of Palestine was a land of barrenness and poverty, but ample evidence exists of the European Jews revitalizing many sections of the region.[5] *Moody Monthly* was one fundamentalist magazine that wrote of "the great reconstruction program in Palestine."[6] On the eve of the First World War, there were approximately fifty Jewish settlements in Palestine and the European Jews tipped the Jewish population in the range of 65,000 to 85,000. There was no turning back for Yishuv.

During WWI, the British gave Arab leaders the impression of future support for Arab independence in Palestine if the leaders sided with Britain against the Ottoman Empire. But the British also reached out to Yishuv. As the British forces engaged the Turkish army in Palestine, British foreign secretary Arthur James Balfour wrote: "His Majesty's Government view with favour the establishment in Palestine of a national home for the Jewish people, and will use their best endeavours to facilitate the achievement of this object." The date of Lord Balfour's letter was November 2, 1917, before the British had even gained possession of Palestine. Arabs viewed the Zionist statement as nothing less than British betrayal. For conservative Christians, Balfour's statement was beyond mere political rhetoric; it "was the hand of God writing a warrant for His people."[7] When A. B. Simpson, founder of the Christian and Missionary Alliance denomination, read the Balfour Declaration to his congregation he could not hold back the tears.[8] One writer in 1918 declared: "The Jews and the land of Palestine are like charts to the mariner. As we study the prophecies concerning 'the people' and 'the land' we hold the key to the mysteries of God's plan and purposes for the world."[9]

Soon after the Balfour Declaration, British military forces took possession of Palestine when the Palestinian Arabs still supported "the (Muslim) Ottoman Empire in its war against the (Christian) Allied powers."[10] At a Bible conference held in Philadelphia, the Rev. A. E. Thompson declared: "The capture of Jerusalem is one of those events to which students of prophecy have been looking for many years."[11] The spoils of victory included Britain formalizing its control of Palestine in 1922 with a League of Nations mandate. The establishment of the British (Palestine and Iraq) mandate in the former Ottoman Empire upset Arabs who viewed the British as the protector of Zionism. A serious problem for the Arabs was the text of the Palestine mandate that approved the Balfour Declaration and recognized "the historical connection of the Jewish people with Palestine and to the grounds for reconstructing their national home in that country."[12] Palestinian Jews looked forward to political independence and they had an advantage in a formal international sense.

As stated in the Palestine mandate document, the Jewish Agency was the public body whose purpose was to cooperate with British officials "in such economic, social and other matters as may affect the establishment of the Jewish national home." The essential goal of the Jewish Agency was to improve the Jews politically by increasing their population and land ownership in the face of Arab opposition. In fact, article 6 of the mandate stated that the British were to "facilitate Jewish immigration" to Palestine.[13] Notably absent from the mandate document was the word "Arab." Of the Jews, the highest concentration resided in Jerusalem. The British census of 1922 recorded 33,971 Jews and 28,112 Arabs living in Jerusalem proper.[14] Despite Arab opposition to the Zionists, the leading Arab families sold land to the Jews up until 1947. The mandate period witnessed the economic rise of the Jewish communities, far outpacing Arab development that lacked the democratic governing institutions of the Jews.[15] The Jews founded their first university (Hebrew University of Jerusalem) in 1925 whereas it was over forty-five years later when the Palestinian Arabs established their first university. After visiting Palestine, American fundamentalist J. Frank Norris predicted in 1920 that the Jews would best the Arabs; while such an outcome was providential, westerners perceived the Jew to be "industrious" and the Arab "lazy."[16]

American Christian Zionists such as George T. B. Davis reprimanded the Arabs for failing to be grateful for the material wealth generated in the region by the Jews.[17] As the Jews increased their land holdings and economic fortunes, there was deadly Arab-Jewish conflict with the worst episodes in the years 1919–1921, 1929, 1933, and 1936–1939. But how did many Arabs in the region respond to the wealth creation in Palestine? Economic opportunity attracts people, and it is interesting to note President Franklin Roosevelt's report that during the 1921–1939 period Arab immigration into Palestine "vastly exceeded" Jewish immigration numbers.[18]

As Jerusalem's grand mufti since 1921, Muhammad Haj Amin al-Husseini played a key role in mobilizing opposition to Zionist goals (in exile during World War II he served the Nazis in Berlin). The Jewish response varied. Jewish defense was the mission of the clandestine organization Haganah, created in 1921.[19] Other smaller groups of Palestinian Jews responded more forcefully to Arab hostility. In 1931, a small group claiming that the Jewish Agency was too accommodating to British officials formed a separate military arm—the Irgun Zvai Leumi (Irgun). An even smaller and more militant group of Jews responsible for various terrorist acts against the Arabs and the British was the Lohamei Herut Yisrael (Stern Gang) which numbered about 300 members.

Despite what the Palestine mandate stated, successive British administrations in Palestine viewed the Zionism of the Balfour Declaration as a monumental error that "muddied the waters between Britain and the Arab World."[20] The British attempted the impossible feat of balancing the causes of the Arabs and Jews, including a 1937 royal commission headed by Lord Peel that recommended partition of Palestine with the Jews getting 20 percent of the land, the Arabs receiving 70 percent, and the remaining 10 percent retained by the British. Arab leaders soundly rejected any "two-state" solution. With a second world war on the horizon, the British made efforts to appease the Arabs at the expense of Palestinian Jews. The Jewish leaders of the 350,000 Jews residing in Palestine found the White Paper of 1939, which limited the total number of Jewish refugees to 75,000 for a five-year period (15,000 per year), unacceptable. However, relations with Britain appeared more promising when Winston Churchill became prime minister in 1940. The following year he wrote: "If Britain and the United States emerge victorious from the war, the creation of a great Jewish state in Palestine inhabitated [sic] by millions of Jews will be one of the leading features of the Peace Conference discussions."[21] During World War II, over 26,000 Palestinian Jews joined the British army to fight with the Allied forces. After the war Churchill was no longer prime minister and the Jews looked more to the United States for political support.

President Roosevelt showed hesitation at times, but he was mostly supportive of a Jewish homeland in the face of State Department opposition to this commitment. One State official warned, "The President's continued support of Zionism may thus lead to actual bloodshed in the Near East and even endanger the security of our immensely valuable oil concession in Saudi Arabia."[22] In a letter to Democrat Senator Robert Wagner, Roosevelt wrote: "There are about one million Jews [in Palestine]. They are of all shades, good, bad, and indifferent . . . 70 million Moslems want to cut their throats."[23]

After Roosevelt gathered with Winston Churchill and Joseph Stalin to discuss postwar plans at the Yalta Conference of January 1945, the president met with King Ibn Saud in Egypt before returning to the United States, a meeting conceived without consultation with Secretary of State Edward Stettinius. Attempting to find some formula to solve the Palestinian issue, Roosevelt told Ibn Saud that he "would take no action . . . which might prove hostile to the Arab people."[24] Roosevelt failed to alter Ibn Saud's unyielding attitude that the Jews must depart from Palestine. Not impressed with talk of the Jews' economic development of Palestinian land, the king claimed that Jewish accomplishments came as a result of American and British capital and that Arabs would see no benefits from Jewish prosperity. Ibn Saud declared that the Arabs would choose death rather "than yield their lands to the Jews."[25] Historians note that Ibn Saud made a major impression on Roosevelt, who attempted to be sympathetic to both the Jews and Arabs. Whereas key politicians encouraged Roosevelt to side with the Jews, the State Department wanted greater sensitivity to Arab concerns. In subsequent years, there was a rift, usually subtle but occasionally glaring, between the bureaucracy of the State Department and politicians accountable to the electorate.

During the years of National Socialist reign in Germany, there was no ambiguity of the mood of Christian Zionists and a good indicator of their support for the Jewish people were their reports of Nazism. Louis S. Bauman, pastor of the First Brethren Church of Long Beach, California was one of the more prolific prophecy commentators who wrote for the *Brethren Evangelist*, *The King's Business*, and *The Sunday School Times*. Bauman provided much more detailed and accurate reports of Jewish persecution during Hitler's reign than was the case of any liberal Protestant writer. Responding to a Hitler speech that spoke of a "Jewish world coalition," Bauman wrote: "Now, if there is any such thing as a 'Jewish world coalition' will someone please tell us where its headquarters are? Who is the head? Wherein has it power? Millions of agonizing, dying Jews would like to know where they can go for a bit of help."[26]

Founded in 1894, *Our Hope* was an American fundamentalist journal writing much about the Jews until and after its merger with *Eternity* magazine in 1958. Concerning Nazi cruelty, *Our Hope* warned: "But there is a day of reckoning coming. God will deal with the enemies of His people and when judgment comes, as it surely will, this modern anti-Semitism will find its ignominious end."[27] The journal gave grim reports of the attacks against Jewish professionals, Kristallnacht, and Jews outside Germany when war broke out and Nazi control expanded throughout Europe. In October 1942, editor Arno Gaebelein declared: "Monster Hitler developed *a devilish mania to persecute and exterminate the entire Jewish race*, an ambition which he has pushed more and more to the front and in which he persists today as never before in his bloody and despicable career."[28] Three years before the world learned the full story of Nationalist Socialist evil, *Our Hope* published a chart stating that the Nazis murdered 2 million Jews and that another 5 million were in danger of extermination. Accounts of German defeats in 1944 and 1945 proved to the dispensationalist writers of *Our Hope* "that those who persecute the Jewish people will be cursed by God."[29]

Historian Paul Boyer writes of the intense interest in prophecy in the United States during the war years. In 1942, the *Christian Digest* wrote: "The Jews are God's index finger when it comes to prophecy." There were a number of prophecy conferences attracting thousands. The 1943 prophecy conference in New York City looked to the future with promise, with one participant declaring: "We all know that the day is coming when Israel is to be restored to the Land of Promise to enjoy what God has covenanted she should have."[30] Although there was a significant amount of prophecy activity in these years, dispensationalism was not the major driver of Christian Zionism. Most American Christians who favored the Jews in Palestine represented a broad spectrum of Christians rather than a subset of fundamentalism. One interesting example was theologian Reinhold Niebuhr, whose liberal theology and position on various issues did not stop his aggressive promotion of a Jewish homeland.[31] Another example was the Baptist in the White House.

When Roosevelt died in April 1945, Jews worried about the future of U.S. government backing, but to their pleasant surprise President Harry Truman's commitment to a Jewish state was stronger than Roosevelt's to the point that Paul Charles Merkley argues that Truman was a modern-day Cyrus.[32] It was King Cyrus of Persia who defeated the Babylonian Empire in 539 BC and encouraged the Jews of Babylon to return to Jerusalem after seventy years of captivity. Special counsel to the president Clifford Clark wrote that Truman was a student of the Bible who "believed in the historic justification for a Jewish homeland" and that "the Balfour Declaration promise constituted a solemn promise that fulfilled the age-old hope and dream of the Jewish people."[33] Truman's Christian Zionism was in line with previous American presidents who approved the "noble ideal" of a Jewish homeland in Palestine.[34] Truman proposed that the British cancel the White Paper plan and immediately allow 100,000 Jewish refugees to settle in Palestine, a proposal that the British and the U.S. State Department disagreed with.

Truman provided some momentum, but the next important step toward eventual nationhood for Palestinian Jews was the establishment in 1946 of a joint Anglo-American Committee of Inquiry consisting of six British and six American representatives. This committee collected data from meetings in Washington and London and fact-finding missions to Egypt, Palestine, and European refugee camps. The final report recommended the immediate transfer of 100,000 Jewish Europeans to Palestine and a proposed binational state composed of an Arab province and a Jewish province administered by the British under the auspices of a UN trusteeship. The final report was pretty much dead on arrival because both the Jews and Arabs rejected it and the British government showed no interest in implementing it. As one condition of support, the British demanded that the Jews surrender their weapons. Considering the hostility of armed Arabs, this was tantamount to the Jews committing suicide, and, thus unrealistic.[35] Christian Zionist Donald Grey Barnhouse predicted Britain's renouncing of her promise to the Jews would result in the decline of the British Empire.[36]

Failing to enforce the law and spending millions of dollars on 80,000 British troops in Palestine, Britain's Labour government turned to the United Nations. There were five Arab member states of the UN and each opposed any plan of dividing Palestine and admitting more Jews to the region. For the Arabs, the 600,000 Jews already there were too many. Conservative Christian leaders insisted on an independent national state for the Jews and that Jewish immigration from Europe increase without limitations. Liberal Protestants were more cautious. The liberal Protestant

Christian Century understood in 1947 that the Palestine issue represented a complex and volatile problem for the UN. Like many within the State Department, liberal Protestant leaders were wary of any statements that might jeopardize relations with Middle East leaders, particularly Saudi strongman Ibn Saud, who controlled "the world's largest unexploited oil reserves."[37]

In April 1947, the United Nations agreed to further study the problem. The United Nations Special Committee on Palestine (UNSCOP), composed of eleven "neutral" member nations, began with the basic outline that division of Palestine between the Palestinian Jews and the Palestinian Arabs was the best option. In 1947, UNSCOP visited the Jewish refugee camps in Europe, met with Jewish and Arab leaders in Palestine, and debated the issue. Jewish representatives made progress since they were able to showcase economic and land improvement and they were well prepared to present their side to UNSCOP whereas the Arabs boycotted meetings, ignored the UNSCOP members who visited Arab villages, and failed to propose any coherent alternative. One UN committee member wrote of UNSCOP's great responsibility: "With our words we eleven men were to decide the destinies of hundreds of thousands of human beings who were blood and flesh, nerves and brains, who, like you and me, worked, struggled, and hoped."[38]

Conservative and liberal Christian leaders knew much was at stake. A Church of England bishop testified to the committee that the Jews had no biblical claim on Palestine, but Pentecostal William Hull wrote to the committee claiming that the great majority of Bible-believing Christians believe "in the ultimate return of the Jewish people to the land which God gave to their fathers."[39] Originally from Canada, Hull lived in Jerusalem from the 1930s to the early 1960s and his book *The Fall and Rise of Israel* (1954), dedicated to Prime Minister Ben-Gurion, was popular with many American conservative Christians interested in the fulfillment of Bible prophecy of the Jews returning to Israel.[40] Interestingly, Ben-Gurion's letter of appreciation was on the jacket of Hull's book. Other evangelicals delivered their Christian Zionist message through evangelical magazines much more popular than liberal ones. Daniel A. Poling of the (Dutch) Reformed Church of America was editor of the *Christian Herald*, a publication with a circulation near 400,000. In response to a reader's inquiry in October 1947, Poling informed his magazine audience: "I am a Christian Zionist who believes that Palestine should become, as promised, the Jewish state." As national co-chairman of the American Christian Palestine Committee, he put action behind his words.[41]

The response in Washington to developments concerning Palestine was less confident. On this issue, policymaking was often reactive and ad hoc; the lack of any unified and preconceived plan suggested confusion.[42] Mostly at odds with the White House, the State Department consistently opposed the establishment of a Jewish state in the face of unrelenting Arab hostility. Palestine desk officer Robert McClinock had little patience for the emotionalism of the Arab, but he understood the danger "of these fanatical and overwrought people" injuring "our strategic interests through reprisals against our oil investments."[43] In August 1947, Fawzi al-Qawuqji—soon to be the head of the Arab Liberation Army (ALA) established in December—warned that if the UN granted the Jews a state, "we will have to initiate total war. We will murder, wreck and ruin everything standing in our way, be it English, American, or Jewish."[44] While living in Nazi Germany during the war, al-Qawuqji recruited Muslim volunteers and broadcasted German propaganda.[45] Many Muslims saw the Arab-Jew conflict as nothing short of a "holy war."

Realism was the "intellectual compass" for State Department officials committed to geopolitics and grand strategy.[46] In a September 1947 memorandum protesting the plan of partition, Loy Henderson, the head of the Near East Division, used phrases such as "undermine our relations with the Arab . . . world," "we shall encounter numerous difficulties," "violent nationalist uprisings," "loss of confidence," "growing suspicion," "lacking in courage and consistency," and "any plan for partitioning Palestine would be unworkable."[47] The language was pessimistic.

The UNSCOP presented its official recommendations to the UN General Assembly on November 29, 1947. There was a majority report from eight members and a minority report from three members. The majority report stipulated the partition of Palestine into two states with the Jewish state having most of the coastal area, western Galilee, and the Negev. The land area of the proposed Arab state was approximately 43 percent; the Jewish state was to be about 56 percent, most of which was desert. Jews recognized two other shortcomings to the partition plan: The Jewish state would have an approximate seven Arabs to ten Jews ratio (which meant that the Arabs would attain a majority within decades), and Jerusalem would be under international control.[48] Conservative Christians believed it was inevitable that the Jewish people would gain additional land, and it made no difference that the Palestinian Jews were overwhelmingly secular. In the *Moody Bible Institute Monthly*, one fundamentalist proclaimed in December 1947 that "the Jews will eventually be given not a portioned Palestine, but the whole of the land, and ultimately the whole of Trans-Jordan as well."[49] When the motion went before the General Assembly, thirty-three voted in favor, thirteen against, and ten in abstention. Opposed were Muslim countries and India (all unwilling to vote against Islam), Yugoslavia, and Greece, but UN Resolution 181 received the necessary two-thirds majority.

Despite the worrisome aspects of the plan, the Jews rejoiced. There was great celebration in packed Jerusalem streets throughout the night of November 29. Many cried out: "Medinath Hayehudim! [Jewish State!] Medinath Hayehudim!"[50] Jews saw the UN vote and support for a Jewish state as representing "a return" rather than a "new creation." Religious

Jews defined it "as God's immutable promise" and secular Jews defined it as fulfillment of historic destiny, but both religious and secular Jews recognized that the November 29 decision "meant a living contact again with an immensely long chain of events in history."[51]

For Arabs, UN Resolution 181 was a great shock and disappointment. All Arab leaders reacted angrily, declaring the plan a nonstarter. The political position of the Arab Higher Committee (the key organization representing Palestinian Arabs) was clear: "The Arabs of Palestine will never recognize the validity of the extorted partition recommendations or the authority of the United Nations to make them."[52] Jamal Husseini, a Palestinian leader, promised: "The blood will flow like rivers in the Middle East." In Arab cities throughout the Middle East, demonstrators demanded "Jihad" in defense of Palestine. For example, the Syrian Muslim Brotherhood announced that the battle represented either "life or death to a nation of 70 million souls . . . whom the vilest, the most corrupt, tricky and destructive people wish to conquer and displace."[53] King Farouk of Egypt went on record that the Arabs would resist partition with military force. Actually, most neighboring Arab leaders were also against the establishment of an independent Palestinian Arab state. King Abdullah of Transjordan, for example, stated that his forces would "occupy every place evacuated by the British."[54]

At the start of the civil war stage (November 30 to May 14) of the War of Independence, the population of Palestinian Arabs was twice the size of the Jewish population. The Arabs had the advantage of populating the high ground whereas the Jews lived mostly in the lowlands. The Jews lacked the safe havens and support offered to the Palestinian Arabs in the neighboring Arab states. Nearby countries were also the source of thousands of volunteers who landed in Palestine to reinforce local militias and join with ALA and Muslim Brotherhood fighters. The head of the ALA reminded his volunteers that "they were going off to Jihad to help the persecuted Arabs of Palestine." Their war was "holy."[55]

The Jews entered the war with fewer than 40,000 fighters (35,000 Haganah, 3,000 Irgun, and 300 Stern members) and they had no tanks, artillery, or combat aircraft. Palestinian Jewish leaders debated whether to concentrate their limited military resources in key areas or adopt a policy of no retreat. David Ben-Gurion favored not retreating from any position, although this was risky in a tactical sense. Jewish military strategy from November to the end of March 1948 was primarily defensive.[56] The British government expected the Jews to lose; the Chief of the Imperial General Staff stated: "In the long run the Jews would not be able to cope . . . and would be thrown out of Palestine unless they came to terms with [the Arabs]."[57] Jewish leaders themselves especially feared the expected invasion of Arab armies from nearby countries, which happened less than seven months later when the British ended their mandate.

As violent clashes between Palestinian Arabs and Palestinian Jews escalated, the British were responsible for law and order, a fact upsetting to Jews knowing armed Arabs crossed over into Palestine seemingly at will from Lebanon, Syria, Transjordan, and Egypt. This included the ALA composed of mainly Syrian, Lebanese, and Iraqi soldiers. Britain continued to arm Arab states according to its treaties. William Hull recounted examples of the British army abusing Jews, even though the British claimed a policy of impartiality. One patrol disarmed four Jewish boys guarding Jewish homes and handed them over to the Arabs: "The next day their bodies were found at St. Stephen's Gate, riddled with bullet holes."[58] Feeling abandoned by the world, Jewish leaders faced the task of defending themselves with limited resources. According to Ben-Gurion, it was "a war against a United Nations Resolution," but the Jews were alone in the fight.[59]

Arab attacks began on November 30, the day after the UN vote with separate attacks on Jewish buses, including one ambush outside Jerusalem which resulted in seven dead. William Hull's good friend lost his wife in this attack.[60] In early December, an Arab mob burned and looted shops in the Jewish city of Tel Aviv with the final result of nineteen Jews and nine Arabs dead. Under the command of Lieutenant Ariel Sharon (future prime minister) one Jewish retaliatory strike hit Arab trucks with Molotov Cocktails. Unclear on whether Jewish military strategy "was working," Sharon wrote: "With every skirmish and every battle the list of the dead lengthened. We hardly bothered ourselves with thoughts of what would happen when the British were finally gone and the real Arab armies invaded. We all knew already we were fighting for our lives."[61]

In mid-December, fourteen died when Arabs ambushed a bus on its way to the Children's Village at Ben Shemen, near Lydda.[62] Other attacks and deaths reduced travel, thus isolating a number of the many sparsely populated Jewish agricultural settlements (approximately 250 rural communities) spread throughout Palestine. Arab control of key roads was a major problem for the Jews. When a Jewish convoy carrying crucial supplies for besieged Jewish communities came under attack, there was almost no place to retreat since the surrounding area usually consisted of unfriendly Arab villages with Jewish settlements far away. The Arabs ambushed Jewish traffic on the Tel Aviv-Jerusalem highway while the Jewish quarter of Jerusalem was in a precarious state since the Arabs destroyed pipes bringing water into the city. A number of ambushes resulted in large numbers of Jews killed. During one week in March, the rate of success of supply trucks reaching Jerusalem was only 30 percent. Hull later wrote of the dozens of wrecked vehicles left along the Road of Valor as a monument to those brave Jewish drivers and fighters killed attempting to bring supplies to Jerusalem.[63]

A particularly tragic incident in mid-January 1948 was the ambush and killing of thirty-five Hebrew University students attempting to provide reinforcements and supplies for the Jewish settlement at Kfar Etzion near Jerusalem. There were reports of the Arabs mutilating the bodies. Traffic to Jerusalem and the city itself were major Arab targets. On February 22, British army deserters dressed in British uniforms drove and parked three British trucks armed with explosives in front of two Jerusalem hotels housing Jewish soldiers. Although the soldiers were out on operations, the huge explosion killed over fifty people (mostly civilians) and destroyed many buildings. The Arabs effectively used bombs in Jaffa and Haifa. One expert Arab bomb-maker learned his craft while serving the Nazis in Germany.[64] But the Jews also committed such bombing acts. The house of William Hull shook when the Jewish Stern Gang bombed a British army lorry, instantly killing five soldiers. Arab fighters across the street held their fire while Hull assisted two wounded British soldiers into his house.[65] With such violence and chaos in Jerusalem, Arab Christians planned to leave the city "but the Muslims threatened to confiscate or destroy their property."[66]

American Christian Zionists viewed events in Palestine as a "David and Goliath contest." But they knew how that story ended. Slowly Jewish fighters made progress in taking control of key highways which allowed the deliverance of much needed supplies to Jews previously cut off for many weeks. Jewish control of the Tel Aviv-Jerusalem road by April was a major achievement. Some historians argue that the Jewish military force was not the underdog portrayed by others. In time, Jewish arms factories (often established in cowsheds and other agricultural buildings) produced a significant supply of essential weapons, particularly mortars, submachine guns, and grenades. The second stage of the civil war (April to mid-May) witnessed a stronger Jewish military as the Jews went on the offensive with better weapons, including secret shipments from Czechoslovakia that allowed the Jews to begin conquering territory including enemy villages.[67]

However, there was nothing to boast about when the Irgun and Stern Gang attacked the Arab village Deir Yassin located along the western approach to Jerusalem. To this day, conflicting interpretations persist on what happened at the village on April 9, 1948. According to Irgun leader Menachem Begin, Jewish troops encountered strong Arab resistance resulting in heavy Jewish casualties—four dead and almost forty wounded. He claimed that on a loudspeaker the Jews exhorted in Arabic for Deir Yassin women and children "to leave their houses and to take shelter on the slope of the hill" before the Jews threw grenades into the interiors of the village homes.[68] Some historians claim that the Jewish van blaring a warning for the villagers to drop their weapons and leave the village overturned in a ditch and many of those staying behind likely did not hear the warning. Others claim that troops shot unarmed civilians execution style. This was a serious charge even in a war where it was the norm for both the Arabs and the Jews to shoot their captured combatants since neither side had proper facilities to house prisoners. Approximately 120 died in the massacre, although others inflated the number for propaganda purposes.[69]

Living in Jerusalem at the time, William Hull wrote that the Jewish Agency disapproved the actions of those who carried out the military operation against the Arab village. In fact, the Jewish Agency sent a formal apology to the King of Transjordan. According to Hull, this "dark blot on the Jewish record" did prove one thing: "that so much was made of it both by the Red Cross, the Arabs and the Jewish Agency showed that it was not the usual practice of the Jews to commit atrocities."[70] Hull was one of many Christian Zionists who saw such acts of violence against innocent Arab people as a rarity. The Deir Yassin massacre also horrified Jews. Harry Levin was a Jew who published a firsthand account of key months of the 1948 conflict; he maintained that Deir Yassin was an inexcusable massacre: "None of the barbarities the Arabs have committed in the past months can excuse this foul thing done by Jews."[71]

Arabs understood the incident as a massacre representative of Jewish barbarism.[72] Champion of the Arab cause Henry Catton acknowledged the Arabs carried out violence, but no one should "make the mistake of equating Jewish with Arab violence." Jewish "terrorism" was to dislodge the indigenous population and conquer the country whereas Arabs resorted to violence in order to retain their historical and legal land.[73]

British John Glubb wrote of the Jewish "terrorists" massacring defenseless old men, women, and children and throwing 250 bodies down the village well.[74] Dr. Stephen Penrose, the president of the American University of Beirut, claimed that the "Zionists made better use of terrorist tactics which they learned only too well at the hands of Nazi taskmasters."[75] For those who suffered unbearable horror and tragedy in Germany such statements cut deep into the heart.

In his account of the refugees fleeing from Jewish forces, Harry Levin wrote that the Arab exit was of "massive proportions." Most of them evacuated themselves on hearing of the Jews' military success; they left their homes—"primitive, backward, filthy; mud walls and grimy floors"—expecting Arab leaders (such as King Abdullah) to take care of them "until the Jews are driven out."[76] William Hull placed most of the blame on Arab leaders who "so multiplied the Deir Yassin massacre and concocted so many other tales without any foundation of fact that the Arabs were terrified of the *terrible* Jews."[77] Other sources indicate that Arab leaders advised many people to leave, specifically women and children. The exodus was to be short term. Historian Benny Morris writes that probably most Palestinians who left "thought of a short, temporary displacement with a return within weeks or months, on the coattails of victorious Arab armies or international diktas."[78]

Ben-Gurion and others apologized for the brutal killing of innocent women and children at Deir Yassin, but the subsequent flight of Arabs from the proposed Jewish state was an advantageous development for Jewish leaders understanding the demographic implications. Nothing could change the reality of a small Jewish population facing overwhelming Arab numbers in the Middle East, but at least Jewish leaders could hinder the growth of the Arab population in a Jewish state. In a letter months later to Chaim Weizmann, Moshe Sharett wrote: "Once the return tide starts, it will be impossible to stem it, and it will prove our undoing. As for the future, we are equally determined—without, for the time being, formally closing the door to any eventuality—to explore all possibilities of getting rid, once and for all, of the huge Arab minority which originally threatened us."[79] Weizmann would become the first president of Israel and Sharett a future prime minister.

Deir Yassin galvanized the Arabs to exact revenge four days later against a Jewish ten-vehicle civilian medical convoy, mostly unarmed, traveling to a Jerusalem hospital. A land mine blew a hole in the road preventing the convoy from proceeding. The attack on the medical non-combatants lasted more than five hours and the death toll was seventy-eight men and women, some of them world-famous doctors and nurses. One of the few survivors, wounded and under a hail of bullets, had rolled into a nearby ditch and crawled to safety before collapsing.[80] Because nearby British soldiers failed to help, Ben-Gurion defined the ambush as "an English massacre." Leo Kohn, a Jewish official, declared that the "British soldiers witnessed at close quarters university professors, doctors and nurses being shot down or roasted alive in the burning vehicles without doing anything."[81]

Approximately one month later, the Arab Legion defeat of the Jewish settlement Kfar Etzion gave Arabs another opportunity to avenge Deir Yassin. After a series of punishing artillery attacks, more than one hundred Jewish men and women surrendered and followed instructions to assemble in the center of the settlement. What followed was a massacre as a mass of Arabs yelling "Deir Yassin" showered the Jews with bullets from all directions. To his credit, one Legion officer did not participate in the massacre, and he saved the life of a Jewish radiowoman by shooting two of his soldiers while they attempted to rape her. Only a few survived the onslaught; the final death toll was grim—one hundred and six men and twenty-seven women.[82]

However, the momentum was with the Jewish fighters as they launched a series of successful offensives, gaining important territory at Tiberias, Haifa, Jaffa, Safad (Eastern Galilee), and western Jerusalem. It was devastating for the Arab civilians fleeing their homes. One Jewish scout in Arab disguise met a distraught Arab elder: "I asked him why he was crying and he replied that he had lost his six children and his wife and did not know [where] they were." Showing kindness, the scout took him to a hotel and gave him money.[83] Hostility ran deep between the Arabs and Jews, but there were acts of human kindness on both sides.

The many violent clashes in Palestine before the departure of the British caused key American figures such as Warren Austin, the U.S. ambassador to the United Nations, to lose faith in a partition solution. Austin related this in his speech to the Security Council, which put Truman in a difficult spot given his earlier supportive pledge to Jewish leaders. He responded in anger: "I'm now in the position of a liar and a double-crosser. . . . There are people on the 3rd and 4th levels of the State Dept. who have always wanted to cut my throat."[84] There was significant criticism of Austin's UN speech in American newspapers and a perplexed Truman attempted to undo the damage.[85]

In the April 1948 *Reader's Digest*, Bayard Dodge's 6,000-word article "Must There Be War in the Middle East?" was representative of a pro-Arab position in some American circles. A liberal Protestant and the first president of the American University of Beirut, Dodge opposed Zionism because it threatened both the work of nonprofit American agencies located in the Middle East and American oil operations. Robert D. Kaplan notes that Dodge "appeared oblivious" to the psychological and historical aspects of the Holocaust and the passion of European Jewish refugees for a Jewish state.[86] Truman received little support from liberal Protestant leaders who believed the United States was guilty of a "tragic blunder in strong-arming the U.N. Assembly into voting for an unworkable partition."[87] As May 15 approached and Arab-Jewish conflict escalated, some liberal Protestants had more concern for protecting sacred sites in Jerusalem than for Jews reaching political goals.[88] The stakes for Jewish leaders themselves were serious; if they failed, they "would be the first the Arab would hang in the middle of Allenby Square."[89]

On May 14, 1948, David Ben-Gurion gathered with Jewish leaders and others at the Tel Aviv Museum and read the Declaration of Independence of the State of Israel: "With trust in Almighty God, we set our hand to this Declaration. . . ."[90] The early Israeli leaders were secular, but with few world leaders giving Israel much hope of surviving, key Jewish leaders understood the powerful force of religion as they advanced the authenticity and credibility of Jewish nationalism that they declared was centuries old. Ben-Gurion's reading of the Declaration of Independence revealed a clear linking of nationhood and religion. The religious flavor in the first part is significant: "In the Land of Israel the Jewish people came into being. In this Land was shaped their spiritual, religious, and national character. Here they lived in sovereign independence. Here they created a culture of national and universal import, and gave to the world the eternal Book of Books." Despite their forced exile "the Jewish people kept faith with their Land in all the countries of their dispersion, steadfast in their prayer and hope to return and here revive their political freedom." Having stayed true to "history and tradition, the Jews in every generation strove to renew their roots in the ancient Homeland, and in recent generations they came home in their multitudes."[91] After the signing of the Declaration of Independence, Jews "wept unashamedly."[92]

As head of the new Provisional Government, Prime Minister Ben-Gurion ushered in an exciting new chapter for the Jewish people. But how would the American government and other key nations respond? After weeks of Washington uncertainty before May 14, Truman set the record straight and the United States immediately extended de facto recognition of Israel—an act described as a "near miracle" by some Israeli leaders.[93] Truman favored the advice of Zionists such as Clark Clifford over the advice of the State Department and military counsels, including secretary of state George C. Marshall, who "was completely tone-deaf to the siren of Zionism."[94] In her response to her bosses' angst, Marilyn Woods, the secretarial help working for the State Department in the 1940s, captures a sense of the divide between State Department managers and many ordinary Americans: "Mr. Wilson, I don't understand why you let yourself get so bothered about Palestine when everyone knows it says in the Bible that the Jews are going back there some day!"[95]

One regular column in *Moody Monthly* was Nathan J. Stone's "Answering Your Questions." A reader asked Stone if the "opening of Palestine to the Jews" meant Christ's return in the next thirty-five to fifty years. First, Stone clarified that the Jews were "returning there in unbelief, striving in their own strength and sufficiency, yet nonetheless heroically, to *gain* what God will only *give*, in fulfillment of His promise." Second, he cautioned against any predictions of what decade Christ might return. There was no message of fundamentalists favoring Israel basically as a means to hasten Christ's return.[96] There was great joy among evangelicals and fundamentalists simply from seeing the fulfillment of Scripture.

For the Christian Zionists who followed the Jewish nation-building process, no other Jewish event since 33 AD was more important. Wilbur Smith referred to it as "this wonderful phenomenon of the twentieth century, the greatest event in Palestine certainly since the destruction of Jerusalem, infinitely more important than the Crusades."[97] From his Jerusalem vantage point, William Hull claimed that Truman's recognition of Israel "was surely the direct leading of God."[98] In a radio address, a teacher at the Bible Institute of Los Angeles described Israel's rebirth as "the greatest piece of prophetic news that we have had in the twentieth century." Other Americans told their children that the day was "the most significant event since Jesus Christ was born." A future Christian Zionist leader, John Hagee remembered at age eight his father response: "Son, this is the most important day of the twentieth century."[99] Certainly for American premillennialists the events leading up to the creation of Israel on May 14, 1948, generated much emotion as they interpreted political events through the lens of prophecy. [100]

American intellectual Norman Podhoretz presents an important Jewish perspective on how Jewish people since the rise of Christianity saw a darker side of Christian political and religious leaders who failed to adequately protect Jews victimized by violent acts of anti-Semitism.[101] Jews remained wary of Christianity despite the improved Christian-Jewish relations of the twentieth century. After World War II, Christians were sympathetic to the suffering of Jews at the hands of the racist and murderous National Socialists. The humanitarian argument had great momentum. However, liberal Protestant leaders were unenthusiastic about the rise of Zionism. Virginia Gildersleeve, president of Barnard College, was one of a number of anti-Zionists who lobbied policymakers not to embrace the cause of Zionism. She became the chairman of the Committee for Justice and Peace in the Holy Land, an organization that later made links with various anti-Israel lobbyists. Other prominent Protestant leaders such as Harry Emerson Fosdick and Henry Sloane Coffin sought to lessen America's commitment to Israel.[102] Such thinking was far from that of Christian Zionists.

Probably most American Jews and Palestinian Jews (and Israelis after May 14), found the stanch support of Christian Zionism puzzling, if they were aware of such support. American Christian Zionists viewed the emergence of Israel as a very exciting event and they rejected arguments that the Jews were unwilling to share Palestine or that the Jews opposed a two-state solution. Certainly, Christian Zionists did not view American support for Jewish statehood as a bad idea or see Yishuv's defense against Arab violence as an act of Jewish expansionist aggression. The success of Zionism in Palestine and the victorious UN vote, in November 1947, for a Jewish state and an Arab state, clarified to Christian Zionists "that the nations were helpless to defy the announced will of God."[103]

That the United States and the USSR officially recognized the State of Israel was a source of wonderment given the Cold War climate in which the Americans and Soviets were rarely in agreement on major issues. Zionism had come a long way since Theodore Herzl, but the new Jewish state faced a daunting task as Arab nations put military might behind the violent rhetoric of Arabs seeking to destroy the Israeli people, who numbered fewer than 700,000. While Ben-Gurion's reading the Declaration of Independence was a momentous occasion, Jewish defenders of the new state had no time for celebration. The Arabs attacked quickly. Christian Zionists paid attention to the next crucial months for the Jewish state as the Israelis fought for the survival of their nation. It was, in Wilbur Smith's words, a "war for freedom."[104]

NOTES

1. Quoted in Morris, *1948*, 395.

2. Merkley, *Those That Bless You, I Will Bless*, 162. Morris, *1948*, 5–6.

3. Poor housing and sanitary conditions were common. See Leslie Stein, *The Making of Modern Israel, 1948-1967* (Cambridge: Polity Press, 2009), 2.

4. Alan Dershowitz, *The Case for Israel* (Hoboken, NJ: John Wiley and Sons, 2003), 17.

5. Dershowitz, *The Case for Israel*, 6, 8, 14–15, 23–4.

6. Arthur W. Kac, "Prophetic Patterns in the World Today," *Moody Monthly*, May 1960, 29.

7. William Hull, *The Fall and Rise of Israel: The Story of the Jewish People During the time of their Dispersal and Regathering* (Grand Rapids, MI: Zondervan Publishing Company, 1954), 122.

8. Kidd, *American Christians and Islam*, 72.

9. Quoted in Boyer, *When Time Shall Be No More*, 186.

10. Morris, *1948*, 10.

11. Quoted in B. Eugene Griessman, "Philo-Semitism and Protestant Fundamentalism: The Unlikely Zionists," *Phylon* 37, no. 3 (3rd Quarter 1976), 204.

12. "Palestine Mandate in Complete Text," *New York Times*, February 28, 1921.

13. "Palestine Mandate in Complete Text," *New York Times*, February 28, 1921.

14. Donald Neff, "Jerusalem in U.S. Policy," *Journal of Palestine Studies* 23, no. 1 (Autumn 1993), 22.

15. Morris, *1948*, 14–15, 83. For the importance of politics in advancing economic success, see Daron Acemoglu and James A. Robinson, *Why Nations Fail: The Origins of Power, Prosperity, and Power* (New York: Crown Business, 2012).

16. Kidd, *American Christians and Islam*, 73.

17. Kidd, *American Christians and Islam*, 84.

18. Stein, *The Making of Modern Israel*, 69.

19. For Arab perceptions of the Haganah, see Sarah Ozacky-Lazar and Mustafa Kabha, "The *Haganah* by Arab and Palestinian Historiography and Media,' *Israel Studies* 7, no. 3 (Fall 2002): 45–60.

20. Shindler, *A History of Modern Israel*, 41.

21. Quoted in Morris, *1948*, 22.

22. Wallace Murray to Joseph Grew, March 20, 1945, *Foreign Relations of the United States* (*FRUS*) 1945, 8: 694–95.

23. Quoted in Evan M. Wilson, *Decision on Palestine: How the U.S. Came to Recognize Israel* (Stanford, CA: Hoover Institutional Press, 1979), 49.

24. Evans, *Decision on Palestine*, 49–51. See Roosevelt's letter to Ibn Saud in Evans's appendixes, 180–81.

25. Allis and Ronald Radosh, *A Safe Haven: Harry S. Truman and the Founding of Israel* (New York: Harper Perennial, 2009), 26–28.

26. Quoted in Robert W. Ross, *So It Was True: The American Protestant Press and the Nazi Persecution of the Jews* (Eugene, OR.: Wipf and Stock Publishers, 1998), 178.

27. Quoted in David A. Rausch, "Our Hope: An American Fundamentalist Journal and the Holocaust, 1937–1945," in *Fundamentalism and Evangelicalism*, ed. Martin E. Marty (New York: K.G. Saur, 1993), 193.

28. Quoted in Rausch, "Our Hope," 197.

29. Rausch, "Our Hope," 199.

30. Boyer, *When Time Shall Be No More*, 187.

31. However, Niebuhr's "neo-orthodox" understanding set him apart from many other liberal theologians. Also, see Kidd, *American Christians and Islam*, 87.

32. Paul Charles Merkley, *American Presidents, Religion, and Israel: The Heirs of Cyrus* (Westport, Conn.: Praeger, 2004). For more on Truman, see Radosh, *A Safe Haven.*.

33. Quoted in Michael J. Cohen, "Truman and Palestine, 1945–1948: Revisionism, Politics and Diplomacy," *Modern Judaism* 2, no. 1 (February 1982), 4.

34. Radosh, *A Safe Haven*, 47–48.

35. Hull, *The Fall and Rise of Israel*, 259–60. According to Hull, the British would only implement it if the illegal armies in Palestine surrendered their arms and that there was significant American assistance.

36. Donald Grey Barnhouse, "Near-East Pressure Cooker," *Eternity*, July 1956, 11.

37. *Christian Century*, April 23, 1947, 515.

38. Quoted in Hull, *The Fall and Rise of Israel*, 272.

39. Hull, *The Fall and Rise of Israel*, 270.

40. From Winnipeg, Manitoba, Hull and his wife spent twenty-eight years in Jerusalem. See "Ruffled Relations," *Christianity Today*, March 29, 1963, 32.

41. Carl Hermann Voss and David A. Rausch, "American Christians and Israel, 1948–1988," *American Jewish Archives* 40 (April 1988), 46.

42. H. W. Brands, *Into the Labyrinth: The United States and the Middle East, 1945–1993* (New York: McGraw Hill, 1994), xiii. Brands states that "American relations with the Middle East were frequently reactive, consisting of ad hoc responses to regional crises."

43. Robert McClintock to Dean Rusk, July 1, 1948, *FRUS* 1948, 5: 1173.

44. Quoted in Morris, *1948*, 61.

45. Morris, *1948*, 69.

46. Michael J. Hogan and Thomas G. Patterson, "Introduction," in *Explaining the History of American Foreign Relations*, 2nd ed., eds. Michael J. Hogan and Thomas G. Patterson (Cambridge: Cambridge University Press, 2004), 3.

47. Wilson, *Decision on Palestine*, 117–18. For a 1946 memorandum written by Wilson promoting a bi-national state, see 79–87.

48. Shindler, *A History of Modern Israel*, 45.

49. T. Decourcey Rayner quoted in Weber, *On the Road to Armageddon*, 168.

50. Hull, *The Fall and Rise of Israel*, 283.

51. F. Dean Lueking, "Hopeful Voices from Israel," *Christian Century*, February 4, 1970, 139.

52. United Nations, General Assembly, United Nations Palestine Commission, A/AC.21/9-S/676, February 16, 1948.

53. Quoted in Morris, *1948*, 50, 70.

54. Sicker, *Israel's Quest for Security*, 13. Abdullah hinted that Arab Palestine be part of Transjordan. Key Palestinian Arab leaders distrusted neighboring Arab leaders. See Morris, *1948*, 46, 67, 72.

55. Morris, *1948*, 81, 85, 90.

56. Sicker, *Israel's Quest for Security*, 14–18; Morris, *1948*, 100.

57. Morris, *1948*, 81.

58. Hull, *The Fall and Rise of Israel*, 288, 295–96.

59. Ben-Gurion, *Israel: A Personal History* (New York: Funk and Wagnalls, Inc., 1971), 66.

60. Hull, *The Fall and Rise of Israel*, 284.

61. Ariel Sharon, *Warrior: The Autobiography of Ariel Sharon* (New York: Simon and Schuster, 1989), 45.

62. Morris, *1948*, 105.

63. Morris, *1948*, 108, 111. Hull, *The Fall and Rise of Israel*, 287.

64. Hull, *The Fall and Rise of Israel*, 298–99; Morris, *1948*, 107.

65. Hull, *The Fall and Rise of Israel*, 300–301. John Glubb, the commander of the Arab Legion, viewed Stern members as murderers, not war soldiers. Glubb, *A Soldier with the Arabs*, 93.

66. Morris, *1948*, 94.

67. Morris, *1948*, 87, 117–18.

68. Menachem Begin, *The Revolt*, Rev. ed. (New York: Dell Publishing Company, 1978), 225–27.

69. Morris, *1948*, 126-27, 153. Also, see Sami Adwan et al., eds., *Side by Side: Parallel Histories of Israel-Palestine* (New York: Prime, 2012), 125.

70. Hull, *The Fall and Rise of Israel*, 309.

71. Harry Levin, *Jerusalem Embattled: A Diary of the City under Siege, March 25th, 1948 to July 18th, 1948* (London: Victor Gollancz Ltd, 1950), 59. Levin wrote: "Most Jews I have spoken with are horrified."

72. Radosh, *A Safe Haven*, 314.

73. Cattan, *Palestine, the Arabs and Israel*, 44.

74. Glubb, *A Soldier with the Arabs*, 81.

75. Quoted in Cattan, *Palestine, the Arabs and Israel*, 43.

76. Levin, *Embattled Jerusalem*, 281-82.

77. Hull, *The Fall and Rise of Israel*, 329.

78. Morris, *1948*, 94–96.

79. Quoted in Shindler, *A History of Modern Israel*, 50.

80. Hull, *The Fall and Rise of Israel*, 308. Levin, *Jerusalem Embattled*, 68–71.

81. Quoted in Morris, *1948*, 128–29.

82. Morris, *1948*, 170.

83. Morris, *1948*, 143.

84. Douglas Little, *American Orientalism: The United States and the Middle East since 1945* (Chapel Hill: University of North Carolina 2002), 85. On Israeli influence on Truman, see Peter L. Hahn, "The View from Jerusalem: Revelations about U.S. Diplomacy from the Archives of Israel," *Diplomatic History* 22, no. 4 (Fall 1998), 513. For Truman's thoughts about the State Department and career officials, see Harry S. Truman, *Memoirs by Harry S. Truman, Volume Two: Years of Trial and Hope* (Garden City, NY: Doubleday and Company, 1956), 164–65.

85. For a good overview of this episode, see Radosh, *A Safe Haven*, 301–309.

86. Robert D. Kaplan, *The Arabists: The Romance of an American Elite* (New York: Simon and Schuster, 1995), 80. Also, Voss and Rausch, "American Christians and Israel," 54–55.

87. *Christian Century*, May 5, 1948, 404.

88. *Christian Century*, May 12, 1948, 456.

89. Shindler, *A History of Modern Israel*, 38–39.

90. Levin, *Embattled Jerusalem*, 155.

91. Quoted in Ben-Gurion, *Israel*, 79. Zvi Zameret writes: "Ben-Gurion refused to define himself as 'secular,' and he regarded himself a believer in God." See Zvi Zameret, "Judaism in Israel: Ben-Gurion's Private Beliefs and Public Policy," *Israel Studies* 4, no. 2 (Fall 1999): 65.

92. Hull, *The Fall and Rise of Israel*, 323.

93. Elihu Bergman, "Unexpected Recognition: Some Observations on the Failure of a Last-Gasp Campaign in the U.S. State Department to Abort a Jewish State," *Modern Judaism* 19, no. 2 (1999), 133; Bruce J. Evensen, "A Story of 'Ineptness': The Truman Administration's Struggle to Shape Conventional Wisdom on Palestine at the Beginning of the Cold War," *Diplomatic History* 15, no. 3 (July, 1991), 358. Chaim Weizmann described Truman's decision as "providential." See Schoenbaum, *The United States and the State of Israel*, 79. For the argument that the U.S. recognition of the new state was of secondary importance to the Truman administration and the Jews in Palestine, see Michael Ottolenghi, "Harry Truman's Recognition of Israel," *The Historical Journal* 47, no. 4 (December 2004): 963–88.

94. Merkley, *American Presidents, Religion, and Israel*, 14. Also, see Radosh, *A Safe Haven*, 325-39.

95. Wilson, *Decision on Palestine*, 5. Approximately one and half years after the CIA predicted that partition was attainable, it acknowledged that "the present state of Israel represents a remarkable accomplishment." Quoted in Schoenbaum, *The United States and the State of Israel*, 69.

96. "Palestine and the Jews," *Moody Monthly*, November 1948, 202–203.

97. Wilbur Smith, *World Crises and the Prophetic Scriptures* (Chicago: Moody Press, 1951), 180–81.

98. Hull, *The Fall and Rise of Israel*, 323, 325. He wrote: "one could almost hear the trumpets sounding, heralding the approach of Messiah."

99. See Boyer, *When Time Shall Be No More*, 187. Clark, *Allies for Armageddon*, 144.

100. Those who closely followed biblical prophecy saw world history unfolding biblically when the Jews returned and reestablished a Jewish state in the Holy Land. One critic of Christian Zionism claimed, "everything was riding on the Jews." See Weber, *On the Road to Armageddon*, 13.

101. Norman Podhoretz, *Why Are Jews Liberals?* (New York: Doubleday 2009).

102. Paul Charles Merkley, *Christian Attitudes towards the State of Israel* (Montreal: McGill-Queen's University Press, 2001), 6–7.

103. Merkley, *Christian Attitudes towards the State of Israel*, 5.

104. Voss and Rausch, "American Christians and Israel," 61.

TWO

The Pan-Arab Invasion

Half a year after the United Nations approved the plan for a Jewish state, Arab leaders still talked about annihilating the Jews. On May 15, 1948, the secretary-general of the Arab League promised the destruction of the Jewish state: "This will be a war of extermination and a momentous massacre which will be spoken of like the Mongolian massacres and the Crusades."[1] Formed in 1945, the Arab League consisted of Egypt, Iraq, Saudi Arabia, Syria, Lebanon, Trans-Jordan, and Yemen. The immediate and serious problem for the new State of Israel was the attacking Arab force of Egyptians, Syrians, Jordanians, Lebanese, and Iraqis which added to the Palestinian Arab fighters engaged in the previous six months of "unofficial fighting." It was now a full-blown war with many of the Israeli soldiers fatigued from the earlier months of fighting.

The equipment and firepower of the four invading armies of May 15 "were far stronger" and Jewish military leaders gave Israel a "fifty-fifty" chance of success.[2] A major problem was weapons: heavy weapons were rare and only 60 percent of the Jewish troops had guns.[3] Yitzhak Rabin, future prime minister, remembered the sense of dread among soldiers as they faced the perilous task of defending Israel: "We were frail corks, being used to stop up hundreds of holes in a leaky dam, that a flood of our enemies might be expected at any time to overwhelm and drown us." The situation remained harrowing because "[t]here were never enough of us, and so many had already been killed. As fast as we stopped one leak, we would be withdrawn and rushed somewhere else to plug another."[4] Representing the thoughts of many, Jewish resident Hagai Horvitz saw the Arab invasion as a continuation of the Holocaust: "We, the Jews of the Land of Israel, were meant to be annihilated. . . . It was obvious that we were fighting for our very existence. . . . [I]f we did not win, we would

be annihilated was one of the foundational experiences of that generation, and so we fought."[5]

Tested repeatedly until the signing of armistice agreements in the first
half of 1949, Israel survived and made territorial gains to its political
borders approved by the United Nations in November 1947. Among
those most enthusiastic about this stunning development were American
conservative Christians. In fact, Christian Zionists were confident from
the beginning that the Jews would see victory. Having experienced firsthand the violence in Jerusalem, Christian Zionist William Hull explained
that "God was with Israel in 1948 as the Arab attack got under way, and
no one could doubt that the side God was on would be victorious."[6]

The Israelis were thankful for the diplomatic recognition by the United States and the USSR, but the new nation faced a serious threat to its
existence as fresh Arab armies fought Jews wearied from fighting Palestinian Arabs and others since late 1947. The loss of 753 soldiers was
significant.[7] Israel needed all able-bodied Jews to contribute in its fight
for survival and among the newer arrivals were World War II Jewish
soldiers from all over the world, many battle-hardened. Examples included Americans and Canadians who fought on the beaches of Nor-
mandy, Danes who fought with the British Royal Air Force, Moroccans
who fought with the Free French, and Poles who fought with the Soviets.
There were many heroic accounts of Jews finding themselves drawn to
the Zionist cause. One story of heroism was a Polish soldier who began
fighting at age sixteen. When the Nazis rolled into Poland with their
blitzkrieg, he fled eastward into the hands of the Soviets, who put him in
the Red Army. At the fierce Battle of Stalingrad where the Soviets turned
the tide against the German invaders, he gained valuable military knowledge, including how an infantryman fought tanks. After fighting on
many fronts, the Soviets transferred him to the Polish Army, where he
became a captain of the Polish Panzer. Two months after his demobiliza-
tion, he heard of the fighting in Palestine. There was nothing to keep him
in Warsaw; his family members were dead, victims of the Holocaust. Like
many other Jews, he answered the call of Zionism.[8] However, the choice
for Jews of all ages was stark: victory or annihilation for Israel.[9]

Although the Arabs saw the military issue differently, believing that
the Jews were militarily stronger and the aggressors, the words and actions of the Jews themselves did not give any evidence of their so-called
military superiority.[10] For Jewish leaders, facing the numerous Arab military operations was a daunting task. Not generally reported in the western press, many Arab fighters had entered Palestine months earlier and
they controlled a number of strategic points. For example, surrounded by
the Arabs, the besieged Jewish quarter of Jerusalem faced hardship for
months as Arabs blocked roads in the area. The shelling of Jerusalem by
King Abdullah's British-trained Arab Legion, known as the best army in
the Arab world, began before the termination of the mandate. British

officials reported the withdrawal of the Legion from Palestine prior to May 15, but William Hull knew otherwise; he saw the Legion in Gaza and Hebron. The commander of the Arab Legion himself wrote that most of his military units were in Palestine before the British departed. Other Arab troops such as the Iraqis were in the Arab city of Jaffa before mid-May.[11]

Consistently hostile to the Jews, King Farouk of Egypt committed his army to defeat the new Jewish state. Overcome by religious fervor, Farouk declared, Arab males "were keen to enter the fray—as the shortest road to Heaven." Muhammad Mamun Shinawi of Egypt's Al-Azhar University stated: "The hour of 'Jihad' has struck. . . . A hundred of you will defeat a thousand of the infidels. . . . This is the hour in which . . . Allah promised paradise." King Abdullah had a similar message for the Arab Legionnaires: "He who will be killed will be a martyr. . . . I remind you of the Jihad and the martyrdom of your great-grandfathers." Muslim mothers shouted to their sons: "God be with you, my son. Don't come back. Martyrdom my son."[12]

The Arab invasion began on midnight, May 16 (the Sabbath) soon after the British Mandate ended. Later in the day, Ben-Gurion went on the radio to tell the people that the nation faced "a titanic political and military struggle" and "a troubled and dangerous time."[13] In his eyes, the earlier UN National Assembly vote to establish the State of Israel appeared forgotten. As Israel's enemies invaded "not one nation lifted a finger to defend the United Nation's decision."[14] Israel's Provisional Government faced grave issues.

Ben-Gurion unified three fighting forces of the Haganah and smaller groups Irgun and the Stern Gang. The Israeli Defense Forces (IDF) consisted of approximately 50,000 soldiers. The IDF faced a Syrian, Lebanese, and Jordanian threat in the north and east and an Egyptian threat in the south. The Israeli position in Jerusalem was precarious. Weeks before the official Arab invasion, Arabs cut off water supplies to the city. The Jews lacked adequate water, food, and fuel for cooking. With rationing, daily food intake was as low as 500 calories.[15] Despite the desperately short supply of trained soldiers, ammunition, water, and food, there were Jewish victories in some parts of Jerusalem. William Hull wrote of the defense of Jerusalem as "a miracle" since the Jews possessed no more than three Bren guns. To fool the Arabs they rushed their Bren guns from one section to another. They also beat large tin cans to give the impression of more guns. The Jewish capture of one Arab district of Jerusalem with two Sten guns, five rifles, and thirty tin cans "was like a repetition of Gideon's victory in Bible days."[16]

However, the attacking Arab forces in mid-May made a major statement. Targeting Israel's largest civilian center, Egypt bombarded Tel Aviv from the air for six straight days, and about 5,500 Egyptian troops attacked isolated Jewish settlements near and along the coast. Whereas one brigade of Syrian (2,750 troops) and Lebanese troops faced fierce Jewish resistance in the north, as many as 6,500 Arab Legionnaires, out of a total force of approximately 9,000, and 2,700 Iraqi troops took control of the West Bank. (By mid-July troops from Yemen, Morocco, Saudi Arabia, and Sudan brought the total number of troops in Palestine to about 50,000.) King Abdullah of Transjordan viewed the early stage of the war in a positive light, pretending to champion the Palestinian cause when in fact he sought to enlarge his kingdom by taking the West Bank. In an early report of the invasion, the *Christian Century* wondered to what degree Arab distrust of other Arabs was behind the military action. [17] Neither the Jordanians nor the Egyptians viewed the Palestinian Arabs as a separate national group. In fact, the majority of Palestinians lacked clear sense of a national identity; not until the late 1960s did strong Palestinian national aspirations captur the attention of the world. Historians note that the Arab states were wary of "one another's territorial ambitions in Palestine," resulting in poor coordination of military tactics. [18] There was much Arab misinformation about the war as Arab leaders sought to bolster their political positions in the eyes of the world. False news reports exaggerated or invented Arab military successes which seemed reasonable to the many journalists who expected the Arabs to triumph militarily. [19]

Israel's most serious military threat was the Arab Legion, a highly mechanized army seeking to score victories in Nablus to the northwest, Ramallah to the west, and East Jerusalem. To the south of Jerusalem, several platoons of Legionnaires, local fighters, Egyptian army troops, and Muslim Brotherhood fighters targeted the Kibbutz Ramat Rachel. After fierce back and forth fighting, the Israelis won and thus were able to protect the Jerusalem-Bethlehem road. Eastern Jerusalem was another matter as Israeli fighters tried to hold ground, in some cases with mostly teenage fighters. The Legionnaires blew up the Hurva Synagogue, the most hallowed Jewish house of worship in the Old City. On May 28, the Israelis surrendered the Jewish Quarter of Jerusalem, unable to withstand the pounding of their position by the Arab Legion. [20]

There was also military failure to the west of Jerusalem. In three battles, the IDF failed to capture the key center Latrun along the Tel Aviv-Jerusalem road. Pinned down by Legion mortar, machine gun, and rifle fire in the first Latrun battle, Lieutenant Ariel Sharon, future prime minister, received serious wounds to his leg and stomach. He wrote: "I felt something thud into my belly, knocking me back. I heard my mouth say 'imah'–mother, and the instant it was out I glanced around to see if anybody had heard. Already blood was seeping through my shirt and from my shorts, where another wound in my thigh had appeared as if by magic." The bullet entered his stomach and exited his upper leg, the strange angle explained by the fact that the Jordanians fired down on the trapped Israelis. Later, as Sharon watched the Arabs looting and mutilating the bodies of the many dead Israeli soldiers, he motioned for his badly-injured men to quietly retreat in the hope that the Arabs would not see them. Unable to walk, Sharon crawled to safety before passing out.[21] Although unable to take Latrun, the Israelis built the "Burma Road"—an alternate supply route to West Jerusalem in full operation by June 10. The Israeli forces benefited with a steady supply of weapons from Czechoslovakia, arms that the IDF badly needed.[22]

From Egypt came deadly air attacks. Spitfires and other aircraft hitting Tel Aviv caused the most damage on May 18 when forty-two civilians died. With its ground attack, the Egyptian army crossed into Palestine on May 15–16, but two smaller forces composed of Muslim Brotherhood and regular Egyptian army volunteers had entered in April and early May. The main Egyptian army progressed north into the Gaza Strip while a portion of the army split off to the northeast, occupying Beersheba, passing through Hebron, and reaching Bethlehem. The Egyptian presence in the Jerusalem region was due to Cairo's distrust of a complete takeover of the West Bank by the Jordanians. In the Bethlehem-Hebron area, quarreling between the Jordanians and Egyptians was common; they even bickered over the size of each other's flags flown in the respective towns they controlled. As for the western coastal region, the Israelis prevented the Egyptians from reaching Tel Aviv, but the price was high for many of the Israelis living in the various settlements which became stubborn obstacles for the Arab forces. When the Egyptians pounded Kibbutz Nitzanim, the settlement opted for surrender after thirty-three died and with no sign of reinforcements. The Egyptians murdered at least two others, including the outpost commander and radiowoman as they approached the victors with a white flag. The Egyptians were not done. A component of their force along the coast drove eastward to connect with the earlier Egyptian invasion force located south of Jerusalem, thereby establishing Egyptian control of a west-east axis, and thus isolating Jewish settlements to the south of the axis.[23]

As for the Arab invasions of the north, participants included Iraqi soldiers numbering approximately 4,500 at the start. Even though their number eventually grew to 18,000 soldiers, they failed in their goal of reaching Haifa. The Syrians had about 10,000 soldiers, of which 2,000 crossed into Palestine from the Golan Heights on May 15 only to fall short in gaining a stronghold in the region south of the Sea of Galilee. Syria did, however, capture the northeast shoreline of Lake Tiberias and a portion of territory west of the Jordan River north of the lake. The goal of the Lebanese army, numbering 3,500 troops, was more modest, owing to the large number of Christians in Lebanon. One Israeli concluded that "in their hearts the [Lebanese] Christians are happy with the establishment of the State of Israel."[24] The only Lebanese military success was conquering the Jewish garrison at al-Malikiya on June 5. After a month of fighting, all the Arab armies were short of their military objectives. The territory occupied by the Jordanians and Iraqis west of the Jordan River and the Egyptians south of Jerusalem was land allotted to the Palestinians Arabs by the 1947 UN report. Israel retained most of its territory and conquered some land set aside for the Palestinian Arabs.[25]

What became a common narrative in the Arab world was that the Israelis were the aggressors seeking to expand their borders. In the *Christian Century*, Yusif El-Bandak saw the actions of the Arabs as defensive: "following the British withdrawal, the Zionist forces swept across the country spreading havoc and destruction among the unarmed Palestine Christian and Moslem citizens."[26] Often ignored or downplayed was the actual reality of an *Arab* invasion in mid-May. Instead, the focus was on the Arabs defending their lands, homes, and historical rights "against an alien invasion." Israel was a foreign occupier assisted by the imperialist forces, Britain first, followed by the United States.[27]

The first break in the war was due to the UN truce of June 11–July 9. The United Nations appointed Count Folke Bernadotte of Sweden as a mediator, but neither the Israelis nor Arabs trusted the UN. At an Israeli cabinet meeting in mid-June, Foreign Minister Moshe Sharret declared that Israel should neither surrender the land given under the November 29, 1947, UN resolution nor any land "conquered in a struggle that was forced upon us." In order to defend the sprawling Jewish settlements, it was vital to control western Galilee and the Jerusalem area. The UN resolution providing a large Arab region between the State of Israel and Jerusalem was now unacceptable. The road to Jerusalem and the western entrance to the city was "one of the territorial changes that we must safeguard at all costs."[28] In essence, the UN resolution of November 1947 was a dead letter. Israeli leaders understood that the political question was now a military one. Ben-Gurion stated: "The political issues will be decided by our ability to triumph militarily should war break out. . . . The war is not yet over; there is only a truce. If war breaks again, it will be a life-death struggle *for us*, but not for them."[29]

The Security Council's truce and the provisions prohibiting the entrance of fighting personnel and war matériel into the region appeared to put the Israelis at a disadvantage to the Arabs, who had stockpiles of weapons and who could recruit for their armed forces from the large in-country manpower reserves.[30] However, the Israelis found a way to replenish their arms supplies with purchases from Eastern bloc countries. The Soviets bypassed the May 29 UN Security Council embargo on arms to the Middle East by way of proxies such as Czechoslovakia. One reason for the Soviet Union's military assistance to Israel was its assessment that Israeli military success would lead to British withdrawal from the region. During the June–July truce, Israel received from Czechoslovakia seventy-five fighter planes (Messerschmidts and Spitfires) and thousands of rifles and machine guns. The Israelis also had the ability to manufacture some of its own weapons, an industry lacking among the Arabs.[31] In acquiring weapons and reinforcing their military positions, both the Arabs and the Israelis violated the truce. However, the Israelis gained the most.

The Arabs' agreement to a truce was a miscalculation. When fighting renewed, Israel, with its strengthened air force, began to bomb Cairo, Amman, and Damascus. Operation Dani resulted in Israeli gains on the central front against the Arab Legion. In the north, Israeli forces defeated the irregular Arab Liberation Army and captured much of Galilee and the large military camp at Sarafand. Hull wrote of Israeli commandos taking Sarafand by lassoing high trees close to the camp and swinging safely above the extensive minefield and barbed-wire defense surrounding the camp.[32]

But the Provisional Government confronted another problem—political instability that slipped dangerously toward civil war as a result of the Irgun being slow to accept a central authority. In June, Ben-Gurion made the difficult decision to attack the *Altalena*, a ship commissioned by the Irgun to smuggle 5,000 rifles, 270 light machine guns, and other weapons into the region. When confronted by the IDF and told to surrender the ship to the government near the coast of Israel, the Irgun refused and insisted it take part in any distribution of the weapons. After two separate violent skirmishes between the IDF and the Irgun there were fourteen dead Irgun and two dead IDF soldiers.[33] In his memoirs Abba Eban explained that Ben-Gurion had no choice: "How could Israel claim the recognition of our own citizens, still less of the outside world, if our army was only one of several militias, each one serving its own political ideology and program?" Rather than May 15, Israeli sovereignty came "on June 28 when an oath of allegiance was taken by all the armed forces and the Irgun ceased to function as a separate force."[34] With the Irgun and the Stern Gang discredited, the IDF could proceed as the unified force for Israel's security.

Hostilities resumed when the Egyptians launched a preemptive strike on July 8 (one day before the end of the first truce). The following day, Israel went on the offensive to break the Egyptian west-east axis south of Jerusalem with inconclusive results. The IDF had better success in the eastern and central theatres with the most important conquests in the regions of Galilee and Lydda-Ramla, all carried out before the UN Security Council imposed a second truce on July 19, which ushered in a three-month period of no major battles.

During this interlude some Americans argued for better accommodation of the needs of Arabs. For example, Daniel Bliss proposed in the *Christian Century* that the only feasible political solution was the formation of a federal union of Jewish and Arab states.[35] Given the violence and the growing number of Arab refugees, many in liberal Protestant circles had little enthusiasm for the Jewish state. It was a waiting game to see what the United Nations recommended. In August, Bernadotte presented his plan to solve the Arab-Israeli conflict: Israel was to repatriate

Palestinian refugees, there was a revision of political borders (Israel would lose the Negev, but gain the western Galilee), and the governing of Jerusalem was to be by an international body. Moshe Sharret saw the plan as "a complete capitulation to Anglo-Arab pressure." And the Arabs rejected the plan for its lack of provisions for a Palestinian state and its stipulation that Arabs recognize and negotiate with Israel.[36] Bernadotte submitted his unpopular plan to the United Nations on September 16. The following day Jewish terrorists murdered him with an automatic pistol as he sat in one car of a three-car UNO convoy.[37] Outraged Israeli officials expressed remorse, but the arrest of 200 Stern Gang members fell short of bringing the actual killers to justice.[38] The *Christian Century* declared that the Israeli government could not evade responsiblity for the assassination since its "propaganda" defaming Bernadotte as "a British tool" encouraged the assassins.[39] In some circles, Israel's government did not receive much credit for seeing that both the Irgun and Stern Gang organizations ceased to exist (although the Herut political party did grow out of the Irgun). However, Gabriel Courier of the conservative *Christian Herald* argued that Israelis leaders were "innocent" of the assassination; the guilty party was the "lawless, barbarously ignorant Stern gang."[40]

The brutal assassination prompted the U.S. State Department to promote Bernadotte's plan with greater vigor; the liberal Protestants of *Christian Century* saw the plan "as equitable as could be devised in the light of the current situation."[41] However, Arab leaders concluded that the assassination was additional evidence of the impossibility of peaceful relations between Jews and Arabs. Arabs became more intransigent. Mushin Barazi, Syria's foreign minister, linked Bernadotte's plan to the "Zionist rape of Palestine."[42] Ben-Gurion also had little faith in any political solution from the United Nations, and in late September he declared: "If we do not take measures ourselves to make territorial adjustments, or at least the most vital ones, they will not be made at all. . . . We must be ready to exploit the military factor whenever and wherever necessary."[43]

During the second truce, the Egyptian expeditionary force grew to 12,000 and three Saudi Arabian battalions joined the mix. Of significant concern for Israeli leaders was Egyptian control of key areas of the Negev, a barren area lacking water, but, nonetheless, necessary for Israel's future settlement and security. And the UN resolution of 1947 had slated this land for a Jewish state. When the Egyptians failed to honor the truce arrangements permitting Israel to send supplies south, the Israelis took action. In mid-October, they began Operation Ten Plagues (named after the afflictions of Egypt told in the Book of Exodus), a plan that saw the Egyptians withdrawal from much of the Negev.[44] Important for the future development of Israel was the Gulf of Aquaba. The town of Eilat was the arrival and departure point for Israeli contact with Africa and Asia.[45]

The UN Security Council established a cease-fire for October 19, something the IDF was in no hurry to respect. But the Arabs were also defiant, obvious in the north when the ALA attacked the IDF west of the Hula Valley on October 22. The Israelis prevailed and by the end of the month the ALA fled to Lebanon.[46] In mid-November, the UN Security Council resolved to establish an armistice for all parties directly involved in the war. But the Egyptians and other Arab refused to enter negotiations with Israel. On December 22, Israel launched another campaign causing the complete Egyptian withdrawal from the Negev. Egyptian defeat in Palestine prompted a Muslim Brotherhood member to assassinate the Egyptian prime minister in late December. Israeli forces also pushed deep into the Sinai Peninsula before being ordered back by Ben-Gurion as a result of British pressure. He took seriously the threat of intervention by the British, who were unhappy with the Israeli territorial acquisitions. Adding to this was the strong warning from President Truman to withdraw; Ben-Gurion was unwilling to jeopardize good relations with the United States. In the end, interventions by the United Nations and the British and Americans prevented the Israeli destruction of the Egyptian army remaining in Palestine.[47]

With the exception of the Arab Legion in control of the West Bank, there were no Arab military forces in what once was Palestine.[48] The Arabs withdrew behind their borders, waiting and planning another day to destroy Israel. Some linked Arab troubles to the shortcomings of Islamic ideas. *Time* magazine stated that "Islam is poor, a sad fate for the only great religion founded by a successful businessman" and "divided and headless, a painful fate for a religion founded by a first-rate practical politician."[49] Looking to the future for better military success, the Syrians and Lebanese wanted the western Galilee, the Egyptians wanted the Negev, and the Jordanians wanted a corridor to the sea.[50] Something had to be done to readdress the 1948 episode that the Arabs called the catastrophe—*al-Nakba*. It was difficult for many Arabs to comprehend Jewish success. Common was the belief that the Arab military forces would prevail over the Jews. Even before May 15, some Arab political and military leaders had selected Tel Aviv homes which they would take possession in the near future.[51]

A major issue in the wake of the war was the plight of Palestinian Arab refugees. One consequence of the Arab attention given to the Deir Yassin massacre was the exodus of thousands of Palestinian Arabs and Christians from their homes in fear of the Jews who increasingly scored military victories in key areas of Palestine. According to Christian Arab Christina Jouzeh, the Arabs saw the West as a Jewish supplier of weapons that the Arabs did not have. In truth, American, British, and other western governments did not supply Israel with weapons in 1948. With no mention of the Arab armies at war with the Jews, Jouzeh wrote of her family driven from their home without their belongings. Although the Jews had used radios and loudspeakers to invite Arabs to stay, "their cruel, sadistic actions" spoke louder than their words: "Only too well do I know the sound and terror of Zionist explosions and bombings, which were contrived in order to scare the Arabs out of the country."[52]

There is wide disagreement of the number of Palestinian refugees for this period; a UN mediator counted 472,000 whereas others put the number in the 520,000 to 900,000 range. Whatever the true number, Christian Zionists such as Hull saw the Arab flight as "mysterious, miraculous." The Arab people left "because their leaders had left and because God put fear in their hearts." The flight was a "tragic disaster" for the Arabs, but it was God's timing that the Jews "should return to their own land."[53]

Immediately after the war, Arab leaders demanded the Israelis allow all refugees to return to their homes in land now part of Israel. Israeli leaders pointed out that it was the Arabs who denied a Palestinian state with their opposition to a two-state solution. Viewing the Arab refugees as a Trojan horse, Israel refused the return of all Palestinian refugees. For security reasons, as Israeli leaders interpreted it, the partition plan of 1947 became a dead document when the Arabs went to war.[54] It was also significant that nearby Arab states were reluctant to absorb the refugees and that the Mufti opposed any return of refugees while Israel still existed. In August 1949, the Israelis did agree to the return of 100,000 refugees, but the Arab states rejected this offer.[55]

Approximately half of the Palestinian population were refugees and they expected the combined Arab armies in the region to recover and again wage war on Israel. But it was never clear if Arab states would allow Palestinian statehood.[56] Actually, even the neighboring Arabs viewed the Palestinian refugees as a security threat.[57] Many Palestinian Arabs were in a sad state. Egypt refused to give citizenship to the 200,000 to 300,000 Palestinian refugees living in the Gaza Strip. Some historians argue that Arab leaders were open to negotiate with Israeli leaders, but the Arab masses viewed the Jews with even greater hatred and hostility after the War of Independence.[58] So why did neighboring Arab states oppose absorbing the Palestinian refugees? Arab apologist Henry Catton wrote that Arab states were economically unable to absorb them and were against the idea of resettling "them against their wishes."[59]

Angry and bitter about their tragic losses, Palestinians were increasingly reluctant to acknowledge that the Holocaust occurred. Seeing themselves as victims, they denied the victimhood of the Jews because it gave Israel "some moral justification." Denial was also a way for Arabs to reconcile their military loss in 1948 to a people who experienced helplessness throughout the Second World War. And denial was a way for the Palestinians to have the world "recognize their national disaster as an equal if not greater tragedy." Actually, a historical revision of the Holocaust began earlier. In May 1945, the Arab journal *Filastin* claimed that the Jews "grossly overstated the number of their victims in Europe, in order to gain the world's support for their imagined catastrophe."[60]

In the period December 1947 to 1949, Israel with a population of 650,000 lost close to 6,000 soldiers and civilians, the equivalent of the United States losing 2 million. Almost half of the Jews who enlisted in the war had arrived from Europe in the 1939 to 1948 period. Their desire for the shelter of their new land "was intense, instinctive and determined" and many of the newcomers who died defending Israel were Holocaust survivors.[61] Recounting the War of Independence, Ben-Gurion wrote: "No other modern state was invaded on the day of its creation, outnumbered 40 to one, and drove back all its enemies."[62] The small nation surprised many in standing against six nations numbering 30,000,000, but Ben Gurion warned in January 1949 for Israel not to be intoxicated with victory: "The enemy forces in the neighboring countries and in the world at large have not yet despaired of their scheme to annihilate Israel in its own land or at least to pare away its borders, and we do not yet know whether the recent war, which we fought in the Negev and which ended in victory for the IDF, is the last battle or not, and as long as we cannot be confident that we have won the last battle, let us not glory."[63]

Although Israel defended itself successfully and did prevent an Arab victory, the conflict concluded with no peace settlement. What followed were four armistice agreements in 1949: Israel signed with Egypt in February, with Lebanon in March, with Transjordan in April, and with Syria in July. For one Syrian journalist, the armistice agreements were a shameful mark to "endure as long as that abominable state, known as Israel, remains within the heart of the Arab world."[64] As for Israel's military capabilities, the UN Security Council embargo on arms shipment to the Middle East practically only applied to Israel because British arms shipments to Arab countries continued after the War of Independence. It was the Israeli hope that the Tripartite Declaration of May 25, 1950, was the answer to this unfair arrangement. The American, British, and French authors of the declaration pledged joint action against a nation in the Middle East acquiring and using weapons for "any act of aggression against any other state." But troublesome for Israeli leaders was that the United States, Britain, and France were willing to sell arms to Arab nations, but not to Israel, thus confirming to the Israelis that they were mostly on their own concerning security.[65]

With this obstacle, Israel explored various avenues to acquire weapons. For example, the Israelis put in a request to the Canadian government for twent-five-pounder artillery and Browning machine guns. The Canadians agreed to sell the "defensive" artillery, but not the "attack" machine guns. One Canadian official explained: "You see, most of the Cabinet Ministers served in the First World War, and they remember how they would emerge from the trenches and go over the top carrying machine-guns to attack the enemy. It's your luck that they didn't go over the top carrying 25-pounders!"[66] Nonetheless, this rare acquisition from a western nation was a bonus. It took creativity and persistence for Israel to acquire necessary weapons typically denied to them.

One Israeli achievement was a diplomatic one when Israel gained admittance to UN membership on May 11, 1949. Political gains followed. On December 13, Israeli leaders chose Jerusalem as the home for the Knesset. The key politician remained David Ben-Gurion, head of the government of Yishuv since 1935 and Israel's first prime minister. By early 1950, the Knesset declared Jerusalem as the capital of Israel, and, in April, Transjordan (renamed Jordan the following month) officially annexed the eastern part of Palestine (the West Bank), previously occupied by the Arab Legion; thus, a ruling minority of Jordanians became the rulers of a Palestinian majority. Israel's Knesset consisted of a one-chamber, 120-member Constituent Assembly. The Israeli electoral system was proportional representation in which Jewish and Arab citizens voted for a political party rather than a candidate. Although only parties with at least 1 percent of the votes qualified for representation, there were numerous political parties resulting in fragile coalitions and frequent downfalls of government over the years. The party with the largest number of votes formed the government. There was a strong socialist presence in Israeli politics, and the second largest party in the first Knesset was Mapam—a Marxist Zionist party. In 1948, the Mapam programme declared support for a "classless socialist society . . . fulfilling the historic mission of the October Revolution." From its beginning and for almost thirty years, Israel's leading party was social democratic.[67] In the 1949 to 1969 period, religious Zionists and the "ultra-orthodox" received only 12 to 15 percent of electoral votes.[68]

The government's best strategy for Israel's security was by building settlements on its expanded borders. Ben-Gurion had no patience with those leftist Israeli leaders who promoted the establishment of a state for the Palestinian Arabs in the West Bank, consistent with the idea of a Jewish-Arab workers' solidarity.[69] For survival, Jewish immigration to Israel was essential. In 1949 and 1950, immigrants, most of them with few worldly possessions, flowed into Israel, resulting in 229 new settlements. For many "tired of being wandering Jews," Israel was home and the land of promise.[70] The government's 1950 Law of Return granted any Jew the right to immigrate to Israel providing that they were not "engaged in an activity directed against the Jewish people" and were not a threat "to endanger public health." The Jewish Law defining a Jew as someone born of a Jewish mother held sway despite opposition by those who preferred a more open definition.[71]

Most Jews in Israel were immigrants from Europe, but immigration patterns changed. One consequence of the Arab defeat in 1948 was the rise of discrimination and persecution of Jews in many Arab nations.[72] For example, an enforced exodus of Jews in Iraq resulted in 93 percent of Iraqi Jews departing, and almost every Jew living in Yemen arrived in

Israel by way of Operation Magic Carpet, a DC-4 Skymasters around-the-clock air campaign. In later years, Jews from Islamic countries accounted for about 80 percent of the annual emigration to Israel. The Arab sympathizers claiming Israel was an intruding outpost of western civilization gave little or no attention to the fact that half of the Israeli population descended from Jews fleeing brutality in Arab nations. More traditional and respectful of religion, the Sephardim (Jews from Arab countries) found European Enlightenment and socialist ideas advanced by the Ashkenazi Jews alien.[73]

American Christian commentators paid close attention to many Israel topics. Henry Sloane Coffin, an editorial writer of *Christianity and Crisis*, viewed Israel as the product of "fanatical Jewish nationalism."[74] Other mainline Protestant magazines, such as *Lutheran* and the *Christian Century*, gave much attention to the humanitarian concerns of Arab refugees.[75] The *Christian Century* provided good analysis and commentary of the Arab-Israeli conflict and several other Israel topics, but its overall message was a pessimistic one. It was unenthusiastic with Truman's decision to recognize the State of Israel; it saw the action as mainly a political move to ensure the New York Jewish vote.[76] The *Christian Century* was also critical of Truman appointing pro-Zionist James G. McDonald as the first American diplomatic representative to the State of Israel. It was "a shocking perversion of the very idea of a diplomatic service" to send someone to Israel unqualified to provide the United States "impartial, dependable counsel."[77] McDonald voiced candid statements, including the observation that the British government and Count Bernadotte colluded on plans unfavorable to the Israelis.[78] At this early stage, liberal Protestants foreshadowed a less than enthusiastic attitude toward any signs of pro-Zionism. Writing in the *Christian Century*, Ernest Lefever of Yale Divinity School was certain that the majority of American Christians living in the Middle East were anti-Zionist: "They regard the establishment of Israel as a grave injustice to the native people of the Holy Land."[79]

Ben-Gurion's policies often received much criticism in the *Christian Century* and liberal Protestant commentary of the war reveals the emergence of specific criticisms of Israel not found in evangelical literature. Worried that the War of Independence threatened "to turn the Holy Land into a shambles," it welcomed arguments for either an Arab-Jewish federal state or a federation of Arab and Jewish states. The latter would have an economic union, common defense arrangements, and Jerusalem as the capital of the federation. The magazine also wanted to see the return of the 300,000-plus Arab refugees.[80] These Arabs "driven from their homes" lacked adequate clothes, food, and shelter: "their just rights will not be assured until they are able to return to their homes and live there in security."[81] In other words, the state of Israel continued to be a mistake and the *Christian Century* wanted to reverse history.

In response to a letter from self-proclaimed Christian Zionist Daniel A. Poling, the *Christian Century* failed to recognize how it was detrimental for Christians to support "pan-Arabism or Moslem fanaticism in its attacks on the Jews of Israel."[82] A weak response is surprising given that Poling's point was not a conservative theological one, for example, the sense of blessings to those who favored the Jews, but rather was the issue of little religious freedom in Muslim nations. Likewise, Karl Baehr, executive secretary of the American Christian Palestine Committee, expected the *Christian Century* to address the issue of religious freedom and consider that there were Christian Arabs "most happy to welcome the Israeli army" in cities such as Nazareth. But much of the focus for the *Christian Century* was the expulsion of Christian Arabs from territories gained by the Israelis.[83]

The *Christian Century* pointed out that Israel, from its very beginning, was dominantly secular, demonstrated early when orthodox Jews led by Rabbi Juda L. Fishman opposed secular politicians on key wording of Israel's Declaration of Independence. The secularists were against the word *Elohenu* (God our Lord), and religious Jews had to accept Ben-Gurion's compromise *Tsur Israel* (Rock of Israel), a religiously neutral literary expression.[84] Interestingly, the *Christian Century*, rather than Protestant fundamentalist writers, took issue with this half measure. Pointing to the secularism of the document which did not mention "God," the liberal magazine wrote that the Jewish nation without God "is an ominous portent."[85] Benjamin Kreitman of London, Connecticut, disagreed with the *Christian Century*, stating that "a religious spirit" permeated the Jewish Declaration of Independence. Had not the "secularists" taken the trouble to convene and seal the document before the Sabbath?[86] Adding another twist to the discussion were the words of Karl M. Chworowsky of the Fourth Unitarian Church in Brooklyn, New York, who suggested that the *Christian Century* got "a huge kick out of [its] persistent needling" of Israel.[87] It seemed odd that the liberal *Christian Century* was under attack on this issue by a representative of one of the most liberal Protestant denominations in America. As it turned out, the *Christian Century* admitted it made an error since the original Declaration of Independence did indeed contain the word "God."[88]

In contrast, the language in Christian Zionist circles was uplifting. In one sense, the creation of the State of Israel was a momentous event that spurred a rebirth of conservative Protestantism, with premillennialists seeking to reshape the difficult and isolated years following the Scopes Trial of 1925 when intellectuals and newspaper reporters ridiculed fundamentalism even though liberals had technically lost the case for evolutionism at the showdown in Tennessee. Shamed in the culture battles of the 1920s, eclipsed by liberal Protestantism in serious debates of the Great Depression, and ignored by the mainstream media, conservative Protestants now were in a better position to be more visible in American culture.[89] The success of Israel provided compelling reassurance that God working in history. Premillennialist John F.Walvoord of Dallas Seminary wrote in 1949 that the previous twenty-five years witnessed a "revolution" in eschatology with even "liberal theologians" giving it more attention.[90] Offering clarity rather than the ambiguity of American policymakers on Middle East developments in 1948, premillennialists could claim they had been closer to the truth all along, even if this message remained mostly at the grass-roots.[91] Writing on the "national regathering" of the Jews, radio Bible teacher M. R. Dehaan declared: "All history stands as proof of the literal fulfillment of the Word of God."[92] In the end, had prophecy believers not been wiser to oppose accommodation with an increasingly secular society that was blind to God's divine plan? After the creation of the State of Israel, it appeared that they might be one step ahead of elite Washington policymakers—the so-called "wise men" and the "best and brightest" who represented the powerful American Establishment.[93]

For Christian Zionists, the rise of Israel promised much, particularly compared to the alleged chaos and anti-modernist mentality of Arab life.[94] One historian states that amid the doom and gloom, premillennial thinking "is, at heart, a Utopian belief system."[95] Stating it would be a "blessing," Ruth Caye Jones of the *American Holiness Journal* encouraged her readers to follow newspapers and keep a scrapbook on the "marvelous prophecy" of Israel.[96] In response to a question from an Ashland, Massachusetts, reader, *Moody Monthly*, a fundamentalist-leaning magazine, wrote of Jewish "strength" in Palestine, "heroically" gaining "what God will only give, in fulfillment of His promise."[97] In contrast, to the buoyant news of the Jews, *Moody Monthly* made reference to "Islamic imperialism" and its fervent "religious totalitarianism."[98] The economic and political development of the Jewish people in comparison to the poor development of the past was obvious to many. The orientalist views common in fundamentalist and conservative Christian circles were bluntly critical of the Arab world, but they clarified who were the chosen people.

The first meeting of the national assembly was on February 14, 1949, a historic day discussed by the *American Holiness Journal*. Ruth Caye Jones noted the importance of Jerusalem being the setting of the first assembly even though old Jerusalem was not yet in Jewish possession. There was a UN commission to decide the future of the whole of Jerusalem, but Jones viewed the issue with confidence. Bible-believing Christians knew "that the future of Jerusalem has been decided by God and prophecied [sic] in His Word and that the disposition of the city is in God's hands, and that no commission of man will have the final say."[99] Of course, there were some shortcomings. Writer Morris Zeidman shared his disappointment with the day's minimal attention to prayer and recognition of God's blessing on such an occasion in Jewish history.[100]

Morris and others addressed the topic of Christ's second coming. Oliver G. Wilson, a Wesleyan Methodist, wrote that "the time is not far distant" when God would pour the spirit of grace on Israel.[101] R. A. Thompson told readers to pray, watch, and be ready for the coming of the Lord: "That God is 'working a work in our day' in the shuffle of the nations, and especially in the establishment of the State of Israel in Palestine, can hardly be doubted by any Bible-believing Christian."[102] Other fundamentalists claimed the Bible gives no clear statement that "the Lord is coming *soon*."[103] Some Christian Zionists commented that the Israelis were capable of taking control of all of Jerusalem, but the inaction of Israel suggested to Wilbur Smith that it was not yet God's timing.[104] While there was a sense of expectation, absent were any signs of Christian Zionists seeking to hasten history to Armageddon.

The centuries-old narrative of Jewish nationalism was consistent with the thinking of Christian Zionists. And exciting aspects of Israel's nation-building were the many economic and social achievements. The *American Holiness Journal* noted Israel ranked first in the world with the most scientists per 1,000 population and the "astounding developments" in science occurring at the Weizmann Institute in Israel.[105] In another article, the journal encouraged young American Jews to consider living in Israel where no "able-bodied man or woman is ever without work."[106]

In *The King's Business*, Louis S. Bauman was one Christian Zionist who forcefully explained the essential role that the Jews played in world history. Even as the world witnessed the early months of the Korean War, Bauman wrote: "What happens in Korea, or in other nations, is of small concern, beside what happens in the land of the Jew!"[107] The important place of Israel in conservative Christian circles was obvious in many ways. One of a number of missionary groups which advertised in *Moody Monthly* was the Friends of Israel Missionary and Relief Society, headquartered in Philadelphia, Pennsylvania. It had a quarterly magazine *Israel My Glory* and the support of many leading fundamentalists such as Lewis Sperry Chafer, Louis Bauman, Harry Ironside, and Wilbur M. Smith.[108]

Soon after the birth of the State of Israel, an advertisement of the International Hebrew Christian Alliance, in *Moody Monthly*, related how one Hebrew Christian widow lost her husband to Hitler when the Nazis occupied Austria. She fled to Hungary and safely hid until the end of the war, after which she learned of the killing of her relatives. The food and clothing packages she received from the International Hebrew Christian Alliance kept her from despair and gave her "new courage and fresh faith." The organization's plea was as follows: "We earnestly ask for your prayers and co-operation in this ministry of seeking to feed the hungry, clothe the naked, console the despairing in the Name of our Lord Jesus Christ. Please remember God's promise, 'I will bless them that bless thee' (Gen. 12:3), and 'they shall prosper that love thee' (Ps. 122:6)."[109] Christian Zionists in the West believed and sought such a blessing. And the economic progress of Israel compared to nearby Arab nations revealed much about God working in history. Even as early as 1949, conservative evangelical Carl F. H. Henry wrote about "Islamic imperialism" as a powerful force opposing western culture.[110] Christian Zionist Wilbur Smith wrote: "Nations must know how to prepare to defend themselves against future enemies, what their ultimate destiny in world history might be, and how to plan their economic life."[111]

As for American politics, behind America's recognition of the State of Israel there were political (domestic vote), moral (Holocaust), and strategic (Soviet threat) motives.[112] In addition, Truman's biblical faith may also be a valid consideration. Isaac Halevi Herzog, the chief rabbi of Israel, told Truman early in 1949 that "God put you in your mother's womb so that you would be the instrument to bring about Israel's rebirth after two thousand years."[113] There is no evidence that Truman was a premillennialist, but as a Bible-believing southern Baptist fascinated with Zionism he responded with emotion to statements linking him to the historic King Cyrus who allowed the Jews to return to their land. Truman knew of the patrimony of Abraham, the struggles of Israel, and God's promises that the Jews would regain the land of Israel.

The "war of extermination" and "massacre" predicted by various Arab leaders failed, and instead Jewish leaders created the State of Israel and began plans to secure western support. Wrestling with issues of insecurity and isolation in a hostile region, Israeli leaders sought closer cooperation with the West in order to be part of western defense plans.[114] While this "desire to belong" theme played out, American Christian Zionists, without the knowledge or at least the recognition of most Israeli politicians, clarified their praise and support for the Jewish state. For the days ahead there were national security challenges but also the promise of economic development.

NOTES

1. A. James Rudin, *Israel for Christians* (Philadephia: Fortress Press, 1983), 52. For a brief account of the war, see Ilan Pappe, *A History of Modern Palestine* (Cambridge: Cambridge University Press, 2004), 131–36.

2. Morris, *1948*, 401. For an opposing argument, see Simha Flapan, *The Birth of Israel: Myths and Realities* (New York: Pantheon Books, 1987), 189–92.

3. Morris, *1948*, 204.

4. Quoted in Shindler, *A History of Modern Israel*, 40.

5. Quoted in Adwan et al., eds., *Side by Side*, 126.

6. Hull, *The Fall and Rise of Israel*, 291.

7. Stein, *The Making of Modern Israel*, 19.

8. Levin, *Embattled Jerusalem*, 267–68. Also, Morris, *1948*, 198.

9. Radosh, *A Safe Haven*, 340.

10. For an example of an Arab assessment of Israel's aggression, see Catton, *Palestine, the Arabs and Israel*, 34. Catton explained it as follows: On May 14, "The Haganah

became officially the army of the new state. Thereupon, military hostilities commenced between Israel and its four neighbouring Arab states." He counted the number of Arab forces at "about 20,000 men."

11. Hull, *The Fall and Rise of Israel*, 333–35. Glubb, *A Soldier with the Arabs*, 89.

12. Shlaim, *The Iron Wall*, 77. Quoted in Morris, *1948*, 183, 209–10, 232.

13. Ben-Gurion, *Israel*, 94–95.

14. Ben-Gurion, *Israel*, 4.

15. Hull, *The Fall and Rise of Israel*, 336–37.

16. Hull, *The Fall and Rise of Israel*, 338.

17. "Israel Offers to Halt War," *Christian Century*, June 2, 1948, 532.

18. Peter L. Hanh, *Caught in the Middle East: U.S. Policy toward the Arab-Israeli Conflict, 1945–1961* (Chapel Hill: University of North Carolina Press, 2004), 52. Also see, Morris, 1948, 195, 205, 207.

19. Hull, *The Fall and Rise of Israel*, 338.

20. Morris, *1948*, 215–19. Stein, *The Making of Modern Israel*, 25–27.

21. Sharon, *Warrior*, 54–61, 63. Also, see Stein, *The Making of Modern Israel*, 29-30.

22. Morris, *1948*, 230–31.

23. Morris, *1948*, 233–35, 242, 244, 314.

24. Morris, *1948*, 245, 248, 251, 258. On Syria's invasion, see Slater, "Lost Opportunities for Peace in the Arab-Israeli Conflict," 82–84. Drawing on new history scholarship, Slater is quite critical of Israel.

25. Morris, *1948*, 263.

26. Yusif El-Bandak, "Palestine's Christians in Peril," *Christian Century*, November 30, 1949,1420.

27. Dershowitz, *The Case for Israel*, 74.

28. Ben-Gurion, *Israel*, 148.

29. Ben-Gurion, *Israel*, 150. Also, Sicker, *Israel's Quest for Security*, 40–41.

30. Sicker, *Israel's Quest for Security*, 38–39.

31. Avi Kober, "Great-Power Involvement and Israeli Battlefield Success in the Arab-Israeli Wars, 1948–1982," *Journal of Cold War Studies* 8, no. 1 (Winter 2006), 36.

32. Kober, "Great-Power Involvement and Israeli Battlefield Success in the Arab-Israeli Wars, 1948–1982," 25. Hull, *The Fall and Rise of Israel*, 341–42.

33. Stein, *The Making of Modern Israel*, 37–38.

34. Abba Eban, *Personal Witness: Israel Through My Eyes* (New York: G.P. Putnam's Sons, 1992), 164.

35. Daniel Bliss, "Justice and Peace in the Holy Land," *Christian Century*, September 8, 1948, 908–10.

36. Hanh, *Caught in the Middle East*, 55.

37. Glubb, *A Soldier with the Arabs*, 182.

38. Hanh, *Caught in the Middle East*, 55.

39. "Bernadotte's Assassination Stuns the World," *Christian Century*, September 29, 1948, 995.

40. Voss and Rausch, "American Christians and Israel," 59.

41. "Bernadotte's Proposals Win British Support," *Christian Century*, October 6, 1948, 1028.

42. Hanh, *Caught in the Middle East*, 56.

43. Ben-Gurion, *Israel*, 274–75.

44. Morris, *1948*, 298. David Ben-Gurion, *Israel: Years of Challenge* (New York: Holt, Rinehart and Winston, 1963), 48–49.

45. Peres, *David's Sling*, 14.

46. Morris, *1948*, 329, 339, 348.

47. Kober, "Great-Power Involvement and Israeli Battlefield Success in the Arab-Israeli Wars, 1948–1982," 26. Morris, *1948*, 404.

48. Shlaim, *The Iron Wall*, 47.

49. Quoted in Jacobs, "The Perils and Promise of Islam," 705.

50. Schoenbaum, *The United States and the State of Israel*, 71.

51. Hull, *The Fall and Rise of Israel*, 340.

52. See her letter to the editor, *Eternity*, October 1956, 34. It is true that years after the war (when she wrote her letter) the Israelis had better success getting weapons from the West.

53. Hull, *The Fall and Rise of Israel*, 312, 329.

54. Sicker, *Israel's Quest for Security*, 55.

55. Shindler, *A History of Modern Israel*, 50–52.

56. Shlomo Gazit, "Israel and Palestinians: Fifty Years of Wars and Turning Points," *Annals of the American Academy of Political and Social Science*, 555, Israel in Transition (January 1998), 84.

57. Schoenbaum, *The United States and the State of Israel*, 71.

58. Shlaim, *The Iron Wall*, 50.

59. Catton, *Palestine, the Arabs and Israel*, 144.

60. Meir Litvak and Esther Webman, "Perceptions of the Holocaust in Palestinian Public Discourse," *Israel Studies* 8, no. 3 (Fall 2003), 125–26.

61. Shindler, *A History of Modern Israel*, 55.

62. Ben-Gurion, *Israel*, 820.

63. Ben-Gurion, *Israel*, 458.

64. Stein, *The Making of Modern Israel*, 151.

65. Sicker, *Israel's Quest for Security*, 60–61.

66. Peres, *David's Sling*, 40.

67. Shindler, *A History of Modern Israel*, 66–68. Also, see Safran, *Israel*, 145.

68. Shindler, *A History of Modern Israel*, 79.

69. Shindler, *A History of Modern Israel*, 71.

70. The idea of Israel as home for Jews born elsewhere continued to be strong even in later decades. See John Scofield, "Israel Land of Promise," *National Geographic* 127, no. 3 (March 1965), 397, 400. It was particularly difficult for those Jews who lost their homes or businesses when forced to leave Arab nations.

71. Shindler, *A History of Modern Israel*, 85–87. In 1970, an amended law added that a Jew could be someone "converted to Judaism and who is not a member of another religion."

72. Radosh, *A Safe Haven*, 353.

73. Shindler, *A History of Modern Israel*, 93–97. In 1983, Joan Peters wrote that "more than half of the people in Israel today are Jews or offspring of Jews who lived in Arab countries and have fled from Arab brutality." See Joan Peters, *From Time Immemorial: The Origins of the Arab-Jewish Conflict over Palestine* (New York: Harper and Row, 1984), 79.

74. For analysis of the impact of Coffin's editorial, see Carenen, *The Fervent Embrace*, 66–67.

75. Carenen, *The Fervent Embrace*, 67–68.

76. *Christian Century*, May 26, 1948, 500.

77. *Christian Century*, July 14, 1948, 701.

78. Stein, *The Making of Modern Israel*, 39–40.

79. "Jerusalem," *Christian Century*, December 14, 1949, 1489.

80. *Christian Century*, September 8, 1948, 900–901.

81. *Christian Century*, September 22, 1948, 964.

82. "Palestine," *Christian Century*, November 10, 1948, 1209.

83. "Nazareth as an Example," *Christian Century*, November 10, 1948, 1211.

84. *Christian Century*, September 8, 1948, 901.

85. "Israel Knows No God," *Christian Century*, June 9, 1948, 565.

86. *Christian Century*, July 14, 1948, 711.

87. *Christian Century*, September 29, 1948, 1012.

88. "Zionist Censor Cut Out 'God,'" *Christian Century*, July 14, 1948, 701.

89. On how survey American history texts portray twentieth-century conservative Protestantism, see John Fea, "An Analysis of the Treatment of American Fundamen-

talism in United States History Survey Texts," *The History Teacher* 28, no. 2 (February, 1995): 205–16.

90. John F. Walvoord, "The Millennial Issue in Modern Theology," *Bibliotheca Sacra* 106, no. 421 (January–March, 1949), 34; Walvoord, "Amillennialism in the Ancient Church," *Bibliotheca Sacra*, 106, no. 423 (July–September, 1949), 291. In one article, Walvoord wrote: "The second World War had a terrific impact on both liberalism and philosophy. A survey of their writings during this period will demonstrate a new appreciation of sin, divine sovereignty, of human weakness, and the recognition of a possible catastrophic end of the world and ultimate judgment of God." See Walvoord, "Postmillennialism," *Bibliotheca Sacra*, 106, no. 422 (April–June 1949), 167.

91. For example, Joel Carpenter states that prophecy beliefs assured fundamentalists "that they and not the [Christian] liberals were right about the state and direction of world civilization." Carpenter, *Revive Us Again*, 244. In "the Private Hopes of American Fundamentalists and Evangelicals, 1925–1975," Watt claims that the emergence of Israel "lent new plausibility to dispensationalists' traditional insistence that the prophecies concerning the last days were not to be fulfilled figuratively by the Christian Church but rather by a literal Jewish state" (160).

92. M. R. DeHaan, *The Jew and Palestine in Prophecy* (Grand Rapids, MI: Zondervan Publishing House, 1950), 11.

93. Walter Isaacson and Evan Thomas, *The Wise Men: Six Friends and the World They Made* (New York: Touchstone, 1988); David Halberstam, *The Best and Brightest* (New York: Fawcett Crest, 1972).

94. One *Moody Monthly* article spoke of terrible future events for Jews, but the foremost theme was Jewish rebirth. Elizabeth Sharp, "Great Earthquake," *Moody Monthly*, May, 1949, 637. One popular prophecy book published a few years later that focuses on the "rise" is Hull, *The Fall and Rise of Israel*.

95. Boyer, *When Time Shall Be No More*, 318.

96. Ruth Caye Jones, "Startling Facts," *American Holiness Journal* 8, no. 10 (April, 1949), 75–76.

97. "Palestine and the Jews," *Moody Monthly*, November, 1948, 202.

98. Carl F. H. Henry, "Evangelicals and the Ecumenical Movement," *Moody Monthly*, May, 1949, 629. In this particular case, Henry's reference was to Africa.

99. Ruth Caye Jones, "Startling Facts," *American Holiness Journal* 8, no. 9 (March 1949), 71.

100. Morris Zeidman, "Rebuilding the Jewish Nation and Temple," *The American Holiness Journal* 9, no. 4 (October 1949), 18–19, 23.

101. Zeidman, "Rebuilding the Jewish Nation and Temple," 18-19, 23. Oliver G. Wilson, "What Time Is It?" *The American Holiness Journal* 8, no. 8 (February 1949), 39.

102. R. A. Thompson, "Watch Therefore," *The American Holiness Journal* 10, no. 2 (August 1950), 14.

103. August Van Rye, "Is Jesus Coming Soon?" *Moody Monthly*, April 1949, 612.

104. Smith, *World Crises and the Prophetic Scriptures*, 235. Writing of the topic of Christ's return in *Moody Monthly*, Elizabeth Sharp mentioned Israel without any hint of believers doing anything to hasten end times. Sharp, "Great Earthquake," 637.

105. "About Israel," *American Holiness Journal* 9, no. 3 (September 1949), 51.

106. "Let's Discuss," *American Holiness Journal* 9, no. 4 (October 1949), 80.

107. Bauman, "Israel Lives Again!" 7.

108. *Moody Monthly*, December 1948, 268.

109. *Moody Monthly* 49, no. 9 (May 1949), 649.

110. Carl F. H. Henry, "Evangelicals and the Ecumenical Movement," *Moody Monthly*, May 1949, 629.

111. Smith, *World Crises and the Prophetic Scriptures*, 43.

112. Isaac Alteras, *Eisenhower and Israel: U.S.-Israeli Relations, 1953–1960* (Gainesville: University Press of Florida, 1993), 3; Michael J. Cohen, "Truman and Palestine, 1945–1948: Revisionism, Politics and Diplomacy," *Modern Judaism* 2, no. 1 (February, 1982): 1–22. For an earlier period, the British blamed its failure to solve the Palestine

problem on Truman's bowing to American Jewish pressure. Arieh J. Kochavi, "British Assumptions of American Jewry's Political Strength, 1945–1947," *Modern Judaism* 15, no. 2 (1995), 161.

113. Quoted in Merkley, *American Presidents, Religion, and Israel*, viii. On Truman and the Bible, Clark Clifford wrote: "As a student of the Bible he believed in the historic justification for a Jewish homeland and it was a conviction with him that the Balfour Declaration promise constituted a solemn promise that fulfilled the age-old hope and dream of the Jewish people." Quoted in Cohen, "Truman and Palestine, 1945–1948," 4. Despite the major rift between Truman's Zionist circle and the State Department, the United States had come through with crucial political support for the new Jewish state caught in a War of Independence that lasted until January 1949.

114. See Elie Podeh, "The Desire to Belong Syndrome," *Israel Studies* 4, no. 2 (Fall 1999), 121.

THREE

On to the Second Arab-Israel War

In the immediate period after the War of Independence, Israeli leaders focused on increasing the population by immigration, modernizing the armed forces, and preventing regional foes from acquiring sophisticated weapons that would give them a qualitative edge over Israel, the last task a daunting one.[1] This focus on security made perfect sense. In addition to the ongoing guerrilla attacks by the Egyptians, Jordanians, and Syrians, Israel had to deal with Egypt's purchase of "weapons of aggression" from the Communist bloc and the Soviets' misinformation that Israel consistently waged a "hostile policy" against its neighbors.[2] Because of Arab bitterness over Israel, there was "a constant danger of a new outbreak of war."[3] From the perspective of Israeli leaders, Arab hostile actions in the months leading to the Suez Crisis of 1956 constituted a virtual act of war. When the Israelis took military action that upset President Dwight Eisenhower, conservative Christian groups continued to voice their support for Israel.[4]

Israeli leaders believed that the Arabs opposed any genuine peace settlement. In 1951, Ben-Gurion told his cabinet: "It is their interest to erase all trace of the Jews from Eretz Israel. . . . . This is [our] terrifying problem. . . . Today designers of Arab policy are willing to make peace with us, [only] if we transfer to Madagascar or elsewhere and forfeit the land."[5] There were only a few episodes of hopeful Arab-Israeli negotiations. After the war of 1948, many Israelis viewed Syria as Israel's most implacable enemy, but there was a promising sign when Colonel Husni Zaim, as a result of a bloodless coup, became the Syrian leader in late March 1949. On July 20, Syria and Israel signed an armistice agreement, but Zaim quickly lost his leadership in a violent military coup. As early as spring 1951 there were serious clashes between Israel and Syria in a demilitarized zone near Lake Huleh. On April 4, the Syrian Army killed seven Israeli soldiers on patrol. There was another clash in early May when the Syrians took control of Tal al-Mutilla, a strategic hill located one mile inside Israel. The Israelis recaptured the hill, but at a high cost of forty soldiers dead.[6] Two years later Syria complained of Israel's project to divert water from the Jordan River.

Essential for Israel's continued existence was a dependable water supply and in July 1953, Israeli leaders approved a project in northern Israel to divert the waters of the Jordan River for usage in southern Israel. The project, however, meant encroaching on a demilitarized zone between Israel and Syria. The canal work began in early September and the UN Armistice Commission and Syria demanded that the Israelis cease construction, as did the U.S. State Department, which threatened to withhold $50 million in funds to Israel. The Americans added additional pressure when President Eisenhower gave the Treasury Department authorization to nullify the tax-deductible status of contributions to Zionist organizations.[7] Ben-Gurion refused to bow to such pressure because he, as Golda Meir explained, did not allow the opposing opinions of others to hinder his focus on Israel's sovereignty and security.[8] Another representative voice of Israel's determination to resist external pressure was Moshe Sharett: "We are a unique state with regard to external assistance which is a vital need for us. . . . but we shall not sell our freedom and independence on behalf of those grants."[9]

The Israeli government abandoned the Jordan River project, but expected an American diversion plan would be a suitable solution to the water issue. Named after special envoy Eric Johnston, the "Johnston Plan" proposed the allocation of 60 percent of the water to Lebanon, Syria, and Jordan and 40 percent to Israel. Accepted by Israel, the Johnston plan worried Arab leaders and thus there was little action for a number of years. As *Christian Century* reported, any cooperative plan between Israel and the Arab states would constitute for the Arabs "intolerable recognition of Israel as a state within its present bounds."[10]

If Syria was the most implacable enemy, Egypt was the most dangerous given the size of its population and the intense hostility toward Israel by various secular and religious leaders. A number of key events proved Israel's disadvantaged position. In late 1949, the Egyptians fortified Sharm al-Sheikh with gun emplacements. With control of the entrance of the Gulf of Aquaba and Israel's sole outlet to the Red Sea and Indian Ocean, Egypt declared a blockade of both Israeli and Israel-bound vessels. In 1951, the UN Security Council ordered that the Suez Canal allow Israeli ships passage, but the Egyptians continued to deny ships sailing to and from Israel. These restrictions on transportation were costly, compromising the security and international rights of Israel.[11]

Israel continued to face additional challenges on the Egyptian frontier. When King Farouk's regime ended with a bloodless coup in the summer of 1952, the Israelis were hopeful of better relations with Egypt. But hope faded. The accession of Gamal Addel Nasser to power on April 17, 1954, suggested more difficulties for Israel. On June 11, 1954, the press reported Nasser's position on Israel that "nobody can force the Arabs to accept peace with Israel or to recognize her as an established state. We believe that we can reverse the position in Palestine to its natural state and return the land to its people and owners."[12] To complicate matters on how Israel might respond to Nasser's aggressive overtones, Israeli leaders received intelligence in 1954 that the United States might act against the Israelis if they invaded Arab territory.[13]

A pressing issue for Israel was Egypt's continued refusal to allow Israeli vessels in the Suez Canal. Israel did not have the best of relations with Britain, but the British presence at the Suez Canal zone was preferable to Egypt having complete control of the canal. Approving the presence of British soldiers at the Suez Canal, the Israelis disliked the planned British withdrawal from the canal that would transfer the canal to Egypt. With the objective of keeping the British there, Israeli military intelligence carried out a sabotage mission in 1954 when a small group firebombed the American libraries in Cairo and Alexandria, causing little damage (no injuries or deaths). The mission was a failure and the Egyptians captured and tortured thirteen members of the operation. Two committed suicide and two received the death sentence in an Egyptian trial. The executions of Moshe Mazzuk and Shmuel Azar hardened the attitudes of Israeli citizens toward Nasser.[14] One notable Egyptian act was the seizure of the Israeli merchant ship *Bat Gallim* and the torture of its crew when it attempted passage through the Suez Canal on September 28, 1954.

Israel experienced many problems with the Jordanians, who ruled the West Bank, including East Jerusalem. The Israelis held secret meetings with the Jordanians, at least until the summer of 1951 before a Muslim assassinated Jordan's King Abdullah outside the al-Aksa Mosque in East Jerusalem for his failure to support Palestinian objectives. Moderate Arab leaders often faced serious threats by extremists willing to use deadly violence to make their voice heard.[15] On the king's murder and the prospect of Jordanian-Israeli talks, Ben-Gurion declared: "With the removal of the Abdullah factor, the whole matter was finished."[16]

Jordanian raids into Israel prompted Israeli responses that were more or less proportional. However, when the violence intensified, the Israeli retaliations were no longer proportional. After a rape-murder incident, Israeli forces retaliated on January 6, 1952, with a raid resulting in the deaths of seven Arabs. Arab incidents of violence on most nights generated much anger in Israel and Ben-Gurion adopted a new deterrent policy. By making the retaliations punitive, Israel hoped the Arabs' costs would be too high and thus discourage attacks on Israeli citizens.[17] It was the primary responsibility of the government and not antiterrorist vigilante groups to act forcefully. In her memoirs, Golda Meir explains that "the children of Israeli farmers in border villages were entitled to sleep safely in their beds at night. And if the only way of accomplishing this were to hit back mercilessly at the camps of the Arab gangs, then that would have to be done." As he fought for security and sovereignty using such measures, Ben-Gurion was one who "regarded world opinion, or even public opinion, as relatively unimportant."[18] Historians sympathetic to the Arabs point out that Arab Legion leadership made serious efforts to prevent West Bank civilians from participating in raids on Israel.[19] This may be the case, but what mattered to Israelis was that there was no stoppage of deadly raids into Israel.

An incident in late 1953 generated ample criticism outside Israel. In October, an Arab raid on a village ten miles from Tel Aviv resulted in the murder of a mother and her two children. The next night Israeli forces targeted the Jordanian village of Qibya. Historian Colin Shindler notes that Israeli leaders disagreed with the retaliation mission at "Qibya." Foreign Minister Moshe Sharett initially opposed the operation while Ben-Gurion approved. With Major Ariel Sharon as its commander, Unit 101 destroyed over forty homes and accidentally killed sixty-nine villagers. But conflicting reports pointed to something more disturbing (killing by small arms fire), and Ben-Gurion's cover story that vengeful settlers were the guilty party did not assuage the anger of the American government.[20]

Many years later in his autobiography, Sharon called the outcome a "tragedy" in which the Israeli soldiers carried out the bombing operation after believing each of the houses were vacant. Sharon and others saw the raid as a turning point in which "Israel's Jews began to feel they were not completely defenseless against" the many attacks reaching every corner of Israel.[21] Arab Legion commander John Glubb referred to the killings as "a major massacre."[22] In his defense of Israel before the UN Security Council, Abba Eban declared that by the records of the Mixed Armistice the Arabs were guilty of 159 armistice violations, many more than the twenty-five by Israel.[23]

One particularly deadly raid on Israel took place on March 17, 1954, when nine Israelis died in an Arab attack of a bus en route to Eilat. But some argue that Israel's retaliatory policy prevented even more incidents and losses to Arab violence from Jordan. The number of Israelis killed in border raids ranged from forty-four to fifty-seven in each of the years of 1951 to 1953, but after Israel's adoption of the punitive retaliatory policy the number of deaths fell to thirty-four in 1954 and another major reduction of eleven in 1955.[24] Two of those killed in 1955 were Israeli tractor drivers; this double murder by Jordanian infiltrators caused a surge of indignation throughout Israel.[25] Having asked the United Nations and the United States for advice on how "to stop the cross-border murders," Ben-Gurion learned that they had no answers. As he declared in September 1954, there was only one path for Israel: "Our blood is not dispensable! There is no other way than by sharp, aggressive reprisal, without harming women and children, to prevent Jews from being murdered by our enemies on the outside, only reprisal—it they are incapable of putting a stop to it."[26] Beyond the issue of deterrence, reprisals also boosted the morale of Israelis living in the border area and placated those demanding revenge.[27]

Behind much of the Arab hostility was the militant position of various Muslim leaders who called for Islamic unity against Israel. Meeting in Jerusalem in December 1953, an Islamic Congress for the Palestine Question urged Muslims throughout the world "to work for the liberation of Palestine." Pacifism was "useless" and peace negotiations with Israel represented "a treasonous act."[28] In the early years of Israel's history it was clear that a strong Israeli military supported by politicians willing to make hard decisions was necessary to secure the confidence of Israeli citizens, many of them new immigrants desiring a level of security lost in Europe as the National Socialists of Germany wrecked havoc on Jews.

As Islamic militants spoke of the annihilation of Israel, American conservative Christians continued to demonstrate their enthusiasm for the State of Israel and prophetic writing that offered "the only explanation of this much talked about 'critical hour.'"[29] But there was also much talk of Israel's economic development. In celebration of Israel's first year anniversary, *American Holiness Journal* praised how the Jews transformed a mostly barren land to one of riches: "Plainly the curse of the Almighty had blighted it, but such is not the story today."[30] Included in one September 1951 *Moody Monthly* article written by Carl Armerding (Wheaton College) is an air view photograph of the bustling Israeli port of Haifa. Under the photograph, the magazine asked: "Is this national revival [nationalism] the forerunner of renewed Messianic hope?" From his study of the Bible and secular news stories concerning Israel, Armerding stated that Israel as a nation was not looking for the Messiah, but he was hopeful that a spiritual revival in Israel was not far in the future. It was heartening to him that the Bible promised the survival of Israel against all forces seeking extermination, and that it was quite possible that the Great Tribulation could occur within thirty years.[31]

In 1952, John F. Walvoord explored what the Bible said about Israel possessing the Promised Land and whether possession depended on human obedience. His conclusion was that God's promises to Abraham were eternal and unconditional and thus "Israel has a bona fide ground for future possession of the land, particularly in the millennial kingdom period." The final "regathering" of Jews was in motion with over 1 million Jews in Israel and this process was to "continue until consummated after the second advent of Christ."[32] American Christian Zionist support for Israel was rock solid and broad, a fact demonstrated repeatedly as Arab-Israeli conflict increased in the mid-1950s. The rise of religiosity in 1950s America, with church memberships reaching an impressively high

69 percent, resulted in greater Christian interest in Israel as Christians and Jews became "partners in a 'Judeo-Christian' civilization."[33]

Political change in Israel did not alter Christian Zionist support. During the period of December 1953 to February 1955, Ben-Gurion left the government and a more cautious Moshe Sharett became prime minister. Ben-Gurion returned as minister of defense for about nine months and then became prime minister on November 2, 1955. The year was a difficult one for Israeli leaders. Radio reports out of Egypt heightened the tensions. For example, Radio Cairo proclaimed in 1955: "The day of Israel's destruction is coming closer. This is our resolve: this is our faith. There will be no peace on the borders, for we demand revenge and revenge means death to Israel!"[34] One set of violent incidents began in January 21, 1955, when an Egyptian army unit targeted an Israeli military outpost, resulting in the death of an Israeli soldier. In February, Egyptian raiders traveled at least thirty miles into Israel and killed a cyclist near Rehovoth.

Egypt viewed Israeli citizens as fair game and in April the Egyptian army began training and assisting Palestinian refugees as *fedayeen* (those who sacrifice themselves) to attack civilian targets. Special bonuses went to those who carried out "wonderful deeds" of murder. Egyptian politician Hassan el Bakuri explained the rationale of the Egyptian government promoting this strategy: "there is no reason why the Fedayeen filled with hatred of their enemies should not penetrate deeply into Israel and turn the lives of its people into hell."[35] Making the point that the term *fadayeen* once had a honourable connotation, E. L. M. Burns, the chief of the UN Truce Supervision Organization, wrote: "I felt that what the Egyptians were doing in sending these men, who they dignified with the name *fedayeen*, or commandos, into another country with the mission to attack men, women, and children indiscriminately was a war crime." In one case, these marauders used their submachine guns to kill four unarmed workers forty-seven kilometers inside the border. This type of "terrorist mission" alienated opinion outside the Middle East; the Egyptians had crossed the line when they supported the targeting of unarmed civilians. Burns declared: "When I realized the extent and character of this campaign I was deeply shocked."[36] Also assisting in the training of Arab terrorists were ex-Nazis. One German newspaper reported that Egypt welcomed 2,000 ex-Nazis, including Arich Altern and Walter Baumann, two high-ranking members, who served as military instructors in Palestinian refugee camps.[37]

Responding to repeated raids from Gaza, Israeli forces attacked Egypt's Gaza headquarters in late February 1955, resulting in thirty-seven Egyptians killed and thirty-nine wounded. Code-named Operation Black Arrow, the devastating Gaza raid was the work of two paratroop companies led by Ariel Sharon.[38] There was a serious incident within a month when a group of Egyptians entered the Negev and attacked, with

automatic rifles and grenades, a wedding celebration of Jewish immigrants from Iran.[39] Although some argue that Operation Black Arrow
caused Nasser to change his policy toward Israel from accommodation to
confrontation, others contend Nasser all along desired war with Israel
because "there could be no room in a Nasserist Middle East for a non-
Arab state."[40] In the wake of the uproar over the Gaza attack, Nasser
proceeded to improve his military, a project assisted by the Soviets, who
provided an impressive quantity and quality of modern weapons
through a Czechoslovakia-Egypt deal announced by Nasser in late September 1955. This development signaled to the Israelis Nasser's eventual
goal of going to war with Israel.[41] Nasser's soothing words of peace
gained traction with some naïve westerners, but others saw him as "an
inveterate liar."[42]

By October 26, a little more than one year before war broke out, Egyptian troops took control of the al-Auja demilitarized zone, after killing
one Israeli and taking prisoner two others. The Israeli response two days
later was a raid on an Egyptian army camp located at Kuntilla in the
southern Negev. When the UN Truce Supervision Organization failed to
convince Egypt to withdraw from al-Auja, the Israelis carried out a more
thorough attack on the Egyptian side of the demilitarized zone on November 2 that resulted in the killing and capture of almost one hundred
Egyptian soldiers. It was the largest Israeli military operation since the
War of Independence.[43] Ben-Gurion held Nasser responsible: "I regret,
too, the fact that fifty Egyptian soldiers were killed, for they were sacri-
ficed not because of their evil intent and will, but because of the aggression of an ambitious dictator who plays with the lives of his countrymen."[44]

To the Knesset in November 1955, Ben-Gurion spoke at length on
Israel's security. His initial words clarified what was at stake: "Our problem is not simply the security of our independence, our territory, our
borders, our regime, but the security of our simple physical survival."
The Arabs opposed more than Israeli territory and independence: "Their
plan, as many of them state frankly, is to throw us all into the sea. Let us
not forget that during World War Two the majority of Arab rulers admired Hitler and looked forward to his victory."[45] Nasser's commitment
to destroy Israel seemed obvious to the Israelis. But did he have the
military power to back up his aggressive rhetoric? Certainly, Israel
viewed Egypt's arms deal with Eastern Europe as a development that
would hasten an Egyptian attack.

The disadvantages for Israel were obvious. The American government
prohibited any sale of arms to Israel. The Egyptians were stronger with
their acquisition of arms from Czechoslovakia, and they had troops stationed in the Gaza Strip not far from Tel Aviv. Israel also had to be more
vigilant of Syria due to a new mutual defense agreement between the
Egyptians and Syrians that placed their troops under a single command.

Israeli leaders believed it important to curb any Egyptian optimism over this new military alliance. In December, soon after the Syrians fired on an Israeli police boat in the northern part of the Sea of Galilee, an Israeli force led by Ariel Sharon carried out a raid that killed fifty-six Syrians, eight of them civilians.[46] One historian claims that the Israeli operation was "an unprovoked act of aggression."[47] But many Americans at the time recognized that Israel had little choice but take action given its precarious security position. Even Alexis Ladas, a UN political officer, reported to UN headquarters "that something has to be done to protect Israel from this deadly threat, and if the West will not provide the shield then Israel will have to cut the hand which wields the weapons."[48]

In February 1956, Egyptian officers stationed throughout the Gaza Strip received a "top secret" field order concerning "the unavoidable war with Israel." The "supreme objective" of the Egyptian troops was to see Israel's "complete destruction," done quickly and "brutally and cruelly as possible."[49] There was much violence throughout the spring with the month of April especially deadly. Acknowledging that "this is a very tense time," President Eisenhower wrote to Ben-Gurion discouraging the Israelis from committing "retaliatory acts." Ben-Gurion's reply to Eisenhower was that "the Egyptian authorities sent gangs of murderers from Gaza to murder innocent citizens, to destroy installations and to spread fear among peaceful villagers. . . . I am certain that no other country would surrender to such a situation without appropriate answer."[50]

In response to the Egyptian firing of mortar shells at Israeli settlements, an Israeli major ordered a heavy rain of mortar fire on the town of Gaza that killed fifty-six Arabs. Among the approximately one hundred wounded were women and children. The Israeli leaders received word that the *fedayeen* would enter Israel from Egypt, Syria, Jordan, and Lebanon on a mission of vengeance for the bombardment of Gaza. There was a large-scale operation, but the entry point was only from Egypt. What followed was the *fedayeen* killing of unarmed Israelis and five schoolchildren at prayer near Ramle.[51] *Christianity Today* later wrote of the "Egyptian *fedayeen* gangs" killing civilians by mining Israel's roads, machine-gunning vehicles, and throwing grenades into buildings. Because of the impotence of the United Nations in response to these commando raids, Israel believed it had no choice but to take the role of policeman.[52] Israel also faced increased violence from Jordanians inspired by the *fedayeen* attacks from the Gaza Strip. One Jordanian politician declared the importance of having an army of Palestinian refugees for going into Israel "to burn, murder and destroy." Shocking was the killing of ten-year-old girl harvesting olives with her mother; the perpetrators severed and took the arm of the dead girl for a souvenir.[53]

Meanwhile, there was no progress on allowing Israel freedom of navigation at the Suez Canal and the Gulf of Aquba.[54] Shimon Peres viewed the Egypt blockade of the Gulf of Aquaba as the primary cause of the

Sinai Campaign that unfolded later in 1956.[55] The report of the chief of the UN Truce Supervision Organization was ominous: "Looking back, one can see that by the spring of 1956 the currents which were bearing the antagonists in the Middle East towards the whirlpool of war were too strong to be stemmed just by diplomatic interventions." It was unrealistic to expect change "by simple mediation by third parties, including the United Nations and its agent the Secretary-General."[56] Israeli anxiety rose when Egypt, in May 1956, received $250 million worth in arms from the Soviets via Czechoslovakia, including some two hundred jet fighters and bombers, one hundred heavy tanks, boats, submarines, and heavy artillery. More problematic, however, was that the arms deal signified that for the first time a major power "aligned itself with an Arab state against Israel."[57]

Egypt's nationalization of the Suez Canal on July 26 heightened tensions in the Middle East. Both Britain and France viewed this development as a serious economic threat. As for Israeli leaders, they understood how Nasser's bold action against the British and French raised his prestige in the Arab world, a development promising more difficult times for Israel. Israeli politicians discussed a plan of action, including the risky option of war. In August, Ben-Gurion was more cautious: "A war which is not forced upon us by others will not solve any of our problems, even if it ends in victory, and there is no assurance that a war initiated by us will end in a victory."[58]

During the 1956 summer and fall months, there was a rise in violence along Israel's borders and the number of Israeli casualties since the War of Independence reached over 1,230, a number comparable (population adjusted) to U.S. casualties in the Korean War.[59] Both the killing of a young Israeli girl on September 24 and the murder of two Israelis at an orange grove on October 10 resulted in separate punitive raids in which the Israelis killed thirty-nine Arabs at a police station near Husan and eighty-three at a police station at Qalqilya, defended by the Arab League. In the wake of the battle at Qalqilya, Jordan and Iraq discussed the formation of a joint Iraqi-Jordanian army.[60]

Meanwhile Ben-Gurion adopted a more aggressive position on the issue of war. On October 17 in the Knesset, he declared: "Most of the time, the most effective way to defend oneself is by offensive actions. And if we are compelled to defend ourselves, we are not going to sit in our homes and defend ourselves." It made sense to "carry the war to the other side and defend ourselves through offensive shock tactics. . . ." Six days later in Paris, at a preliminary meeting with the French, Ben-Gurion explained it was vital for Israel to destroy the Egyptian military bases in the Sinai and the Gaza Strip because they represented the staging area for a major Egyptian assault. Ben-Gurion saw the situation as grim: "We cannot allow the fedayeen to bleed us to death over the years; nor can we permit ourselves to become the victims of a surprise attack from which we might not recover."[61]

In a meeting later in the day with both the French and the British, Ben-Gurion and General Moshe Dayan agreed with their proposal to dislodge the Egyptians from their control of the Suez Canal. Known for his haw-kish views, Dayan spoke in April 1956 at the funeral of a young farmer murdered by Arab mauraders: "The only choice we have is to be pre-pared and armed, strong, and resolute, or else our sword will slip from our hand and the thread of our lives will be severed."[62] The previous year he told Israeli military leaders that the "solution to Israel's worsen-ing security problem is the overthrow of Nasser's regime in Egypt."[63] However, lost in any analysis of such aggressive Israeli rhetoric is the point that it was a French initiative rather than an Israeli one to go to war.[64]

While Israel, Britain, and France plotted in secrecy, the Arabs made plans to work together to take military action against Israel. On October 27, the official publication of the Egyptian military government wrote of the establishment of the unified command of Egypt, Jordan, and Syria, viewed as "a supreme effort to tighten the death noose."[65] More trou-bling news for Israeli leaders was the possibility of the Soviets sending "volunteers" to fight with the Egyptians and conducting bombing raids on both civilian and military targets in Israel.[66] Following the agreed-upon plan with the French and British, Israel struck first with a bold paratrooper drop forty-five miles east of the Suez Canal on October 29, followed by Israeli offensives by land into the Sinai. The Israelis scored key military victories in early November that resulted in their control of the Sinai including along the Suez Canal.[67]

As secretly planned, these developments "forced" the British and French to issue an ultimatum on October 30 for the Egyptian and Israeli troops to withdraw from the Suez Canal. Of course, Nasser ignored the ultimatum and the British and French response was bombing Egypt and landing paratroopers to take control of the canal. The complicated mili-tary operation against Egypt was a military success but a diplomatic disaster because President Eisenhower responded with fury, pressuring Britain and France to accept a cease-fire.[68] Also on November 7, Eisen-hower demanded Israel's withdrawal to the armistice lines: "It would be a matter of the greatest regret to all my countrymen if Israeli policy on a matter of such grave concerns to the world should in any way impair the friendly cooperation between our two countries."[69] His subsequent threat of economic sanctions against Israel did not go well with many Americans, including Republican Senate minority leader William Know-land, who, critical of the double standard applied to Israel, threatened to resign as a UN delegate if sanctions went through.[70]

There were cooler relations between the United States and Israel dur-ing the Eisenhower years. The Eisenhower administration understood that the pro-Israeli domestic vote heavily favored the Democrats, and Eisenhower did not view "Israel as in any special sense a work of God in history."[71] He admitted in May 1953, that had he been president in 1948 he might not have supported establishing the State of Israel.[72] Christian Zionists received no proof from Eisenhower, raised in a fundamentalist River Brethren church, of having any sympathy for Israel's favored place in Bible prophecy. Beyond his focus on Cold War politics, it is possible that his parents' conversion to the Jehovah's Witnesses, seen as a cult with peculiar end-times teachings and restrictions on military service, caused Eisenhower to respond disdainfully to any notions of Bible prophecy and religious zealotry.[73]

Israeli politicians found other ways to explain the weak support of the Eisenhower administration. In private correspondence, Moshe Sharett wrote that "if a comparison is made between Eisenhower and Truman with respect to the heart and [John Foster] Dulles and [Dean] Acheson with respect to the brains then the descent is rather steep."[74] Eisenhower and Dulles preferred a detached, rational, even-handed approach, but impartiality was not equality: "to Eisenhower the Arabs offered assets, while Israel constituted a liability to American interests." Two and half years before the Suez Crisis, assistant secretary of state Henry Byroade declared that the Eisenhower administration "would back no state, including Israel, in a matter of expansive aggression."[75]

Adhering to orientalist stereotypes, the Eisenhower administration believed that Arabs, particularly leaders such as Nasser, were irrational, resentful, and dangerous. But the military action taken by the British, French, and Israelis was unacceptable from every geopolitical angle. Applying economic pressure, the United States forced the British and French to withdraw from Egypt, and the Israelis from the Sinai and Gaza. It was important to the Eisenhower administration to maintain stability in the Middle East by keeping pro-western regimes in the Middle East strong while opposing colonial thinking, and limiting revolutionary change and Soviet encroachment, confirmed by the subsequent Eisenhower Doctrine that pledged economic and military aid to any Middle East nation prepared to fight communism.[76]

Eisenhower used television on February 20, 1957, to explain to Americans that if Israel did not vacate conquered Arab territory, the United States would support UN sanctions. This was shocking to Israeli leaders not expecting such strong-arm tactics.[77] The following day, Ben-Gurion told the Knesset: "For eight years the United Nations had permitted acts of hostility, boycott, blockade, and murder by the Egyptian government against Israel. The people of Israel cannot submit to discrimination in international relations." He appealed to the Americans to stand with Israel as it sought "sovereign equality, peace, and security."[78]

In a March 1957 letter to Eisenhower, Ben-Gurion informed the Americans of Israel's withdrawal from the Gaza Strip. It was not an easy decision: "During the last few months the inhabitants of our villages in the South and Negev could, for the first time in eight years, live in peace, knowing that grenades would not be thrown into their homes at night, and that they would not be ambushed on their way to work in the fields during the day."[79] Moreover, when the Israelis received from the United States, France, and Britain a guarantee of "free and innocent passage" in the Gulf of Aqaba, they evacuated Sharm al-Sheikh. Equally important was these countries' recognition that Israel had the right to use force to re-open the passageway if Egypt imposed another blockade.[80]

Israeli leaders remained bitter that the United Nations pressured them to withdraw from Sinai, the Gaza Strip, and Sharm al-Sheikh. The United Nations Emergency Force oversaw the cease-fire and withdrawal, but it lacked authority to prevent any future Egyptian military mobilization of the Sinai. Israeli leaders had little confidence in vague UN promises of maintaining order and preventing the Egyptians from using the territories for hostile acts once Israel evacuated.[81] Vexing to Israeli leaders was "the Russian threat via Syria and Egypt."[82] At any rate, Israel made some important steps as a result of its military success during the brief war. Gone was the immediate threat of an Egyptian attack, broken was the Egypt-Syria-Jordan military alliance, and gained was Israeli shipping through the Straits of Tiran and the Gulf of Aquaba.[83]

American liberal Protestants had more faith in the UN in the months leading up to the invasion of Egypt and they were quite critical of Israel. Axel Christensen of the Lutheran World Federation declared his opposition to the State of Israel: "Israel is founded on an act of injustice and nothing good can ever come of it."[84] American Jews and conservative Christians were aware of the significant amount of liberal Protestant criticism. For example, as Rabbi Stanley Rabinowitz of the Adath Jeshurun Synagogue, Minneapolis, Minnesota, observed, the *Christian Century* gave the impression that it did not "accept the reality of the state of Israel."[85] Concerning the violent clashes along the Israel-Jordan border, the *Christian Century* called Israel's response a policy of "massive retaliation." One example given was the approximately fifty Arab men, women, and children "slaughtered" at Kibya years earlier, a response for the killing by "infiltrators" of an Israeli mother and her two children: "The old law of an eye for an eye has apparently been supplanted in Israel's ideology by a more savage rule: a head for an eye." The editorial writer asked, is Israel "deliberately trying to provoke Jordan into a war?" Perhaps Israel's purchase of some jet planes from Canada meant "she need no longer fear her neighbor."[86]

Christian Century analysis of why the American government cancelled aid to Egypt for the Aswan Dam project in August 1956 dismissed the Arab theory that the administration "succumbed to Zionist pressure for fear of election year reprisals." Instead, the cancellation was more due to congressional resistance to any foreign aid in general, and, to a lesser degree Nasser's attempt to play the West and the Communists against each other. However, the *Christian Century* argued that the United Nations should ensure that the "poverty-stricken" Egyptians received financial assistance from the Americans and Soviets for the project.[87] Two weeks later the magazine stressed the importance of the UN to deal with Nasser, "an emotional leader," and the British and French. While hints of orientalism remained in liberal Protestant discourse, the *Christian Century* was on guard against what it saw as colonialism. Any solution to the Suez crisis that by-passed the United Nations was a mistake: "The time has come when domination by a few great powers has ceased to be good for the world."[88]

Theodore A. Gill's report "The Sometime Holy Land" offered a window to the thinking of a liberal Protestant journalist who took a short visit the Middle East. Gill began with an engaging, vivid description of the physical beauty of the region before launching into a pessimistic account of political realities. He questioned the sanity of the statesmen "who ever dreamed a country as little as Palestine could be divided so arbitrarily and exist." Did not such a "monstrous arrangement" give credibility to suggestions "of dark plot and illicit coercion that make the old Protocols of Zion canards look tame?" Despite Israeli attempts to defend the cause of their country, the fact remained that the "land was brutally divided, terror was instituted, property was stolen, a million residents of ancient landholdings were driven into the wretchedness and squalor of refugee camps around the rim of their former homeland." Was it not immoral that these refugees lived in poverty while Jews from abroad confiscated their apartments, houses, and ancestral homesteads? Gill hoped that no one seriously sought biblical texts for any justification for this "mess." For him, it made sense that the refugees had no desire to find new homes; what matter was for them "to go *home*."[89] Some Americans thought Gill's article represented "a much needed corrective" to the one-sided, pro-Israel reporting in American newspapers, but others believed he should have spent some time on the "Israeli side of the fence" before writing his article.[90]

Another article by Gill also generated contrasting responses. One statement in particular on Israel's War of Independence annoyed some readers: "The sanctioned Israeli invasion of the Arabian Palestine united the peoples of the Arabian nations in one fury."[91] This prompted I. D. Unna, an information officer of the Consulate General of Israel, to clarify that "no such invasion ever took place but that, on the contrary, the Arab states invaded and attempted to destroy the state of Israel." Gill's blaming of Dulles for the Suez Crisis did gain the support of one divinity school dean. Sherman E. Johnson of the Church Divinity School of the Pacific, Berkeley, California, found Gill's reporting "accurate and temperate."[92] John R. George of Martinez, California, suggested that Gill's twisting of facts on Dulles made him a perfect person to return to the United

States and "stump the country for the Democrats." He used sarcasm to criticize Gill's overall approach: "We should for free build the [Aswan] dam so Egypt should be strong enough to destroy Israel, a creation of the U.N.! We should subsidize her schools because they are 85 percent illiterate. True the schools must teach only the Mohammedan religion. How cruel the Christian world is not to rush in and establish schools!"[93]

As the threat of war in the Middle East loomed large, every issue of the *Christian Century* offered editorial comment on the Suez Crisis. In late October, it identified another problem in the region when it argued that Israeli attacks on Jordanian strategic outposts were an overreaction to "comparatively small outrages against Israeli citizens by infiltrating Arabs." The Israeli attacks on Jordan, "whose population consists largely of Palestinian refugees," caused greater political instability for Jordanian leaders.[94] At the first signs of Israeli military movement in late October, the *Christian Century* suggested that an agreement among Arab states to give Egypt full command of military operations if war broke out was not a sufficient reason for Israel's complete mobilization. The magazine was also critical of Israel advancing across the Egyptian border and into the Sinai peninsula—a clear rejection of Eisenhower's warning to Ben-Gurion not to take any "forceful initiative." In another report, the *Christian Century* made the astute observation that the timing of the Israeli thrust into the Sinai was likely as a result of the United States being preoccupied with the presidential election and the Soviet Union absorbed with the Hungarian Revolution. Without saying so explicitly the *Christian Century* saw the Israelis rather than Nasser as the ones guilty of aggression.[95] If there was any confusion on where the magazine stood, one week later it blamed Israel for starting the war.[96]

In its report on the United States election results, the *Christian Century* praised Dulles for his "courageous" resistance of "heavy Zionist pressure for arms for Israel." Noticeably missing from this report and most other reports is any mention of Israel's desire for peace with its hostile neighbors. The magazine seemed to believe that Israel received too much favorable treatment and not enough criticism for its actions. For example, the problem with the Democratic Party was its vain attempt "to criticize American policy without imputing the slightest wrong to Israel."[97] As the *Christian Century* wrote in an editorial, the assault on Egypt by the Israelis, French, and British was "evil."[98] One British woman who had worked with Palestinian refugees in Jordan called it "old-fashioned imperialism," something Arab states would not tolerate.[99]

Too many Arabs suffered, such as the 10,000 Egyptians forced to evacuate from the canal zone. Sadly, the New York press boycotted efforts to raise money and supplies for these Arabs, according to the *Christian Century*.[100] Because Israel defied Eisenhower and ignored the United Nations, the state of affairs in the Middle East was "highly dangerous." In fact, Israel's capture of $50 million worth of weapons during the Suez campaign was nothing to cheer about.[101] Elsewhere, the *Christian Century* called for Israel to return land to the Arabs that it acquired back in 1948. Some Americans would not approve, but allowing the UN to redraw the border in the southern Negev, where Israel took Arab land not granted by the boundaries established by the UN in 1947, was the proper thing to do.[102]

Overall, liberal Protestants presented four major points on the Suez crisis: Israel was too aggressive, the British and the French could not escape their colonial mindsets, there was inadequate attention to Arabs problems, and the United Nations was the best hope for peace. The split between liberal Protestants and evangelicals on these points was significant. For example, Irving E. Howard of New York City approved *Christianity Today's* criticism of the United Nations: "I fear the identification of UN with a New England town meeting, which you prove to be a false identification, is something that is being propagated by left wing influences in the hope that they can eventually make the UN a world government."[103] The *Christian Century* offered astute political analysis, but rarely mentioned any religious dimension.

One exception was when the topic was missionary activity in the region. One unfortunate consequence of the Suez Crisis was the "serious setback" of Christian missions. Some missionaries in Egypt were under house arrest and many family members of missionaries left the country. Hostilities also resulted in the eviction of some missionaries from Syria. It was a gloomy topic for Roland Scott, secretary of the National Council of Churches' Near East committee, and the approximately 300 board executives and missionaries who met at Buck Hill Falls, Pennsylvania, for the 1956 annual meeting of Protestant mission boards.[104]

Evangelical discussion of Israel and the Arab world included much about religion. For example, various evangelical organizations embraced the objective to win more Jews to Christ. The goal of the Philadelphia-based Million Testaments Campaign was to hand out its prophecy edition of the New Testament to Jews in the United States, Canada, and Israel. An advertisement in *Eternity* displayed a photo of a Jewish woman at her doorstep receiving a New Testament from a young man. The caption read: "Never before have the Jews been so willing to read the New Testament. Now is the God-given time to place God's Word in their hands."[105] Discussing in *Moody Monthly* the opposition of orthodox Jews to Christianity and how many unreligious Jews feared "that the Christian faith might disturb their national cohesion," Victor Buksbazen looked forward to the day when Israeli Christians would increase their impact and "be a living testimony to their unbelieving brethren."[106]

Other evangelical commentary was on how Muslim leaders hated Israel and its economic success because it could "eat away at the foundations of their religious system." With Muslim clerics involving themselves in politics, Arab politicians gave much support to the Quran and its teachings. Only boys received an education, and the predominant subject was Islam, putting the Arabs at a disadvantage to better educated Israeli boys and girls. Since the Quran teaches that Allah controls the fate of Muslims, it made little sense to attempt to better oneself: "If he is poor, then it is the will of Allah." But the improved standard of life in Israel for both men and women represented a threat in that Muslim women would get modern ideas and expect equal treatment with men. And the Arab "feudalistic economy" that favored landowners over the masses would appear wanting compared to an economy built more on "the trade of machines and ideas." According to *Christianity Today*, these differences explained the reason for the Muslim clerics' holy war against Israel. Arab states "controlled by one-man or one-family regimes" likewise saw Israel as a threat.[107] Democratic ideas were dangerous to such regimes.

One article in *Christianity Today* entitled "Israel—Fulfillment of Prophecy?" outlined the impressive agricultural development and population rise of Israel's first ten years. The influx of immigrants to Israel was important to dispensationalist Christians because they interpreted it as a sign of the second coming of Christ. And yet there was much work to do since there were only 160 Christian churches in Israel and very few Hebrews professing Christ. There was greater hope for evangelism with the building of a new Israel-American Institute of Biblical Studies.[108]

Christianity Today articles by Oswald T. Allis, critical of Israel, and W. M. Smith, supportive of Israel, generated much discussion.[109] One response to Allis came from the Israel's in Washington. H. Y. Orgel took exception to Allis's statement that the establishment of the Israeli state was "highly dangerous to the peace of the world." There was aggression and bloodshed, but it was the Arabs who defied the UN Partition Plan and initiated the war. For the past decade, the Arabs had carried out border violence, economic warfare (blockades and boycott), and arms deals with the Soviets. Choosing a state of war with Israel, they showed no interest in negotiating "any settlement with Israel which would ease the tension and lead towards a lasting peace in the area."[110]

While the issue of Arab refugees was a problem, it was the result of Arab aggression: "The Arabs cannot first declare a war of destruction and then wash their hands of any responsibility for its outcome." Quoting Edward Atiyah, director of the Arab League Propaganda Office in London, Orgel wrote that many Arabs left, "encouraged by the boasting of an unrealistic Arabic press and the irresponsible utterances of some of the Arab leaders, that it could be only a matter of weeks before the Jews were defeated by the armies of the Arab states." Allis's direct response to Orgel made his anti-Israel position clear: "The present partitionment of the land is a monstrosity as every intelligent person must admit. The recent explosion over Suez and the extreme reluctance of the Israeli government to evacuate the territory which it had over-run is a clear indication of what Israel proposes to do as soon as a more favorable opportunity arises."[111]

Christian Zionists found such a conclusion incorrect and a diversion from more important issues. The International Hebrew Christian Alliance advertisements in *Moody Monthly* informed readers of the material needs of "Hebrew Christians" in the Holy Land. There were reports of organizations such as Million Testaments Campaigns, Inc. sending Jewish translated New Testaments to Israel to reach the large number of immigrants "pouring into their ancient homeland."[112] One article in *Moody Monthly* told the story of Auguste Kluehe, who at age sixty-two went to Israel to witness for Christ. Without knowing the language or much of the country, her months spent among the Israelis in 1952 was a "story of obedience and soul-winning."[113] Another *Moody Monthly* report in 1956 cited an Israeli poll revealing that 85 percent of Americans who visited Israel desired to visit again. The overwhelming majority of them "found the progress of the new state the most interesting feature of their visit."[114]

HIS was another evangelical magazine giving readers vivid accounts of Israeli successes despite the actions of Arab enemies not reconciled to the idea of a permanent Israel. In October 1956 before the Suez operation, Maurice Moyal wrote of the experiences of Jewish settlers living in Revivim located in the Negev approximately thirty miles from the Gaza Strip. For six months in 1948, Revivim was the target of daily bombing by the Egyptians. Only about one hundred settlers had defended it against two Egyptian infantry attacks. Eight years later, young people worked together behind barbed wire to prepare defenses against "suicidal Egyptian terrorists" who stole across the Gaza border most nights "creating a permanent state of insecurity in this vital border area." The tactics of these intruders included ambushing buses, killing shepherds, and blowing up farmhouses and cisterns. Many nights crackled with gunfire and rockets as Revivim settlers slept under guard of sentries knowing that the Arabs were intent on driving the Israelis "into the sea." But Israel was here to stay. Moyal concluded his article with an inspiring message from a Revivim leader: "We've fought off droughts and locusts. And our 20th century showpiece Israel, in the midst of medieval, miserable Arab lands, has cost us much sweat, tears and blood. Israel is thus doubly ours, by virtue of our sacrifices and efforts, and the promise made by God more than 4,000 years ago to Abraham."[115]

Another Christian Zionist wrote of "the unconditional covenant God made with Abraham," declaring Israel's right to claim all the land from the Nile River to the Euphrates River. While Israel's earlier disobedience resulted in the worldwide dispersion of the Jewish people, any acts of disobedience since did not nullify the prophetic promises of a Jewish homeland: "The Arab . . . has no divine title to a single inch of the land . . . no power can exterminate Israel, as Nasser and his supporters will find out. Those who bless Israel, God will bless. Those who curse her, God will curse."[116] Anglican bishop W. M. Jackson explained that the creation of the state of Israel "may have been done selfishly, or even without any intent or purpose of aiding the plan of God. Yet it is a fact, along with many other historical interpositions, sanctified to the establishment of God's ancient people."[117] Supporting the doctrine of the second coming of Christ, the *American Holiness Journal* was another publication proclaiming the importance of "the remarkable recovery of the Jewish nation."[118]

It is no surprise that the evangelicals most fervently supportive of Israel were those deep into Bible prophecy. In November 1955, Calvary Baptist Church in New York City was the site for the second International Congress on Prophecy, sponsored by the American Association for Jewish Evangelism. Under the leadership of the Rev. A. B. Machlin and the Rev. Herman B. Centz, the event had thirty-four speakers including Wilbur M. Smith, John S. Wimbish, Frank E. Gaebelein, Allan A. MacRae, V. Raymond Edman (president of Wheaton College), and Hyman J. Appleman. The lectures more or less continued where the first congress had stopped in 1952.

A common theme of the prophecy congress was how Scripture provided the correct roadmap for understanding the darkness of the world and the radiance of Jesus Christ. Smith warned of American politicians becoming too uncritical of the United Nations and the idea of world government. He feared this pointed to "the coming World religion prophesied in Scripture, which will have as its author and ruler, Satan, the god of this world and the prince of the powers of the air." Wimbish spoke of the dominance of godlessness as the world approached "the last hour of human history." Gaebelein took issue with the errors of Arnold Toynbee's understanding of history, notably his bitterness toward Jewish Zionism: "let us step outside this massive field of human scholastic opinion that is Arnold Toynbee's work and breathe the pure fresh air of biblical truth." In the last days, MacRae explained, only through the Lord Jesus Christ will there be "a reign of peace and security such as man with all his modern learning and ingenuity has never been able to attain." Edman underscored the importance of biblical prophecy in light of recent events linked to the Jews' return to the "Promised Land." Seeing Israel as the fulfillment of prophecy, Appleman urged Bible leaders to "understand the times and press for evangelism now as never before to both Jew and Gentile—'the Lord is at Hand.'"[119]

Citing a number of church observers, *Moody Monthly* saw the Suez crisis as proof of Arab nationalism and resurgent Islam "coming out in open aggression against Christian forces." Behind Nasser's "protestations of independence," one missionary official wrote, "lies all the emotional drive of the Arab renaissance of the past thirty years. And with this must be seen a widespread effort to promote a revival of Islam as a religious force which can unite the Muslim peoples of the world in a political bloc able to negotiate with strength."[120]

As for the actual Israeli military operation into the Sinai, Christian Zionists articulated their support for Israel and their criticism of

American pressure tactics on Israel. George T. B. Davis asked: "Is the oil of the Middle East more important than the blessing of God?"[121] In the *Sunday School Times*, Davis appealed to readers to pray earnestly for American politicians to support Israel "and so bring blessing to our own beloved land." The words Abraham received from God and recorded in Genesis 12:3 was the "promise that changed history." Davis gave many examples in world history of how nations received blessings or decline depending on whether they opposed or supported the Jews.[122] Writing for *Moody Monthly*, Sidney Correll, director of United World Mission, understood why Israel was reluctant to relinquish the Gaza Strip, "the base for Fedayeen suicide raids." When the Israeli army evacuated on March 7, 1957, border settlers watched grimly, knowing that "this portion of the Promised Land, again would be 'Fedayeen country.'"[123]

It was essential for Christians to understand that Islamic hostility to the Jews went deeper than any analysis from the United Nations or Washington: "even the hoped-for settlement will by no means remove the root-causes of future conflict."[124] For American Christian Zionists, God's blessings went to those who blessed Israel and curses to those who cursed Israel. Prophecy writer Donald Grey Barnhouse stated: "When Britain formally renounced her promises to Israel a few years later, I wrote in these pages that we could well expect the break-up of the British Empire."[125] Soon after the Suez War, Wilbur M. Smith wrote of the "prosperity and plenty" that Israel witnessed in her first eight years and the "greatest glory" yet to unfold. Using hard-hitting language, he wrote: "Anyone who saw the pitiful barrenness and poverty of that land even thirty years ago, and has seen the land more recently, recognizes that the Arab was a curse to the land."[126] In the 1950s, Israel's Gross National Product increased on average 10 percent every year.[127]

Some wrote of the Middle East and the signs of "the near culmination of our age in the Great Tribulation followed by the Second Advent."[128] In its report on the realignment of nations in the Middle East, particularly Egypt joining Syria to form the United Arab Republic (UAR), *Christianity Today* reminded readers that many Christians supported the biblical prophecy of the Middle East being the location of history's "ultimate denouement."[129] Various writers gave more nuanced political analysis as was the case with *Christian Herald's* Gabriel Courier, who discussed how the UAR threatened both Israel and Jordan.[130]

In Washington, American policymakers found the mob violence of Arab nations unsettling, and they recognized difficulties in negotiating with Arab leaders who had to heed the potential inflamed views of ordinary Arabs.[131] The events of late October and November 1956 angered Eisenhower, and his response to Israeli military action against the Arabs caused a further rift between the White House and Israeli leaders. The American evangelical response to the Second Arab-Israel War suggests one more rift. Although they voted for Eisenhower in large numbers, they stood strong for Israel and adopted a more supportive stand for Israel than almost any other group.

The language of evangelicals and liberal Protestants differed significantly. Typically, liberal Protestant commentators demonstrated some sympathy for Israel's security concerns, but their advice that the Israelis be more accommodating to neighboring Arab leaders revealed a lack of appreciation of what was at stake. Israeli leaders refused to believe that American politicians would be so accommodating if American citizens on American soil experienced numerous attacks causing loss of life and property. American evangelicals appeared to understand this better than liberal Protestants. Evangelicals had few idealistic notions that Israeli concessions would appease Arab leaders. As *Christianity Today* explained the conflict, Israel's population of "1,600,000 set in a sea of 50,000,000 Arabs" simply sought survival whereas the Arabs saw the western-supported Israel as a threat to their economy and "ancient way of life."[132] One unfortunate outcome for Israel was that newly created Third World countries typically courted the favor of Arab nations, thus this trend spelled fewer friends for Israel at the United Nations.[133] But Israel could always count on American Christian Zionists who saw no moral equivalence between Arab terrorism and Israeli responses.

With the Second Arab-Israeli War, President Eisenhower's pressure tactics were upsetting to Israeli politicians and to American conservative Christians aware of the persistent Arab hostile acts inflicted on Israel. It was true that Jews from Europe were prone to link Christianity with anti-Semitism, but this was an issue that conservative Christian leaders sought to correct. Victor Buksbazen wrote in *Moody Monthly* that "many Jews today realize that not every Gentile is a true Christian and that earnest Bible-believing Christians are generally friendly disposed toward the Jews."[134] Whether or not Buksbazen's optimism was accurate, for those paying attention there was ample evidence in conservative Christian literature of American Christians consistently standing with Israel.

NOTES

1. Sicker, *Israel's Quest for Security*, 59–60.
2. Ben-Gurion, *Israel*, 470. Nadav Safran writes: "Israel's shape is awkward and vulnerable. . . . The clumsy frontiers, the result of the freezing of the battle lines of the 1948 war, look as through they had been drawn to achieve the maximum length and unmanageability." See Safran, *Israel*, 69.
3. Smith, *World Crisis and the Prophetic Scriptures*, 203.
4. The American Christian Palestine Committee was one organization linked to mainline Protestantism that was supportive of Israel.
5. Quoted in Uri Bialer, "Top Hat, Tuxedo and Cannons: Israeli Foreign Policy From 1948 to 1956 as a Field of Study," *Israel Studies* 7, no. 1 (Spring 2002), 8.
6. Shlaim, *The Iron Wall*, 68, 72. An issue for the Syrians was the Israeli project to drain Lake Huleh for cultivation.

7. Yaacov Bar-Siman-Tov, "The Limits of Economic Sanctions: The American-Israeli Case of 1953," *Journal of Contemporary History* 23, no. 3 (July 1988), 426–28.

8. Golda Meir, *My Life* (New York: G.P. Putmam's Sons, 1975), 284–86.

9. Quoted in Bar-Siman-Tov, "The Limits of Economic Sanctions," 438.

10. "Israel's Quest for Water," *Christian Century*, April 7, 1965, 424. For the later years, see Moshe Shemesh, "Prelude to the Six-Day War: The Arab-Israeli Struggle Over Water Resources," *Israel Studies* 9, no. 3 (Fall 2004): 1–45.

11. Sicker, *Israel's Quest for Security*, 61–62. Even liberal Christians supported Israel's right to passage in the Suez Canal. See the *Christian Century*, October 17, 1956, 1189.

12. Quoted in Sicker, *Israel's Quest for Security*, 66.

13. Kober, "Great-Power Involvement and Israeli Battlefield Success in the Arab-Israeli Wars, 1948–1982," 27.

14. Shindler, *A History of Modern Israel*, 112–13.

15. Shlaim, *The Iron Wall*, 45, 62, 66–67. Jacobs, "The Perils and Promise of Islam," 718–19, 721.

16. Quoted in Shlaim, *The Iron Wall*, 68.

17. Sicker, *Israel's Quest for Security*, 62–63.

18. Meir, *My Life*, 284.

19. Shlaim, *The Iron Wall*, 85.

20. Shindler, *A History of Modern Israel*, 107. Also, Stein, *The Making of Modern Israel*, 158.

21. Sharon, *Warrior*, 89–90.

22. Glubb, *A Soldier with the Arabs*, 310.

23. Sicker, *Israel's Quest for Security*, 63–64.

24. Sicker, *Israel's Quest for Security*, 63–64, 66.

25. Shlaim, *The Iron Wall*, 116.

26. Quoted in David Tal, "Israel's Road to the 1956 War," *International Journal of Middle East Studies* 28, no. 1 (February 1996), 67.

27. Many UN officials viewed illegal border crossings as nonthreatening to Israel's vital interests. Hahn, *Caught in the Middle East*, 159.

28. Jacobs, "The Perils and Promise of Islam," 726.

29. *Moody Monthly*, November 1951, 145.

30. "You Should Be Interested," *American Holiness Journal* 8, no. 12 (June 1949), 8–9.

31. Carl Armerding, "The Fig Tree and Its Branch," *Moody Monthly*, September 1951, 18–19, 35–36.

32. John F. Walvoord, "The Abrahamic Covenant and Premillennialism," *Bibliotheca Sacra* 109, no. 435 (July–September 1952), 217–18, 224.

33. Michelle Mart, *Eye on Israel: How American Came to View Israel as an Ally* (Albany: State University of New York Press, 2006), 85i86.

34. Ben-Gurion, *Israel*, 448.

35. Quoted in Stein, *The Making of Modern Israel*, 165.

36. E. L. M. Burns, *Between Arab and Israeli* (Toronto: Clarke, Irwin and Company Limited, 1962), 84–89. In *David's Sling*, Shimon Peres wrote of other incidents of murdered Israeli citizens in 1955 (88). The Egyptians reported that one Israeli retaliatory raid resulted in thirty-six dead, but due to the international backlash against *fedayeen* terrorism the Security Council did not condemn the raid. See Sicker, *Israel's Quest for Security*, 69. Also, Tal, "Israel's Road to the 1956 War," 62, 69.

37. Stein, *The Making of Modern Israel*, 166.

38. Shlaim, *The Iron Wall*, 124.

39. Shlaim, *The Iron Wall*, 129. One young woman died and twenty others in the party were wounded.

40. Sicker, *Israel's Quest for Security*, 68–69.

41. Stein, *The Making of Modern Israel*, 167. Tal, "Israel's Road to the 1956 War," 76.

42. Stein, *The Making of Modern Israel*, 169.

43. Sicker, *Israel's Quest for Security*, 71. Shlaim, *The Iron Wall*, 147.

44. Quoted in Sicker, *Israel's Quest for Security*, 71.

45. Ben-Gurion, *Israel*, 447.

46. Sicker, *Israel's Quest for Security*, 73.

47. Shlaim, *The Iron Wall*, 149.

48. Quoted in Donald Neff, *Warriors at Suez: Eisenhower Takes America into the Middle East* (New York: Linden Press, 1981), 119.

49. Sicker, *Israel's Quest for Security*, 73. Also, Stein, *The Making of Modern Israel*, 171.

50. Quoted in Ben-Gurion, *Israel*, 474-75.

51. Burns, *Between Arab and Israeli*, 141–42. Tal, "Israel's Road to the 1956 War," 73. Stein, *The Making of Modern Israel*, 171.

52. "Report from Israel," *Christianity Today*, December 10, 1956, 29. The grenade incident happened at a synagogue with children present.

53. For other disturbing acts of violence, see Stein, *The Making of Modern Israel*, 172–73.

54. Sicker, *Israel's Quest for Security*, 73.

55. Peres, *David's Sling*, 15.

56. Burns, *Between Arab and Israeli*, 143.

57. Sicker, *Israel's Quest for Security*, 70–71. Zach Levey, "Israel's Quest for a Security Guarantee from the United States, 1954–1956," *British Journal of Middle Eastern Studies* 22, no. 1–2 (1995), 56.

58. Quoted in Sicker, *Israel's Quest for Security*, 76.

59. Schoenbaum, *The United States and the State of Israel*, 105.

60. Sicker, *Israel's Quest for Security*, 77–78.

61. Quoted in Sicker, *Israel's Quest for Security*, 79.

62. Quoted in Shlaim, *The Iron Wall*, 101.

63. Quoted in Shlaim, *The Iron Wall*, 141.

64. Tal, "Israel's Road to the 1956 War," 75.

65. Sicker, *Israel's Quest for Security*, 81.

66. Kober, "Great-Power Involvement and Israeli Battlefield Success in the Arab-Israeli Wars, 1948–1982," 27.

67. On the various Israeli military offensives, see Chaim Herzog, *The Arab-Israeli Wars: War and Peace in the Middle East* (New York: Random House, 1982), 120-44. Also, Stein, *The Making of Modern Israel*, 192–97.

68. For a concise account, see Peter L. Hahn, *Crisis and Crossfire: The United States and the Middle East Since 1945* (Washington, DC: Potomac Books, 2005), 30–33.

69. Quoted in Ben-Gurion, *Israel*, 509–10.

70. Alteras, *Eisenhower and Israel*, 260, 265–66.

71. Merkley, *American Presidents, Religion, and Israel*, 27.

72. Alteras, *Eisenhower and Israel*, 30. In October, 1953, the Eisenhower administration imposed sanctions on Israel because it refused to halt a plan to divert waters of the Jordan River to the Negev, a project in a demilitarized zone. See Bar-Siman-Tov, "The Limits of Economic Sanctions," 425–43. On the refusal of the Eisenhower administration to provide Israel with weapons or a security guarantee, see Levey, "Israel's Quest for a Security Guarantee from the United States," 43–63.

73. Merkley, *American Presidents, Religion, and Israel*, 29. Merkley believes that Eisenhower was aware of end-times teachings but "came to despise them" in connection with his great embarrassment about his parents' acceptance of the Jehovah's Witnesses (that prohibited giving allegiances "to the earthly kingdom in any form" such as military service). On the Jehovah's Witnesses, see Walter R. Martin, *The Kingdom of the Cults* (Minneapolis: Bethany Fellowship, Inc. Publishers, 1965). In his memoirs, Abba Eban's observations about Eisenhower suggest that Eisenhower was ignorant of the notion of Jews playing a special role in history. Eban, *Personal Witness*, 225. A recent article states that Eisenhower "generally avoided specific allusions to the Christian apocalyptic tradition." Moreover, for Eisenhower "spiritual values required a practiced restraint of all emotions, including 'hysteria' and 'complacency.'" See Ira Chernus, "Operation Candor: Fear, Faith, and Flexibility," *Diplomatic History* 29, no. 5 (November 2005), 786, 800. It is interesting that the conservative Protestant magazine

Eternity named Eisenhower its "Man of the Year" in its January 1956 issue, which included an article on prophecy. The author wrote that prophecy demanded more attention in "light of the Israeli-Arab question and the rise of Israel as a separate nation, in direct fulfillment of ancient prophecies long scoffed at by the skeptic and seldom emphasized by the Church at large." Walter R. Martin, "The International Congress on Prophecy," *Eternity*, January, 1956, 19.

74. Quoted in Hahn, "The View from Jerusalem," 521.

75. Steven L. Spiegel, *The Other Arab-Israeli Conflict: Making America's Middle East Policy, from Truman to Reagan* (Chicago: The University of Chicago Press, 1985), 53, 55; Tal, "Israel's Road to the 1956 War," 68.

76. Little, *American Orientalism*, 180-81. In "The Perils and Promise of Islam," Jacobs claims that U.S. Middle East specialists had "a deeply flawed interpretation" of Islam; there were those oblivious to the nuances of Islam and others who saw Islam as less significant than the force of secular Arab nationalism (736–38). For a recent discussion of the Eisenhower Doctrine, see Salim Yaqub, "Imperious Doctrines: U.S.-Arab Relations from Dwight D. Eisenhower to George W. Bush," *Diplomatic History* 26, no. 4 (Fall 2002): 571–91. Also Alteras, *Eisenhower and Israel* and Salim Yaqub, *Containing Arab Nationalism: The Eisenhower Doctrine and the Middle East* (Chapel Hill: University of North Carolina Press, 2004).

77. Douglas Little, "The Making of a Special Relationship: The United States and Israel, 1957–68," *International Journal of Middle East Studies* 25, no. 4 (November 1993), 553–54. Also see Alteras, *Eisenhower and Israel*. Alteras argues that the Eisenhower administration "viewed Israel as a burden and a hindrance to U.S. interests in the Middle East" (xiv).

78. Quoted in Ben-Gurion, *Israel*, 529. Also, see Zach Levey, "Israel's Quest for a Security Gurantee from the United States," 43.

79. Ben-Gurion, *Israel*, 533.

80. Peres, *David's Sling*, 16.

81. Burns, *Between Arab and Israeli*, 243–44. Sicker, *Israel's Quest for Security*, 91–92.

82. Little, "The Making of a Special Relationship," 565.

83. Sicker, *Israel's Quest for Security*, 82.

84. "Act of Injustice," *Christianity Today*, May 27, 1957.

85. *Christian Century*, November 14, 1956, 1331.

86. *Christian Century*, October 10, 1956, 1155.

87. *Christian Century*, August 1, 1956, 891.

88. *Christian Century*, August 15, 1956, 942–43.

89. "The Sometime Holy Land," *Christian Century*, October 10, 1956, 1158–59.

90. *Christian Century*, October 31, 1956, 1265.

91. "The Eye of the Storm," *Christian Century*, September 26, 1956, 1117.

92. *Christian Century*, October 24, 1956, 1235.

93. *Christian Century*, October 31, 1956, 1265.

94. *Christian Century*, October 24, 1956, 1219. "Muslim agitators" were also guilty of causing political instability

95. *Christian Century*, November 7, 1956, 1283–84. It declared: "An appeal was filed with the United Nations Security Council, presumably for a finding as to who was the aggressor—as if there was any doubt."

96. "The Election Results," *Christian Century*, November 14, 1956, 1315.

97. "The Election Results," 1315.

98. *Christian Century*, November 14, 1956, 1316. Interestingly, the magazine had placed Britain on a higher moral stand: "It was evil for the Russians to blast the Hungarians and for the French and Israelis to violate their commitments under the U.N. Charter. But the world expected a higher level of international morality from Britain."

99. *Christian Century*, December 5, 1956, 1413.

100. *Christian Century*, December 5, 1956, 1412.

101. *Christian Century*, November 21, 1956, 1347.

102. *Christian Century*, December 5, 1956, 1415.

103. "U.N. Town Meeting," *Christianity Today*, April 29, 1957, 24.

104. *Christian Century*, December 12, 1956, 1445.

105. George T. B. Davis, "A Forward Movement to Win More Jews to Christ," *Eternity*, April 1956, 5.

106. Victor Buksbazen, "Israel and Her Hebrew Christians," *Moody Monthly*, December 1956, 22–23, 32, 35.

107. *Christianity Today*, October 15, 1956, 25.

108. "Israel—Fulfillment of Prophecy?" *Christianity Today*, May 26, 1958, 28.

109. See the opposing non-premillennialist and premillennialist positions: Oswald T. Allis, "Israel's Transgression in Palestine" and Wilbur M. Smith, "Israel in Her Promised Land," *Christianity Today*, December 24, 1956.

110. *Christianity Today*, November 25, 1957, 26.

111. *Christianity Today*, November 25, 1957, 26–27.

112. *Moody Monthly*, December 1951, 257, 259.

113. Auguste Kluehe, "Fishing in Israel," *Moody Monthly*, October 1956, 18.

114. "Expect More Christian Tourists in Holy Land," *Moody Monthly*, June 1956, 6.

115. Maurice Moyal, "The Desert is Rejoicing," *HIS* 17, no. 1 (October 1956), 7–9, 23.

116. *Christianity Today*, November 25, 1957, 26.

117. *Christianity Today*, November 25, 1957, 26.

118. I. F. McLeister, "Why We Believe in the Second Coming of Christ," *American Holiness Journal* 16, no. 9 (March 1957), 13.

119. Martin, "Then International Congress on Prophecy," 19, 34.

120. "Suez Seen as Part of Larger Islam Pattern," *Moody Monthly*, November 1956, 7. Also, see "Islam and the Suez," *Eternity*, November 1956, 16.

121. *Christianity Today* was broad in its initial criticism of the Suez Crisis: "Our modern statesmen no longer quote the Living God and his commands. They walk where Moses walked but, instead of seeing the bush of God aflame, they toy with the flame throwers of another world conflagration." See "International Crisis on the Sandy Wastes of Sinai," *Christianity Today*, November 12, 1956. The editorial did state that Eisenhower's criticism of England and France was "forthright and courageous." Davis quoted in Weber, *On the Road to Armageddon*, 177. According to Weber, one premillennial explanation was that denunciation of Israel's attack was consistent with the end-times scenario: "Possibly the isolation and widespread condemnation that Israel experienced after its invasion of Sinai was part of the divine plan too. After all, the prophets had predicted that in the last days Israel would find itself surrounded on every side by hostile powers and that the decisive battle of Armageddon would include nations intent on destroying Israel once and for all."

122. George T. B. Davis, "A Divine Promise That Changed History," *The Sunday School Times*, March 16, 1957, 1–2, 18.

123. "At the Gaza Strip," *Moody Monthly*, May 1957, 5.

124. "Rehearsal in the Middle East," *Moody Monthly*, December 1956, 11.

125. Donald Grey Barnhouse, "Near-East Pressure Cooker: Israel in the Fire Surrounded by Hostile Sons of Ishmael and Esau," *Eternity*, July, 1956, 11. On British resentment toward Israel, see Miriam Haron, "Britain and Israel, 1948–1950," *Modern Judaism* 3, no. 2 (May, 1983): 217–23.

126. Weber, *On the Road to Armageddon*, 177. Smith, "Israel in Her Promised Land," *Christianity Today*, 24 December 1956, 11. The media attention that the Sinai Crisis received in the United States prompted Wilbur Smith to study and write a book on Egypt as it related to biblical prophecy. See Smith, *Egypt and Israel*, ix.

127. Stein, *The Making of Modern Israel*, 131.

128. "Signs of Vitality," *Christianity Today*, December 23, 1957, 21.

129. "Realignment of Nations in the Middle East," *Christianity Today*, March 3, 1958, 23. Also, "First Impressions," *Christianity Today*, March 31, 1958, 34.

130. Voss and Rausch, "American Christians and Israel," 60.

131. See Yaqub, "Imperious Doctrines," 577.

132. "Mechanized March by Children of Israel," *Christianity Today*, November 12, 1956, 28. A common device in the American media was to compare the tiny population of Israel to the tens of millions of surrounding Arab enemies. See Yaqub, "Imperious Doctrines," 580.

133. Stein, *The Making of Modern Israel*, 145.

134. Victor Buksbazen, "A Christian Look at the World's Religion: Judaism," *Moody Monthly*, June 1956, 59.

FOUR

The Sixties and the Six-Day War

For the ten-year period after the Second Arab-Israel War there were only a few large military operations between Israel and neighboring Arab states, but it was obvious that Israel could not relax its guard given the ongoing Arab terrorist raids and military flare-ups. When *Christian Century* writer Kyle Haselden asked Jordanian representatives if there could be compromise with Israel, the answer was, "Never! We cannot compromise issues with a state which does not exist."[1] And Jordan was the so-called "moderate" Arab nation.[2] In 1967, fundamentalist John F. Walvoord, president of Dallas Theological Seminary, wrote that Israel was "an armed camp." If the Arabs could, they "would drive every Israelite into the Mediterranean Sea and kill them. . . ."[3]

The Arab "fanatical opposition" to any peace negotiation prevented any worthwhile settlement. Scholar Michael B. Oren identifies Arab populist forces and clarifies what was at stake for Israel: "The vast array of Arab forces on all of Israel's borders, combined with the anti-Zionist frenzy sweeping the Arab world, produced a momentum for Israel's destruction that no Arab leader could resist."[4] Arab apologists absolved Arabs of any wrongdoing. For example, some claimed that it was Israel's commitment to aggressive acts that forced Egypt to close the Straits of Tiran, the key passageway for Israeli ships to the Indian Ocean. Henry Catton actually argued that Israel possessed no legal right of passage through the Straits of Tiran.[5] More critical of Israel than traditional Israeli historians, "new historian" Avi Shlaim writes that Israeli aggression with Syria "was probably the single most important factor in dragging the Middle East to war in June 1967." Overall, Arabs saw the war as one of Israeli expansion. But to Shlaim's credit, he admits that the war was a "defensive war" to safeguard Israel's security rather than a war to expand its territory.[6]

In the years that followed the 1956 war, more Americans took notice of Israel. The Jewish state—built on a mostly secular foundation—offered a stark contrast to the apparent economic and political stagnation of neighboring Arab nations. One 1964 study noted that the record of industrial expansion in the Middle East was "sobering."[7] In a broader context, many followers of Islam identified Israel as western and foreign. Anti-western sentiment, including strong opposing views of Christianity, was common.[8] The Islamic militant groups Hezbollah and Hamas did not exist in this period, but the Society of the Muslim Brothers was in operation in Egypt since 1928 and on a number of occasions played a role in stockpiling weapons and training members to fight Jews. Bernard Lewis gives a clear picture of the anti-western hatred of the Muslim Brotherhood with his analysis of Sayyid Qutb, an Egyptian Muslim Brotherhood activist whose preaching and writing warned of the decadency of western life.[9]

To defend itself, Israel sought better relations with western nations, particularly those willing to sell sophisticated weapons. For years, the Israelis searched for weapons, having no success with the United States due to its embargo on arms shipments to Israel. The Americans did authorize Canada to transfer F-86 jets to Israel in 1956, but the Canadian government was too slow to approve the deal and the Israelis scored the purchase of advanced weapons from France, a country that experienced cooler relations with Arab states due to Egyptian and Arab League support for rebels in France-controlled Algeria. Later, Israel received from France dozens of Mystére 2 and Mystére 4A aircraft, 450 Ouragan fighter-bombers, and dozens of tanks and transport and combat trucks.[10]

The Israelis also sought ground-to-air missiles to counteract the Soviets' supplying Egypt with the MiG-17 fighter, the MiG-19 fighter, and the TU-16 bomber. In February 1960, the Israeli government wanted to buy Hawk ground-to-air missiles from the United States, a request refused by the Eisenhower administration. After Egypt launched a successful ground-to-ground missile in July 1962, Ben-Gurion wrote to President John Kennedy: "We are confronted with a unique security problem. It is not our democratic system, or our borders and independence alone which are threatened, but our very physical existence is at stake."[11] Historians note Kennedy's awareness of the Jewish vote playing a significant role in his razor-close victory over Nixon in the election of 1960.[12]

The following month Kennedy approved the sale of Hawks, the first American president agreeing to a major arms deal. But earlier in the year, the Kennedy administration showed its displeasure at an Israeli reprisal against Syria by instructing the U.S. ambassador to the United Nations to echo other Security Council members and condemn Israel's actions.[13] Kennedy sent Joseph Johnson to broker a deal between Israel and the Arabs, proposing that Arab refugees be allowed to return to Israel or receive compensation. In the Knesset, Ben-Gurion clarified the problem of Johnson's proposal: Israel "categorically rejects the insidious proposal of freedom of choice for the refugees, for she is convinced that this proposal is designed and calculated only to destroy Israel." [14]

As was the case with Eisenhower, Bible prophecy commentators found no sign of biblical understanding behind Kennedy's actions. Premillennialism was likely foreign to Kennedy for two reasons: he had little interest in any religious doctrine and he was Roman Catholic. The roots of Christian Zionism are in puritanism, not Roman Catholicism. [15] The Roman Catholic Church favors amillennialism, the position that disputes the idea of a literal millennial kingdom of Christ on earth, sees prophetic Scripture concerning the Jews as allegorical allusions to the Church, and, thus denies any special role for Israel. [16] Nonetheless, although official Vatican recognition of Israel did not come until 1993, there were many Catholics across America who supported Israel. [17]

Justification for the decision to supply the Israelis with ground-to-air missiles was in part because the Hawk was a "defensive" weapon. The Israelis also argued that there was no fear of an arms race in the Middle East since the Egyptians had a "fifteen-to-one superiority in manpower and superior weapons." [18] With the Algerian war winding down and France returning to its "traditional pro-Arab stance," it was important for Israel to have the United States as its major supplier of arms. The Israelis did not take delivery of the Hawks until 1965, but the earlier approval was a symbolic victory for Israel. Arab nationalism, Soviet intrusion in the Middle East, and concern over Israel's nuclear program prompted the American government to act in favor of providing Israel with better military assistance. [19]

On the topic of nuclear weapons, the *New York Times*, on December 20, 1960, wrote of Israel's nuclear program. Three days later Nasser publicly threatened Israel with war if there was Israeli production of nuclear weapons: "It is inevitable that we should attack the base of aggression even if we have to mobilize four million to destroy it." [20] Scholars suggest that Israel's decision to develop them came sometime in 1962, the timing unclear due to a "policy of nuclear ambiguity" in which Israel did not formally admit possession of nuclear weapons. [21]

As was the case with Kennedy, the goal of the Lyndon B. Johnson administration was to honor the United States' commitment to Israel's sovereignty without worsening Cold War tensions with the Soviets. In May 1964, Johnson clarified his policy to Myer Feldman and Frank Sloan, the two emissaries he sent to Israel: "The United States regards itself, and all the Arabs do, too, as consistently the staunchest supporters of Israel. But we have felt it necessary to maintain at least an appearance of balance between Israel and the Arabs, because of our wide interests in the area and desire not to thrust Arabs into the arms of Moscow." [22] But Johnson, who regarded the Arab world as backward, had an even stronger relationship with Israel, going further than Kennedy and approving the sale of tanks and fighter jets, offensive weapons crucial in the future.[23] Eventually siding more openly with Israel than the State Department recommended, it was Johnson "who defined America's special relationship with Israel."[24]

A closer relationship between Israel and the American government was timely. In addition to the Egyptian threat, Israel faced serious problems along the Israel-Syria border where there were over four hundred attacks from late 1956 to early 1962. Most of these incidents against both Israeli army patrols and citizens involved regular Syrian army forces.[25] The Syrians were particularly angry over Israeli projects to divert water from the Jordan River to the Negev, thus advancing Israel's political goals, economic independence, and absorption of masses of immigrants. Various Arab leaders viewed Israel's diversion work as "the greatest danger threatening the Palestinian Arabs' rights since the *nakba* [the castastrophe of the Palestinians] in 1948."[26] In January 1962, the Syrian army commander-in-chief saw the Mediterranean Sea as an avenue to annihilate Israel: "To strangle and destroy Israel, the Arabs must pluck out Israel's sea lung by means of a naval combat force that will constitute a wall of steel in the sea and deny air to this monstrous state."[27] Conflict escalated in 1964 when the Syrians began construction to divert waters of the Jordan River with the planned outcome of preventing water to flow into the Sea of Galilee, the freshwater reservoir Israelis depended on for water supply. The water issue played a significant part in the Israelis and Arabs going to war in 1967.[28]

Acts of violence in other parts of the country were from the activities of the Palestinian Liberation Organization (PLO), formed in June 1964. For years, the Arab media promised Palestinian refugees they would return to their land; Palestinian literature and school textbooks were full of "We Shall Return" slogans. One 1964 study of Palestinians found that refugees refused attempts to raise their standard of living, fearing improvement would be a sign of accepting permanency. By the 1960s a "revolution generation" pushed for more action toward the goal of the "Return." The organization *Fatah* (the Arabic translation "conquest"), founded in 1959, eventually took control of the PLO establishment and gave direction to the idea of armed struggle. It launched its first Israel raid on January 1, 1965. Members of the PLO operated without any formal constraints placed on them by Arab states. In fact, the PLO was fine with the idea of provoking a general outbreak between the Israelis and other Arabs. Shimon Peres wrote of *Fatah* operating "in anarchy, taking no account of the losses and damage suffered by the Arabs or by the countries from which it launches its attacks."[29]

When Arab nations failed to meet the needs of the Palestinian refugees, Palestinian solidarity strengthened. As was the case with many Palestinians, Fawaz Turki, living in Lebanon, saw himself as a "stateless person" who did not feel a kinship with other Arabs. There were Palestinians living in refugee camps who refused to move to nearby Arab cities; they feared isolation and alienation in a new environment.[30] One *Fatah* booklet claimed that "the persecution of the Palestinians in the Arab countries contributed to the preservation of the Palestinian personality and non-absorption in the immediate environment."[31] Social alienation encouraged a national awakening that in turn fuelled calls for violent strategies to realize the return to the Palestinian homeland.

For many Arab refugees, the enemy was the American government for sending weapons to Israel. In the refugee camps, one idea with traction was that material assistance to the refugee camps was "blood money" sent from "guilt-ridden people who give much more to his enemies."[32] Israel's Arabs, however, made "great strides" economically and socially. According to Dwight L. Baker of *Christianity Today*, Arabs living in Israel enjoyed a higher material standard of living and had better health services and education than other Arabs.[33] Other publications such as the *Pentecostal Evangel*, the principal organ of the Assemblies of God (the largest Pentecostal denomination), wrote of Israel's achievements and "good" national health. Regardless of how one assessed the appropriateness of Israeli or Arab tactics, the *Pentecostal Evangel* clarified that the Jews were the chosen people: "We cannot endorse all their actions either in the State of Israel or in the various lands of their dispersion . . . nevertheless, we love . . . Jews because God loves them." In contrast to the miracle of Israel and the transformation of the land, Pentecostals wrote of "the judgment of God" and the economic desolation of Palestinian Arabs of previous years.[34]

Controversy over Arab refugees surfaced at the New York World's Fair, 1964–1965. Located in the Jordan Pavilion was a wall-sized mural of a poem and Arab refugee holding a child in her arms. The nine-stanza poem did not mention Israel, Jordan, or "refugee," but the political message was difficult to miss: Palestinians had suffered because of Israel.[35] The poem informs readers that until the arrival of "strangers" (European Jews) Palestine was a land of "peaceful harmony." One stanza glosses over the Arab violence that responded to the United Nations's plan of Palestine partition and the creation of Israel: "What followed then perhaps you know, Seeking to redress the wrong, our nearby neighbors, Tried to help us in our cause, And for reasons, not in their control, did not succeed." The next stanza presents the dire consequences: "Today, there are a million of us. Some like us but many like my mother, Wasting lives in exiled misery, Waiting to go home." Viewing it as a clear case of propaganda, opponents argued that the mural was a violation of the spirit of the World's Fair. Despite the pressure from New York politicians and various Jewish organizations, Fair officials ruled against any action to remove the mural.[36]

For the early 1960s period, assessments of the Arab-Israeli conflict by American liberal Protestants are instructive. In July 1960, one *Christian*

Century commentator wrote of the internal cohesion of Israeli society despite its composition of diverse people from around the world. Out of this kaleidoscope of cultural differences emerged homogeneity of purpose: "It is easy for a society to know what it wants when what it wants is something as uncomplicated as physical and economic survival." Sealing Israel's "messianic urge" was the "continuous militant hostility from the surrounding Arab states." According to Gabriel Gersh, one problem with this single-mindedness was the Israelis' difficulty in facing "the Palestine Arab refugee problem with the humility which the rest of the world expects of him." There was evidence of Israeli "short-sighted contempt" directed to the "self-doubt and confusions of more complex societies." Gersh believed Judaism played a role in boosting Israeli identity, but it had less of an impact on the majority of Israeli young people. As one Hebrew University student declared: "Whatever it may still be to the Jews of the Diaspora, to us it has become a religion pure and simple. It has given us principles to guide us in our daily life, but not a formula by which to shape the state and fit it to modern needs."[37]

The analysis of Israel in Christian Century was a mixture of criticism and some admiration. Sam E. Salem argued that American politicians and the media were too supportive of Israel and not appreciative enough of the difficulties Arabs faced.[38] Supporting his point was that only a minority of Christian Century writers generally sided with Israel in their attempt to offer balance. Without making a link to God's work in history, a few acknowledged the impressive economic and technological advances by the Israelis.[39] After having traveled in Lebanon, Syria, Jordan, and Israel, Methodist bishop Gerald Kennedy of the Los Angeles area wrote "that what has happened cannot be undone and that both sides will gain more from peace and cooperation than from war. The Israeli accomplishment should not be allowed to disintegrate." It was imperative to find peace and "save these mighty achievements of courage and religious faith."[40]

Reform rabbi Balfour Brickner explained that "alleged discrimination" against Arab Christians was due to their ethnic background rather than to their faith.[41] There were some reports in the Christian Century hinting of the "spiritual" element of Israel. Kyle Haselden wrote of the shaping "this little country into a people, a nation" faster "than the forty years required by Moses for a similar project."[42] Haselden also shared information on Arab improvements as a result of the Israeli government. He quoted the mayor of Nazareth discussing how the Israelis were "doing all that we can in health, education, employment and government to give Arabs first class citizenship."[43] Haselden was one who saw the existence of Israel as a "good" and who viewed Arab longings for 1947 as "politically naïve." Israel as a sovereign state was here to stay and "Arab demands that conflicts be resolved on grounds which presume the nonexistence of Israel require of Israel a political suicide which few nations in history have been willing to commit."[44]

Critical reports of Israel covered a wide variety of subjects. In spite of Prime Minister Ben-Gurion's plea for understanding, the *Christian Century* found no justification for Israel's revengeful and illegal kidnapping of Adolf Eichmann in Argentina, clearly a violation of Argentine sovereignty and an act more akin to international gangsterism.[45] Captured on May 11, 1960, by Israel's secret service organization Mossad, Eichmann was a wanted Nazi fugitive for the key role he played in the Holocaust. After a trial lasting from April to December 1961, an Israeli court found him guilty of "crimes against the Jewish people and crimes against humanity." Fascinating was the disclosed evidence of the warm association between Eichmann and Haj Amin Al-Husseni, head of the Palestinian national movement. In May 1962, Eichmann's death sentence was by hanging.[46]

One *Christian Century* writer believed Orthodox Judaism did not accept "the basic concepts of democracy," evident in the limitations to freedom of worship and assembly in Israel. Church activity by Protestants received close scrutiny, and when Billy Graham visited Israel in 1960 one condition of his use of a Tel Aviv hall was for him to avoid any mention of Jesus Christ. A request for Graham to return to Israel for a preaching mission went nowhere, much to the frustration of the Israelis "embarrassed by their country's fear that Judaism cannot stand on its own feet against all comers."[47] The treatment of Graham was regrettable, but as Balfour Brickner pointed out, the decision was by a board of directors of a semiprivate institution who acted independently of the government. At least Israel allowed Graham entry into the country, unlike some Islamic nations.[48] In the 1960s, evangelicals witnessed more signs of the Muslim world barring Christian missionary efforts.[49]

However, there were notable cases of Christians in Israel experiencing restrictions on their religious freedom. For years, groups such as the International Hebrew Christian Alliance sought donations from American and Canadian evangelicals to assist Christians in Israel. One advertisement in *Eternity* showed a photograph of an Israeli family who faced serious hardship. Shortly after his baptism, the father received a severe head injury when Israeli "fanatics" stoned him. This led to epileptic attacks and his inability to do heavy work. The message was clear: "Hebrew Christians are discriminated against."[50] *Christianity Today* acknowledged there was a lack of productive dialogue between evangelical Christians and Jewish religious leaders and there were significant prejudices against missionary activity in Israel. Some of the problems Orthodox Jews identified with Christian evangelism included the belief that some Jews converting to Christianity left Israel, and that Christian missions were a threat to Israeli "unity" and "have produced anti-Semites."[51]

Covering every phase of life, Orthodox Judaism (the only religious group Israel legally recognized) embraced the teachings of the Torah (first five books of the Bible) and the Talmud. Among Orthodox believers there were various groups including the small Neturai Karta (Guardians of the Wall) who had "nothing to do with the government," the Hasidium, and others. Conservative and Reformed Jews held more liberal understandings of Judaism. The main Orthodox groups had their own political parties to represent them in the Knesset.[52]

At times, evangelicals in Israel asked for trouble by failing to be sensitive to the teachings and ways of Orthodox Jews. Christian Zionist William Hull wrote that one missionary church affiliated with the U.S. denomination Churches of Christ was too brazen in its methods to induce Jewish children living in an Orthodox district to attend its meetings. He agreed that the Orthodox response of stoning the church was over-zealous, but he claimed that there was more religious freedom in Israel than had been the case in Palestine under the British mandate.[53] In the early 1960s, there were only about 50,000 Christians (mostly Arabs) out of Israel's population of 2,400,000. In February 1964, Prime Minister Levi Eshkol told the Cabinet that there were only eleven Jewish children baptized as Christians over a period of thirteen years.[54] Nonetheless, Orthodox Jews felt the threat of Christian evangelism and they occasionally responded with violence.

Actually, the Orthodox community scored a victory in the courts when Israel's Supreme Court ruled that Jews ceased to be Jews (in the national sense) if they converted to another religion. This ruling meant that the Law of Return giving automatic Israeli citizenship to Jews arriving from elsewhere did not apply to Christian Jews known also as Hebrew Christians (there was no problem if one was an atheist).[55] Stating that a person's religion "is irrelevant to the interpretation of the Law of Return," the one dissenting judge argued that "religious laws are applicable to matters of marriage and divorce only." There was much press attention to the case of war hero Oswald Rufeisen (Father Daniel), a Roman Catholic monk of Jewish origin denied Law of Return citizenship. Jacob Jocz, a Lithuanian Jew teaching at an evangelical seminary in Toronto, found it troubling that the secular court was acting as a religious court with too little attention to democratic values: "As the Jew was the acid test of Western Christianity, so the Hebrew Christian has become the acid test of Israeli society."[56] Were Hebrew Jews entering Israel to become illegal immigrants? Was Israel a true democracy?

Other evangelicals commenting on the court decision expressed their unhappiness with the "anti-Christian" thinking of various Israeli intellectuals. Addressing the issue in a letter to *Christianity Today*, Jacob Gartenhaus wrote: "The State of Israel came into being with the help of Christians. There was little if any help from non-Christian countries or individuals, and up to date the State has been kept intact only with the help of

Christians." According to Gartenhaus, Israeli leaders were aware that "[o]nly Christians who believe in the Bible as the Word of God also believe that the Jews have a right to possess the Land of Israel." This fact was important to counteract statements by the court judges that revealed the persistence of anti-Christian "falsehoods" within the Israeli intelligentsia. Blaming today's evangelicals for the deeds of Christians living centuries ago was only "pushing the people back into medievalism."[57]

Christian support for Israel did not stop some Orthodox religious factions from more forceful action against evangelicals. In early 1963, along Jerusalem's Street of the Prophets, students of a Jewish Talmudic school attacked missionary institutions. The Israeli government was careful not to upset Christians with talk of an anti-missionary law, but reports quoted minister of religious affairs Dr. Zerah Wahrhaftig favoring voluntary anti-missionary actions. After William Hull retired from twenty-eight years of missionary work in Jerusalem, *Christianity Today* wrote that one reason that he left Israel was the "mounting Orthodox-sponsored pressure against proselytizing activities."[58] During the summer, Orthodox students threw stones at buses transporting tourists, including Baptist youths returning from a world youth conference in Beirut, Lebanon.[59] In September, students of the Yeshiva religious sect targeted the Beth El Children's Home and School in Haifa. Dr. Solomon Birnbaum, the school's director, had to be vigilant with repeated Orthodox Jewish attacks.[60] Other raids took place against Christian schools in Jerusalem, Tel Aviv, and Jaffa. In the four cities, police arrested 130 involved in the attacks. Some of the Orthodox students had distributed pamphlets titled: "The Cross Completes What the Swastika Left Unfinished."[61]

Two years later in Haifa, young followers of Yeshiva broke into the home of the Gutkinds, a Hebrew Jewish family representing the American Board of Missions to the Jews. The youths' destruction of family property and threats against the occupants to cease Christian evangelism was troubling. Peter Gutkind, the sixty-two-year-old father, claimed harassment of his family went on for ten days.[62] In early 1965, the Knesset enacted an anti-conversion law prohibiting direct attempts to convert Jewish children unless both parents provided written consent. Although Orthodox rabbis wanted a tougher bill, some Christians feared the legislation provided Jewish zealots with "a handle with which to cause trouble."[63] Disturbing as these reports were for a number of American Christians, conservative Christian support for Israel showed no signs of diminishing.

Evangelical publications noted incorrect and unfair statements from politicians who were critical of Israel. As reported in *Christianity Today*, American Jewish leaders demanded an apology from Democratic Senator William Fulbright, who suggested that Israel was "the most corrupt of all nations" because total U.S. government aid was $310 million for a population of only two million.[64] A significant focus of conservative Christian publications was the health and security of Israel.

Astute Israeli politicians understood the sincerity of Christian Zionist support. Visiting Israel to discuss the arrangements for a Bible Lands Prophetic Pilgrimage to take place in April and May 1959, J. Palmer Muntz and Abraham B. Machlin of the American Association for Jewish Evangelism met with Prime Minister Ben-Gurion, President Itzhak Ben-Zvi, and other Israeli officials. Both Ben-Gurion and Ben-Zvi received a copy of Arthur W. Kac's *The Re-Birth of Israel*. The Americans learned that the government-owned radio broadcasting station promised to provide news coverage of the event.[65] In December 1959, John F. Walvoord wrote that approximately 2 million "Israelites" had returned "to their ancient home"—the "greatest movement of Israel" since Moses.[66] What Israeli politician would have a problem with any statement supportive of Israel?

Others remembered that it was a southern Baptist president who came through for Israel. While visiting New York City in 1961, Ben-Gurion met with Harry Truman and told him, "as a foreigner I could not judge what would be his place in American history; but his helpfulness to us, his constant sympathy with our aims in Israel, his courageous decision to recognize our new State so quickly and his steadfast support since then had given him an immortal place in Jewish history." Truman's eyes filled with tears. Rarely seeing "anyone so moved," Ben-Gurion gave Truman time to regain his composure before facing reporters waiting outside the hotel suite.[67] In this period, President Kennedy spoke of a "special relationship" between the United States and Israel.[68] At the same time, Bible prophecy literature became more abundant with books on the market such as John F. Walvoord, *Israel in Prophecy* and Arthur W. Kac, *The Rebirth of the State of Israel—Is It of God or of Men?*[69]

American evangelicals such as Carl Henry marveled at the economic development of Israel while recognizing the major issue of national security; the number of Arabs in the nations bordering Israel outnumbered Israelis fifteen to one.[70] By the mid-1960s, the Jordan-Israel border witnessed a rise of violence as Arabs carried out a number of incursions into Israel from the Hebron area; among those involved in acts of sabotage were *Fatah* members. In November 1966, the Israelis inflicted a punishing raid on the villages of Samu, Khirbet Markaz, and Khirbet. A fierce battle with Jordanian police and guards resulted in fifty Jordanian deaths.[71] The Israeli attack of the Jordanian border settlement Samu on November 13, 1966 "proved to be a decisive moment in the march to war," mainly due to the rupture of the spirit of détente between Israel and Jordan and King Hussein ibn Talal ibn 'Abdallah shifting his foreign policy to favor Egypt. For Hussein personally, the alliance with Nasser was distasteful, but he had to act on his perception that Israel sought to take the West Bank from Jordan.[72]

There was also the Palestinian reaction throughout the West Bank against the Jordanians days after Israel's successful military campaign at Samu. For example, 10,000 pro-Nasser demonstrators gathered in Nablus, where they inflicted heavy damage to government buildings. These demonstrations deepened the distrust between the Jordanian government and the West Bank Palestinians aligned with Egyptian and Syrian leaders. Since the 1950s, Jordan's King Hussein believed that competing Arabs causing political upheaval on Jordanian territory would give Israel reason to seize the West Bank. One notable crisis in the West Bank occurred in 1963 when Palestinian protesters, hostile to the Jordanian authority, demonstrated their support for Nasser in a number of violent demonstrations. In clashes with the Jordanian army, thirteen protestors died and about one hundred required medical treatment.[73]

In 1966, there were increased threats to Israel from the Syrians and Egyptians. A left-wing military coup in Syria in February resulted in the rise to power of President Nureddin al-Atassi. The new leader called for a "people's war" of sabotage and terror against the Zionists. Rhetoric turned to action one month later when the Syrians fired upon Israeli settlements located on the eastern bank of the Sea of Galilee. After an Israeli unit retaliated with an attack on Syrian soil, Syria appealed to the UN Security Council, which passed a condemnation of Israel on April 9. The following month Atassi persisted with his message: "We raise the slogan of the people's liberation war. We want a total war with no limits, a war that will destroy the Zionist base." The Syrians were serious and by late 1966 they took part in hosting, supporting, and training *Fatah* units.[74] As the *National Geographic* described it, "the thunders of border war have been commonplace beside the Sea of Galilee. Farmers in Israel's frontier kibbutzim worked their fields with rifles slung on their backs and operated their tractors from armored cabs."[75]

The Syrians had pulled out of the United Arab Republic (1958–1961), but once again the Syrians worked together with the Egyptians to defeat Israel. On April 7, 1967, the Syrians, from their positions on the Golan Heights, fired artillery, mortar, and tank cannon on the settlements of Ein Gev, Gadot, Haon, and Tel Katzir. The assault came to an end when the Israeli air force bombed the Syrian batteries and shot down six MiG-17s.[76] Soviet weapons in the hands of Arab clients remained a major concern for the Israelis, as did the possibility of direct Soviet Union military intervention. According to some scholars, the Soviets sought to destroy Israel's nuclear development and, thus, they pressed for the Arabs to war against Israel. THe Soviet course of action included giving the Egyptians disinformation on May 13 that Israel had positioned thirteen brigades on the Syrian border.[77]

On May 16, 1967 the Egyptian military demanded the UNEF to withdraw from the Sinai immediately, a fact denied by Nasser apologists. Three days later, U Thant told the General Assembly of the withdrawal in process. Within days, the Egyptian force in the Sinai grew to about 80,000 men. On May 22, Nasser declared that no Israeli-flag ships would be permitted passage through the Aqaba Gulf: "Our armed forces and all our people are ready for war, but under no circumstances will we abandon any of our rights. This water is ours." Both Egyptian and Israeli leaders understood "this was tantamount to a declaration of war."[78] Historian Michael Oren paints a bleak picture of what would happen if the Arabs were victorious; even Hussein and Nasser lacked "the power to rein in their forces once they vanquished the Israel Defense Forces and occupied Israeli territory."[79] In late May an increasing number of American Jews voiced their fear for Israel's survival. Abraham Heschel, professor of Jewish ethics, wrote: "The darkness of Auschwitz is still upon us, its memory is a torment forever. In the midst of that darkness there is one gleam of light: the return of our people to Zion. Will He permit this gleam to be smothered?"[80]

Christianity Today reported how the Egyptians were flexing their military muscles, notably blocking Israeli shipping at the Straits of Tiran. It wrote of Muslim support for Nasser to attack the "Zionist menace."[81] In the Sinai, there were seven Egyptian divisions apparently massed for attack. Egyptian General Mourtagi declared: "In five days we shall liquidate the little State of Israel." A Syrian general predicted that "Egypt and Syria will be able to destroy Israel in four days at the most." Time was running out. A worried Abba Eban, Israeli foreign minister, took stock of the situation: "We looked around and saw the world divided between those who were seeking our destruction and those who would do nothing to prevent it."[82]

But it was the Israelis who struck first, an action Christian Zionists defended. On the morning of June 5, Israeli bombers flying extremely low to evade Egyptian radar reached Egypt and destroyed most of its airforce in a surprise attack. In a remarkable achievement, Israel began the war with 90 percent of its planes operational.[83] Next was the spectacular victory by Israeli ground troops, who took control of the Gaza Strip and the Sinai Peninsula from the Egyptians. Egyptian media boasted the success of the Egyptian military, including one story of Arab fighters in the streets of Tel Aviv "spreading death."[84] All such stories were fiction. Israel experienced stunning victories on all fronts.

In the Gaza Strip, a twelve-year-old Palestinian boy, Izzeldin Abuelaish, assumed the Israeli soldiers would force everyone to jump into an empty waterhole and shoot them. To his surprise, the Israelis only arrested a few young men and told others to return to their homes and respect a 6:00 p.m. to 6:00 a.m. curfew until the war was over: "Almost no one had behaved the way I'd expected them to behave—not the parents who'd run off without their children, not the soldiers who I'd presumed were there to kill us. The knowledge unsettled me."[85]

Although there was a preemptive attack on Egypt, Israel used all channels to assure King Hussein of its peaceful intentions with Jordan unless the Jordanians attacked Israel. Hoping to avoid war with Jordan, Israel endured three hours of Jordanian shelling and tank movement toward northwest Jerusalem before it made the decision to counterattack.[86] Oren explains that Hussein had no other reasonable options: Jordan's Palestinian majority demanded action and a Nasser defeat of Israel without Hussein's would likely mean Hussein's death by the Egyptians. After a brief spell of war fever, Hussein correctly assessed the hopelessness of Jordan's military position.[87] Dramatic was the Israeli defeat of the Jordanians and consequent acquisition of East Jerusalem and the West Bank. Before the war ended on June 10, the Israelis also captured the Golan Heights from the Syrians.[88] To make sense of such a humiliating loss, many Arabs believed that the United States assisted Israel to defeat the "revolutionary Arab regimes which had refused to be a part of the Western sphere of influence."[89]

The Six-Day War received much attention in American Christian magazines. One *Christian Century* article commented on the desperation motivating Israeli soldiers who understood the slim chance of decent treatment once captured by the Arab enemy. The Arab propaganda telling of the destruction of the Jewish people was the cause of many "unbelievable acts of heroism." One example was the story of two Israeli soldiers who, without tank support, continued to climb a mountainside with Syrian bombs, mortars, and howitzer shells raining on them. Their reward was Russian weapons left behind by fleeing Syrian soldiers. Additional acquisitions were useful in other ways. One placard captured from an Arab read, "Yes, Adolf, we will finish your glorious task." Someone thought it clever to hang the placard "on the wall of a urinal at a rest stop in Negev."[90]

There were also many tragic stories. Born in Galilee, Solomon Mattar was an Arab who became a Christian and married a Christian Arab. In 1953, he became the warden of the Garden Tomb, where many believed Christ had laid and risen. Over the years, he shared with visitors the good news of Christ's resurrection. Mattar's reading of the Bible and God's promise to Abraham was that Israel one day would take possession of the land. The seventy-five-year-old Mattar would not witness Israel claiming any additional land. Upon hearing the warning sirens in Jerusalem on June 5, Mattar, his wife, and a female worker sought shelter in the tomb. The shelling and shooting continued throughout the day and there was concern that the three might die in the tomb. As stated in *Moody Monthly*, Mattar's response was: "I am ready to die! I am ready to meet the Lord!" When the shooting lessened, he left the tomb and sought coffee and breakfast in his home. After preparing some water, he went outside where he saw and greeted Israelis soldiers with "Good morning." There was a brief conversation and then someone fired shots, killing

Mattar. Someone also fired shots into the tomb and Mrs. Mattar felt a bullet enter the blanket wrapped around her. Fortunately, she escaped injury. Other Israelis arrived, but they went away.[91]

Christian Zionists commenting on the sad story accepted the Israeli government's apology and explanation for the killing of Mattar. Jordan had a gun emplacement at the top of the hill overlooking the tomb and Israeli soldiers expected Jordanian soldiers in Mattar's house and area. This was a reasonable assumption given that Israeli troops fighting across old Jerusalem had discovered other holy places fortified by the Arabs. Stating that her husband never showed resentment to anyone, Mrs. Mattar declared: "We can only accept God's will in it all. . . . Through all these events I can see God's love."[92]

Another Israeli error was the attack on the American intelligence ship USS *Liberty*, monitoring the conflict while in the Mediterranean Sea near the Sinai coast. On June 8 there was a major explosion at al-'Arish that the Israelis concluded was due to Egyptian shelling from the sea. The subsequent attack on the *Liberty* by two Mirages followed by a squadron of Mystères and torpedo boats resulted in thirty-four dead and 171 wounded. Some American officials found the attack inexcusable and an act of premeditated murder. In the short term, mortified Israeli leaders sent apologies for the tragic accident, in the long term there was a full Israeli inquiry and eventually the Americans received a $12 million compensation package.[93]

In contrast to the sadness of the *Liberty* episode was the joy of Israeli possession of Old Jerusalem. Defense Minister Moshe Dayan visited the Wailing Wall and upon leaving the Temple Mount area he declared: "We have returned to the holiest of our sites, and will never again be separated from it. To our Arab neighbors, Israel extends the hand of peace, and to the peoples of all faiths we guarantee full freedom of worship and of religious rights."[94] In the previous years, the Jordanians dynamited all but one synagogue of thirty-five in the Old City and they removed many thousands of tombstones from an ancient cemetery to use for construction purposes. A Catholic priest declared: "There appeared to be no limit to the sacrilege."[95] In late June, the barriers in Jerusalem separating Arab and Jewish sections came down. Israeli troops destroyed sniper nests and walls, dismantled checkpoints, and cleared barbed wire and land mines. It was the first time in Jerusalem since 1948 that Arab and Jewish residents faced each other in open space.[96] To the UN Security Council, Abba Eban explained that the Israeli's control of all Jerusalem provided "the inhabitants of all parts of the city social, municipal, and fiscal services."[97]

The Knesset's imposition of Israeli law in East Jerusalem was the first step in securing complete and absolute sovereignty in East Jerusalem. But the annexation was a major offense to Arabs and many in the international community. A later American proposal was for Israel and Jordan to share the civic administration of Jerusalem. Not convinced, a *Christianity*

Today editorial concluded that this solution only made sense "in a dream world free from sin."[98] One strategy of the Israelis was to respect the freedoms of peaceful Arabs. An editor of an Arabic newspaper in East Jerusalem spoke of his positive living experience: "In the winter I go to Jericho to get warm. In summer I go to the beach at Natania to swim. My paper is not subject to any political censorship. Israelis visit me in my house and I visit them in theirs."[99]

This kind of information was rare in liberal Christian publications such as *Christian Century*. Explaining its stand on Israel, the magazine opposed any unilateral and military intervention by the United States. One editorial scolded American Jews, notably Rabbi Pesach Z. Levowitz and Rabbi Balfour Brickner, for arguing that too many Christians failed to raise their voice in defense of Israel. According to *Christian Century*, it was wrong to sign a blank check for Israel without a better understanding of both sides of the story. Both the *Christian Century* and the National Council of Churches opposed Israel's annexation of the Old City of Jerusalem.[100] Two months after the war, Cecil Northcott, a *Christian Century* editor, expected the Israeli government to return East Jerusalem to the Jordanians if it genuinely desired "a settled peace."[101] Articles by liberal Protestants such as J. A. Sanders of Union Theological Seminary and Willard G. Oxtoby of Yale University echoed the *Christian Century* editorial position.[102] American Jewish leaders found statements by liberal Protestants troubling. Also problematic was what liberals were not saying. Why were Christian leaders silent about Jordan's expulsion of Jews from East Jerusalem nineteen years earlier? Why silence on the Arab destruction of synagogues and the banning of Jews from the holy sites since 1948?[103]

Whereas a *Christian Century* editorial disapproved Israel's unilateral annexation, stating a joint Israel-Jordan administration of the city would be preferable, *Christianity Today* reported that Jewish possession of all of Jerusalem "was a great moment in religious history."[104] Other conservative Christians found Israel's victory exhilarating, especially its control of all of Jerusalem.[105] In a *Christianity Today* article titled "Unfolding Destiny," L. Nelson Bell, Billy Graham's father-in-law, wrote that the Jewish possession of Jerusalem "gives a student of the Bible a thrill and a renewed faith in the accuracy and validity of the Bible." Discussing the outcome of the war, Bell looked to God's providence to explain the "unbelievable" and "fantastic" success of the Israeli fighting force such as its "pinpoint accuracy" in destroying Arab planes and Egyptian tanks at the Mitla Pass in Sinai.[106] In one *Christianity Today* advertisement, the American Board of Missions located in New York City stated: "Astounding was the only word for it! A historical re-acting of the story of David and Goliath in which the characters were nations . . . tiny Israel stood in the role of victor because God promised and gave the victory." Seeking others to reach Jews for Christ, the organization offered a free study course on biblical prophecy.[107] *Christianity Today* also noted that ardent supporters of Israel included Roman Catholic Archbishop Paul J. Hallinan of Atlanta and Monsignor George Higgins of the U.S. Catholic Conference. A series of pro-Israel articles in the *Pentecostal Evangel* was proof of Pentecostal enthusiasm for Israel's military victories.[108]

After four days of fighting, Chicago's Christian radio station WMBI broadcast a two-hour program with two Bible professors and a radio pastor, all three from Moody Bible Institute. For Dr. Alan Johnson, the war confirmed the literal interpretation of Bible prophecies such as the prophecy of the Jews regaining control of Jerusalem. There were obvious links between the war and Old Testament prophecy, but Johnson cautioned against overexaggerating "the meaning of events." As a typical Christian Zionist, Johnson gave no evidence of wanting to hasten Armageddon and he took the issue only so far: "We do not necessarily look for signs to precede the rapture of the Church, but the coming events of the tribulation period certainly are well able to cast their shadows beforehand." Dr. Louis Goldberg likewise advised against using Scripture to explain every little detail conclusively. It was problematic comparing one detail to "a corresponding line of Scripture to say in effect, 'Well now, this is it.'" It was more important to look at the big picture on how the story of Israel gave "strong evidence for the validity of the Word of God." While also telling Christians to guard against making specific claims about prophecy, Robert J. Little stated that "present events may be of a preparatory nature." He agreed that the signs of the times were "not needed for the rapture of the Church." Moreover, Israel is God's "prophetical clock," but it is not clear when "God is dealing *directly* with Israel in their land."[109]

In both popular and academic publications, John R. Walvoord discussed Israel's dramatic victory over the Arabs, the most stunning fulfillment of Bible prophecy in 1,900 years: "Surely this is the finger of God indicating the approaching end of the age."[110] In *Bibliotheca Sacra*, he wrote on Israel's "complete possession" of Jerusalem and how this outcome was "a matter of tremendous Biblical and prophetic importance." While cautioning against any hasty interpretations, he declared that this new phase in Israel's history "may be the last preparatory step prior to the important sequence of events that lead to the second coming of Jesus Christ."[111]

Israel's military success and acquisitions of the Gaza Strip and the West Bank generated much excitement. Even though most Israelis viewed the occupation of these territories as representing expansion, many conservatives saw it as land long due to Israel.[112] Certainly, many conservative Christians gave little credence to emerging Palestinian nationalism.[113] Christian Zionists were aware of the hardships among the Palestinians, but this was an unavoidable fact. For its part, Israel's "enlightened military government" sought to avoid any unnecessary interference with the local West Bank population. Israeli leaders desired better economic and trade relations, which included employment in Israel for West Bank residents. West Bank Palestinians had free entry into Israel, Israeli soldiers were to treat West Bank residents with respect, and there was no "restriction on listening to and viewing Arab radio and television broadcasts." Israel's policy on Palestinian terrorism was to focus only on those directly responsible for terrorist acts.[114] As Moshe Dayan explained, "On no account will we turn the entire local population against us by penalizing innocent persons. On no account should we expect the local population to take up our fight against terrorism."[115] The policy of treating West Bank inhabitants with respect and targeting only those involved in terrorism looked good on paper, but was very difficult to practice.

As for the American Jewish community, the Six-Day War caused an "abrupt, radical" change of mood for many as more Jews than ever before saw Israel as a source of pride. Liberal author Amos Oz understood the Arab-Israeli conflict was not a simple case of misunderstanding: "It is based on full and complete understanding: we returned and offered the Arabs good-will, good neighbourliness and co-operation, but that was not what they wanted from us. They wanted us to abandon the establishment of the Jewish State of the Land of Israel, and that is a concession we could not make and shall never be able to make."[116] Many other well-known Jews clarified their allegiance to the Zionist cause. Notable was the transformation on college campuses as Jewish students, often described as apathetic and alienated, "felt their identification with and their responsibility for the people of Israel to the very depth of their being."[117] This positive student reaction was in sharp contrast to the leftist attacks from the Student Non-Violent Coordinating Committee (SNCC). In its summer newsletter, SNCC linked Jewish capitalism to the "conspiracy" of creating the State of Israel. It also declared that "Zionists conquered the Arab homes and land through terror"—a theme embraced by leftist activists who began to speak more aggressively about so-called imperialistic Zionist wars.[118] Having sided with liberal-left causes for decades, the American Jewish establishment could not escape the rise of anti-Semitic rhetoric from the New Left. And also eye opening for American Jews were the acts of persecution against Jews living in Arab nations in the days after the Six-Day War.

Lawrence Grossman traces the transformation of the American Jewish Committee (AJC) that for decades maintained its distance from Zionism and Israeli affairs in general. Founded in 1906 and the oldest existing Jewish defense and community-relations organization in America, the AJC feared Jewish nationalism would leave American Jews vulnerable to the attack of being disloyal Americans. In 1964, AJC president Morris Abram did not use the term "Jewish people." He instead referred to himself as "a Jew and an American—period." Moreover, the common attitude of the AJC toward Israel's government was paternalistic, believing it knew better than Israeli politicians what was best for Israel. The stunning Israeli military victory transformed the thinking of the AJC; "almost overnight" it became an ardent defender of Israel.[119] The approval of American military support for Israel unfolded despite the inconsistency of American Jewish opposition to the Vietnam War. Frightened by the precarious position of Israel but elated with the latest news of Israeli military success, Abram at a June 8 Israel-support rally in Washington stated "we did not foresee that tiny, encircled Israel would be able to overcome multiple fanatical adversaries equipped with Soviet arms. But the people of the Book have proved the verities of the Book: 'Not by power, nor by force, but by the spirit, sayeth the Lord.'"[120] Additional confirmation of a transformed AJC came in the summer when it refused a White House request to help put pressure on Israel concerning Middle East negotiations.[121]

Interestingly, the AJC collected research on the Christian response to Israel's war crisis and found weak support for Israel from national church leadership. Particularly disappointing was the reluctance of the National Council of Churches and National Conference of Catholic Bishops to commit unequivocally to "Israel's survival."[122] Although at the grassroots there was good all-around Christian support for Israel, Rabbi Marc Taneubaum, director of interreligious affairs, understood the need for a new focus explaining to non-Jews the "centrality of the Land of Israel within Judaism."[123] Given that conservative Christians represented one group well aware of the centrality of Israel, the work most needed was with mainline Protestant churches which in recent decades had distanced themselves from the inerrancy of the Bible.

G. Douglas Young, Beldun Menkus, and William LaSor were three of a number of evangelical writers participating in an entire issue of *Eternity* on the subject of Jews and evangelicals. As the director of the American Institute of Holy Land Studies (Jerusalem), Young wrote that Israel's existence was reason for Christians to heed the Bible "where it is clear that God has a continuing interest in the Jews." In Israel one could see "that everything points (as biblical prophecy should lead us to expect) to the time when once again 'the law shall go forth from Zion, and the word of the Lord from Jerusalem.'" There were many important lessons to learn from "the values that God enabled Jews to perpetuate, the values He intends to keep on using." Young explained that "conservative Protestants" represented a minority and they could learn from the Jews who as a minority survived persecution by working together, looking after each other, stressing the importance of education, and not allowing the state to control religion.[124] Evangelicals respected Young, who with his wife Georgina moved to Israel in 1963. *Christianity Today* spoke highly of the work of the American Institute of Holy Land Studies, "especially in the light of the prophetic Scriptures."[125] Evidence of the Israelis' appreciation for Young's impact was his appointment to civic and municipal commissions and his receiving the title "Worthy of Jerusalem," the city's highest honor.[126]

In discussing the sensitive issue of evangelism and the Jews, frequent *Eternity* contributor Belden Menkus was prudent to state "that our submission to Christ does not make us morally or religiously superior to anyone else, especially to our Jewish neighbors." It was likely true, as Rabbi Guther Plaut suggested, that "Christian fundamentalists" outnumbered Jews in believing "that the re-establishment of Israel was an expression of God's love in fulfillment of the ancient covenants." One concern for Menkus was that there were Christians who knew much about biblical prophecy but remained ignorant or indifferent to the issues important to today's Jews. It was essential for evangelical Christians to reach out to Jews with sincerity: "If our witness fails to win our Jewish neighbors but we are better neighbors in the process, we will not have totally failed our Lord."[127]

William LaSor, professor of Old Testament at Fuller Theological Seminary, discussed biblical prophecy and the stunning success of the Israelis in the Six-Day War. Only one month before the war erupted, LaSor addressed members of a Holy Land Tour on whether the State of Israel was a fulfillment of prophecy. After the war, his discussion of Israel became even more pressing as Christians pondered Israel's expansion. From his biblical understanding of the land-promises to Abraham, he identified "the Promised Land" as all of Israel, Lebanon, the West Bank, most of the Sinai, and part of western Syria. However, he cautioned that all of these lands were not "God's promise to the modern State of Israel." LaSor was unwilling to state that modern Israel and the biblical Israel was identical, but he thought it "likely that the regathering of the Jews to Palestine, the establishment of the State of Israel, and the almost incredible military successes of Israeli armies against what appeared to be overwhelming odds, are somehow to be related to God's promises."[128]

When Israel scored its impressive military victory and claimed Jerusalem, American bookstores quickly sold out prophetic books as many Americans turned to Bible prophecy.[129] One *Christianity Today* editorial explained: "To Christian observers, the cresting confusion in international affairs make it increasingly obvious that the world needs a summit conference with the transcendent God. True, nobody is proposing a locale. But the Book of Revelation reminds us long ago God scheduled one in Armageddon."[130] Raising "volumes of excited comments among students of Bible prophecy," the war was the top news story for 1967 according to *Moody Monthly*.[131] Having visited Israel weeks before the war, Wilbur M. Smith completed his prophetic book project in time for publication in 1967. In *Israeli/Arab Conflict in the Bible*, Smith included two photographs of Jerusalem's Wailing Wall: one showing an Israeli army chaplain celebrating with other soldiers and the other of Prime Minister

Levi and General Uzi Narkiss walking at the base of the Wall.[132] In 1968, there was a second printing of the book.

The rhetoric of Christian Zionists scored high marks with Christians appreciative of a message that appeared to offer clarity, steadfastness, and promise.[133] Subtleties tended to get lost, but the message was pregnant with emotion, certainly more exciting and optimistic than the cold deliberations of power politics. Christian Zionists cared about the restoration of Israel, which confirmed the accuracy of their views, and they took seriously the declaration that those who favored Israel would be blessed. However, prophecy believers faced obstacles. While prophecy literature in newsletters, articles, and books was expanding, prophecy voices lacked mainstream media visibility and a political base.[134] Fundamentalists were "reluctant warriors" in the political forum in the sense that they believed worsening world conditions brought them closer to the Rapture. Only the seriousness of fighting Satan overrode their reluctance to get involved, although this caused some cognitive dissonance.[135]

Prophecy popularizers rarely had the educational background and institutional network of Washington policymakers. For example, Wilbur M. Smith began his college education at Moody Bible Institute after being denied a seat at Dartmouth College.[136] Many prophecy leaders were the products of Dallas Theological Seminary, where John F. Walvoord taught. Beyond the periphery of America's most prestigious colleges, there were the numerous conservative Bible schools and seminaries, which produced pastors for conservative churches from coast to coast.[137] However, one did not need to be a dispensationalist to have an interest in and appreciation for the linkages between the Bible and the unfolding of history in Israel. Smith himself wrote that "a superficial reading of the prophetic writings of the Old Testament" was enough for one "to believe that God has promised to finally restore Israel to her land where she will permanently abide, never again to be rooted up."[138] The certainty of Christian Zionist literature was appealing.

For many ordinary Americans, the rhetoric from Washington on the proper relations with Israel was often ambivalent or conflicting. Beyond the common acceptance of certain Cold War truths—keeping the Middle East stable being foremost—policymakers struggled to provide a more unified and consistent position on Israel. They inherited and preserved the culture of geopolitical realism. Although their task was not easy, the key policymakers benefited from private schools such as Groton and college education at Yale, Princeton, Harvard, and other great national institutions. In favoring rational and secular thinking, they connected with like-minded thinkers, including most Israeli leaders and officials.[139]

President Johnson was no Harvard or Yale man. His religious roots were the fundamentalist-leaning Church of Christ (Disciples) and his education was at a small Texas college. But Johnson had distanced himself from the literalist teaching of conservative Christianity. His attachment to

Israel "was essentially sentimental" rather than theological.[140] Johnson's support for Israel's stunning victory was due to domestic pressure, the desire to see Nasser humiliated, and the belief that a strong Israel would be more willing to compromise with moderate Arabs such as Jordan's King Hussein and would be less inclined to become a nuclear power.[141] However, to an audience of the B'nai B'rith in 1968, Johnson declared: "Most, if not all of you, have very deep ties with the land and with the people of Israel, as I do, for my Christian faith sprang from yours. The Bible stories are woven into my childhood memories as the gallant struggle of modern Jews to be free of persecution is also woven into our souls."[142] Such thinking reveals another type of Christian Zionism not based on a complicated Bible prophecy interpretation.

Israel needed loyal friends on the international scene and Israeli leaders like Ben-Gurion understood the power of religious ideas.[143] In a November 1967 letter to French President Charles de Gaulle, Ben-Gurion wrote: "While it is true that for two thousand years we have believed in the vision of our Prophets and many among us still believe in the coming of the Messiah who will bring Jews, dead and living, to the Holy Land from all corners of the world, we have never had a 'burning conquering ambition' but a burning faith in the vision of peace of our Prophets: for 'nation will not bear sword against nation, and neither shall they learn war any more' (Isaish 2:4, Micah 4:3)."[144] National security was paramount. During the twentieth anniversary celebrations of Israel, Ben-Gurion told the Knesset that "The bitter truth is that if, God forbid, the Arab armies defeat us only once, say in the fifth war, or the tenth, it may well be final because the Arab leaders' aspiration, like Hitler's, is to wipe us off the face of the earth." For him, Israel's major tasks were "to attract and absorb immigration at an ever-growing rate, and to be a select people. Only in these ways can our security be assured and our State fulfill its historic mission."[145]

Newell S. Booth, Jr., associate professor of religion at Miami University, argued that there was no middle position on the Arab-Israeli issue. Neutrality was impossible and, thus, the Arabs and Israelis who understood this were "more realistic in their intransigence than their outside advisers." Unlike Americans or others who expected a diplomatic solution, the thinking of the majority of Arabs and Israelis was "not confused by the desire to appear reasonable." In the end, one had to decide whether to side with the Arabs or the Israelis, any other choice was an illusion.[146]

It was an easy decision for the overwhelming majority of American evangelicals. Like other evangelical writers, Raymond Cox reacted with amazement at Israel's many accomplishments in agriculture, industry, and the military. The Israelis faced a serious security challenge, but Cox looked to the Bible for answers on whether Israel could survive. He asked, "If God has begun resettling the sons of Isaac in Israel, can the sons of Ishmael dislodge them? The Bible seems to indicate an emphatic negative answer. Israel will survive." [147] American evangelicals unsettled by the encroachment of liberalism in public schools, the media, Hollywood, and the rise of anger seen on college campuses and disregard for traditional values found reassurance when they marveled at the recent events in Israel. God was in control of history.

Judith Klinghoffer writes: "There are linkages between history and ideology, as well as between history and theology. The Six-Day War united Jews the world over. It also presented them with a new powerful enemy: the USSR, her allies and sympathizers." [148] By criticizing Israel, many American leftists proved "their 'anti-imperialist' credentials." [149] Fortunately, the Six-Day War also sparked the interest of the many Americans with Christian Zionist sensibilities. Having been staunch anticommunists throughout the Cold War, conservative Christians nurtured the special relationship between the United States and Israel. Israel's democratic success in a region inhospitable to western ideals was impressive, and many American Christians lauded Israel's military achievements, particularly inspiring relative to America's efforts in Vietnam. Christian Zionists believed that it was the Arabs rather than the Israelis who started the Six-Day War. They did not see the Israelis as aggressive expansionists who occupied territories without justification.

The argument that Israel's only legitimate borders were the ones in place on June 4, 1967, made no sense to Christian Zionists. [150] History told them that wars and conquest often meant revised borders. Often ignored by those who promoted Palestinian nationalism was the Jordanian acquisition of the West Bank in 1948 that prevented the creation of a Palestinian Arab state as planned by the United Nations in 1947. A close examination of history was inconvenient for Christian anti-Zionists. Liberal Christians were less enthusiastic about Israel's gains, with some questioning Israel's right to exist as a state. [151] In time, there would be a growing number who embraced aspects of liberation theology that linked Israel with "colonialism" and "oppression." [152] From the standpoint of conservative Christians, Israel's place in God's plan was more obvious than ever. Their support for Israel became stronger and more visible, indicative of the increasing polarization of liberal and conservative Christian leaders on major foreign policy issues.

NOTES

1. "'And See the Land, What It Is,'" *Christian Century*, March 24, 1965, 361.

2. Sadly, the Jordanian educational curriculum was disturbingly hostile. For example, in one high school textbook a writing exercise went as follows: "Israel was born to die. Prove it." See Peters, *From Time Immemorial*, 79.

3. Walvoord, *The Nations in Prophecy*, 114.

4. Oren, *Six Days of War*, 119, 337.

5. Catton, *Palestine, the Arabs and Israel*, 92, 104–105.

6. Shlaim, *The Iron Wall*, 235, 241–42.

7. Georgiana G. Stevens, ed., *The United States and the Middle East* (Englewood Cliffs, NJ: Prentice-Hall, Inc. 1964), 61. This book was reviewed and recommended for "America's evangelical Christians" by *Christianity Today*, June 19, 1964, 26–27.

8. On this point, see Francis Rue Steele, "Islam: The Continuing Threat," *Christianity Today*, July 31, 1964. 19. Steele wrote: "From its inception and throughout its history Islam has been anti-Christian, often violently so."

9. Lewis, *The Crisis of Islam*, 76–81.

10. Levey, "Israel's Quest for a Security Gurantee from the United States, 1954–1956," 61. Sicker, *Israel's Quest for Security*, 73–75. Kober, "Great-Power Involvement and Israeli Battlefield Success in the Arab-Israeli Wars, 1948–1982," 38.

11. David Tal, "Symbol Not Substance? Israel's Campaign to Acquire Hawk Missiles, 1960–1962," *The International History Review* 22, no. 2 (June 2000), 307, 313.

12. For example, see Merkley, *American Presidents, Religion, and Israel*, 52.

13. Little, "The Making of a Special Relationship," 568.

14. Quoted in Don Peretz, "The United States, the Arabs, and Israel: Peace Efforts of Kennedy, Johnson, and Nixon," *Annals of the American Academy of Political and Social Science* 401 (May 1972), 119. Also see Warren Bass, *Support Any Friend: Kennedy's Middle East and the Making of the U.S.-Israel Alliance* (Oxford: Oxford University Press, 2003), 166 and Spiegel, *The Other Arab-Israeli Conflict*, 114–15.

15. Arthur M. Schlesinger, Jr. *A Thousand Days: John F. Kennedy in the White House* (New York: Fawcett Premier, 1971), 106. Merkley, *American Presidents, Religion, and Israel*, 53.

16. John F. Walvoord, "Amillennialism from Augustine to Modern Times," *Bibliotheca Sacra* 106, no. 424 (October–December 1949), 420; Walvoord, "Amillennialism as a Method of Interpretation," *Bibliotheca Sacra*, 107, no. 425 (January–March 1950), 43. For further discussion of amillennialism, see Walvoord, "Amillennialism as a System of Theology," *Bibliotheca Sacra*, 107, no. 426 (April–June, 1950): 154–67; Walvoord, "Amillennial Eschatology," *Bibliotheca Sacra*, 108, no. 429 (January–March, 1951): 7–14. In 1948, *L'Osservatore*, the semi-official Vatican newspaper, declared, "Modern Israel is not the heir to biblical Israel. The Holy Land and its sacred sites belong only to Christianity: the true Israel." Quoted in "Evangelicals and Israel," *Center Conversations* 25 (November, 2003), 5. On relations between the Vatican and Israel in the early 1960s, see F. Michael Perko, S.J.,"Toward a 'Sound and Lasting Basis': Relations between the Holy See, the Zionist Movement, and Israel, 1896–1996," *Israel Studies* 2, no. 1 (Spring, 1997), 8–9.

17. For example, in her study on the American response to the Yom Kippur War, Judith Hershcopf Banki wrote of "a widespread expression of identification with, and sympathy for, Israel from Catholics in every part of the United States . . . ." See Judith Hershcopf Banki, *Christian Responses to the Yom Kippur War* (New York: The American Jewish Committee, 1974), 12.

18. Tal, "Symbol Not Substance?" 311.

19. Tal, "Symbol Not Substance? 312, 317. On the Kennedy administration's attempt to restrict Israel's nuclear development see Zaki Shalom, "Kennedy, Ben-Gurion and the Dimona Project, 1962–1963," *Israel Studies* 1, no. 1 (Spring 1996): 3–33. Also, Bass, *Support Any Friend*, 186–90.

20. Ariel E. Levité and Emily B. Landau, "Arab Perceptions of Israel's Nuclear Posture, 1960–1967," *Israel Studies* 1, no. 1 (Spring 1996), 39, 54.

21. The timing was late 1962 or early 1963. See Zeev Maoz, "The Mixed Blessing of Israel's Nuclear Policy," *International Security* 28, no. 2 (Fall 2003), 46–47.

22. Quoted in Arlene Lazarowitz, "Different Approaches to a Regional Search for Balance: The Johnson Administration, the State Department, and the Middle East, 1964–1967," *Diplomatic History* 32, no. 1 (January 2008), 35.

23. On Johnson's distrust of Nasser, see Little, *American Orientalism*, 31.

24. Lazarowitz, "Different Approaches to a Regional Search for Balance," 54.

25. Sicker, *Israel's Quest for Security*, 92.

26. Iraqis and Syrians saw blocking Israel's water project a central issue. Shemesh, "Prelude to the Six-Day War," 7, 9.

27. Quoted in Ben-Gurion, *Israel*, 652.

28. Shemesh, "Prelude to the Six-Day War," 137.

29. Moshe Shemesh, "The Palestinian Society in the Wake of the 1948 War: From Social Fragmentation to Consolidation," *Israel Studies* 9, no. 1 (Spring 2004), 91–93. Peres, *David's Sling*, 14, 260. Also, Stein, *The Making of Modern Israel*, 255–56.

30. Shemesh, "The Palestinian Society in the Wake of the 1948 War," 95–96.

31. Quoted in Shemesh, "The Palestinian Society in the Wake of the 1948 War," 96.

32. "Arab Refugees Dread White Christmas," *Christianity Today*, December 20, 1968, 32.

33. "Communist Star Rises Over Nazareth," *Christianity Today*, December 17, 1965, 35.

34. Malachy, *American Fundamentalism and Israel*, 95–98, 100.

35. Emily Alice Katz, "It's the Real World After All: The American-Israel Pavilion–Jordan Pavilion Controversy at the New York World's Fair, 1964–1965," *American Jewish History* 91, no. 1 (March 2003), 131–32.

36. Katz, "It's the Real World After All: The American-Israel Pavilion–Jordan Pavilion Controversy at the New York World's Fair, 1964–1965," 139–41.

37. Gabriel Gersh, "Young Israelis in Transition," *Christian Century*, July 27, 1960, 874–75.

38. Sam E. Salem, "Toward Arab-Israeli Peace," *Christian Century*, August 29, 1962, 1028–29.

39. Gabriel Gersh, "Notes on a Visit to Israel," *Christian Century*, October 11, 1961, 1201–02. Garbiel Gersh, "Israel After Fifteen Years," *Christian Century*, April 17, 1963, 487–89.

40. Gerald Kennedy, "Israeli Notebook, Updated," *Christian Century*, February 24, 1965, 237–38.

41. "Appraisals of 'Opportunity in Israel,'" *Christian Century*, January 25, 1961, 118.

42. "'And See the Land, What It Is,'" 361.

43. "E Pluribus Israel," *Christian Century*, March 31, 1965, 391.

44. "Abraham's Children," *Christian Century*, April 14, 1965, 456.

45. *Christian Century*, June 22, 1960, 741.

46. Stein, *The Making of Modern Israel*, 231–35.

47. Marguerite Harmon Bro, "Opportunity in Israel," *Christian Century*, December 14, 1960, 1466–467. Also, see William Martin, *A Prophet with Honor: The Billy Graham Story* (New York: William Morrow and Company, Inc., 1991), 265.

48. "Appraisals of 'Opportunity in Israel,'" 120.

49. See "The Isolationism of Islam," *Christianity Today*, March 27, 1964, 38.

50. *Eternity*, October 1956, 44.

51. "The Christian Witness in Israel," *Christianity Today*, July 31, 1961, 22–23; "The Christian Witness in Israel," *Christianity Today*, August 28, 1961, 18–19.

52. "The Goldbergs Discover Israel: III. Religious Life in the New Nation," *Moody Monthly*, November 1968, 73–75.

53. "The Messiah," *Christianity Today*, October 13, 1961, 45. For a report on the incident, see "Jewish Mobs Stone New Church in Jerusalem," *Christianity Today*, July 31, 1961, 26.

54. "The Conversion Rate," *Christianity Today*, March 27, 1964, 40. For additional discussion of discrimination against Christianity in Israel, see "Appraisals of 'Opportunity in Israel,'" 118, 120–21.

55. "The Loss of Identity: Who Is a Jew?" *Christianity Today*, January 4, 1963, 25. "The Alternate Course," *Christianity Today*, January 18, 1963, 33–34. Itamar Rabinovich and Jehuda Reinharz, eds., *Israel in the Middle East: Documents and Readings on Society, Politics, and Foreign Relations, 1948–Present* (New York: Oxford University Press, 1984), 40, 151–54.

56. Jacob Jocz, "A Test of Tolerance," *Christianity Today*, March 29, 1963, 6–9. Also, see "Law of Return Excludes Brother Daniel," *Christian Century*, December 19, 1962, 1553 and Leonard R. Sussman, "A Judaism for All Seasons," *Christian Century*, April 3, 1963, 427–29.

57. "Brother Daniel's Exclusion," *Christianity Today*, March 15, 1963, 15–16.

58. "Ruffled Relations," 32.

59. "Zealots in the Holy Land," *Christianity Today*, October 11, 1963, 33.

60. "Israel Enacts Anti-Conversion Law," *Christianity Today*, April 23, 1965, 49.

61. "Zealots in the Holy Land," 33.

62. "Harassment in Israel," *Christianity Today*, August 27, 1965, 53.

63. "Israel Enacts Anti-Conversion Law," *Christianity Today*, April 23, 1965, 49.

64. "Zionist Lobbying," *Christianity Today*, June 6, 1960, 27.

65. "Israeli Officials Aid Preparation for Bible Lands Prophetic Pilgrimage," *Moody Monthly*, February 1959, 43, 46.

66. John F. Walvoord, "Russia and the Middle East in Prophecy," *Moody Monthly*, December 1959, 26.

67. Radosh, *A Safe Haven*, 346.

68. Little, *American Orientalism*, 96; Little, "The Making of a Special Relationship," 569. Also, see Yaacov Bar-Siman-Tov, "The United States and Israel since 1948: A 'Special Relationship'?" *Diplomatic History* 22, no. 2 (Spring, 1998): 231–62.

69. John F. Walvoord, *Israel in Prophecy* (Grand Rapids, MI: Zondervan Publishing House, 1962); Arthur W. Kac, *The Rebirth of the State of Israel—Is it of God or of Men?* (Chicago: Moody Press, 1958).

70. "Israel: Marvel Among the Nations," *Christianity Today*, September 11, 1961, 14–16.

71. Sicker, *Israel's Quest for Security*, 95–96.

72. Clea Lutz Bunch, "Strike at Samu: Jordan, Israel, the United States, and the Origins of the Six-Day War," *Diplomatic History* 32, no. 1 (January 2008), 56, 60, 72, 75.

73. Moshe Shemesh, "The IDF Raid on Samu': The Turning-Point in Jordan's Relations with Israel and the West Bank Palestinians," *Israel Studies* 7, no. 1 (Spring 2002), 142, 144, 154, 162.

74. Sicker, *Israel's Quest for Security*, 93–95.

75. Howard La Fay, "Where Jesus Walked," *National Geographic* 132, no. 6 (December, 1967), 739.

76. Sicker, *Israel's Quest for Security*, 96.

77. Isabella Ginor and Gideon Remez, "The Spymaster, the Communist, and Foxbats over Dimona: The USSR's Motive for Instigating the Six-Day War," *Israel Studies* 11, no. 2 (Summer 2006), 88.

78. Sicker, *Israel's Quest for Security*, 98, 100–101.

79. Oren, *Six Days of War*, 336–37.

80. Quoted in Judith A. Klinghoffer, *Vietnam, Jews and the Middle East: Unintended Consequences* (New York: St. Martin's Press, Inc., 1999), 160. While on a fact-finding mission in Israel in early May, White House troubleshooter Harold Saunders discovered that the Israelis viewed "Arab terrorism as the greatest threat to their security today." See Little, "The Making of a Special Relationship," 577.

81. "Middle East Crisis: A Biblical Backdrop," *Christianity Today*, June 9, 1967, 38, 40.

82. All three statements quoted in Robert St John, *Eban* (London: W. H. Allen, 1973), 445–46.

83. Stein, *The Making of Modern Israel*, 291–92. Safran, *Israel*, 241. An excellent and comprehensive study on the war is Oren, *Six Days of War*.

84. Stein, *The Making of Modern Israel*, 293.

85. Of course, the Israeli tanks rolling into the Gaza Strip were terrifying. See Isseldin Abuelaish, *I Shall Not Hate: A Gaza Doctor's Journey* (Toronto: Random House Canada, 2010), 44–45.

86. Eban, *Personal Witness*, 409–10. St John, *Eban*, 452–53.

87. Oren, *Six Days of War*, 337–38.

88. On the "unexpected Soviet passivity in 1967," see Kober, "Great-Power Involvement and Israeli Battlefield Success in the Arab-Israeli Wars, 1948–1982," 28–32.

89. Fawaz A. Gerges, "The 1967 Arab-Israeli War: U.S. Actions and Arab Perceptions" in *The Middle East and the United States: A Historical and Political Reassessment*, 2nd ed., ed. David W. Lesch (Boulder, CO: Westview Press, 1999), 186. For a tally of the Arab losses, see Oren, *Six Days of War*, 305–306.

90. "Messianic Times," *Christian Century*, September 13, 1967, 1150

91. Louis Goldberg, "The Man Who Kept the Tomb," *Moody Monthly*, April 1968, 9, 23. For another version of this death, see "Mideast: Weighing the Effects," *Christianity Today*, July 7, 1967, 31.

92. Goldberg, "The Man Who Kept the Tomb," 23.

93. Oren, *Six Days of War*, 263–70.

94. Moshe Dayan, *Moshe Dayan: The Story of My Life* (New York: William Morrow and Company, Inc., 1976), 16.

95. Stein, *The Making of Modern Israel*, 149.

96. Neff, "Jerusalem in U.S. Policy," 32.

97. Quoted in Neff, "Jerusalem in U.S. Policy," 32. Neff is very critical of Israel's claim on all of Jerusalem and America's reluctance to constrain Israel.

98. "Beleaguered Israel," *Christianity Today*, January 16, 1970, 26.

99. Quoted in Peres, *David's Sling*, 269.

100. "Israel and the Christian Dilemma," *Christian Century*, July 12, 1967, 883–84; "Israel Annexes Old Jerusalem," *Christian Century*, July 12, 1967, 884–85. "Comment on This Issue," *Christian Century*, July 26, 1967, 954.

101. "Israel's Finest Future," *Christian Century*, August 23, 1967, 1062.

102. "Urbis and Orbis: Jerusalem Today," *Christian Century*, July 26, 1967, 967–70. "Christians and the Mideast Crisis," *Christian Century*, July 26, 1967, 961–65. One dissenting and pro-Israel article was A. Roy and Alice L. Eckardt, "Again, Silence in the Churches: I. The Case for Israel," *Christian Century*, July 26, 1967, 970–73.

103. Joshua Michael Zeitz, "'If I am no for myself . . . ': The American Jewish Establishment in the Aftermath of the Six Day War," *American Jewish History* 88, no. 2 (June 2000), 270.

104. "Israel Annexes Old Jerusalem," *Christian Century*, July 12, 1967, 885; "Jews in Old Jerusalem! A Historic Re-Entry," *Christianity Today*, June 23, 1967, 37–38. Some liberal Protestants such as Reinhold Niebuhr also voiced their support for Israel. See Merkley, *Christian Attitudes towards the State of Israel*, 38–37.

105. On the important temple issue, see John F. Walvoord, "Will Israel Build a Temple in Jerusalem?" *Bibliotheca Sacra* 125, no. 498 (April, 1968): 99–106.

106. "Unfolding Destiny," *Christianity Today*, 21 July 1967, 28–29.

107. "A Modern David and Goliath," *Christianity Today*, September 15, 1967, 48.

108. Malachy, *American Fundamentalism and Israel*, 112.

109. "Bible Prophecy and the Mid-East Crisis," *Moody Monthly*, July–August, 1967, 22–24, 59, 66.

110. John F. Walvoord, "The Amazing Rise of Israel!" *Moody Monthly*, October 1967, 25.

111. John F. Walvoord, "The Times of the Gentiles," *Bibliotheca Sacra* 125, no. 497 (January 1968), 3, 9. In another article, he writes "the end of the age may be very near." See John F. Walvoord, "Will Israel Build a Temple in Jerusalem?" *Bibliotheca Sacra* 125, no. 498 (April 1968), 106.

112. Shindler, *A Modern History of Israel*, 148. Menachem Begin also held this position.

113. Clark, *Allies for Armageddon*, 3.

114. Gazit, "Israel and the Palestinians," 87–89.

115. Quoted in Gazit, "Israel and the Palestinians," 89

116. Quoted in Sicker, 8.

117. A B'Nai B'Rith Hillel Foundation statement quoted in Zeitz, "If I am no for myself . . . ", 259–60.

118. Zeitz, "If I am not for myself . . . ", 260–61, 267–68. Also, see Milton Himmelfarb, "In the Light of Israel's Victory," *Commentary*, October 1, 1967, 54–55.

119. Lawrence Grossman, "Transformation Through Crisis: The American Jewish Committee and the Six-Day War," *American Jewish History* 86, no. 1 (1998), 26–28, 36, 51.

120. Grossman, "Transformation Through Crisis," 44, 48.

121. Grossman, "Transformation Through Crisis," 51.

122. Zeitz, "'If I am no for myself . . . ," 268.

123. Judith H. Banki and Eugene J. Fisher, ed., *A Prophet for Our Time: An Anthology of the Writings of Rabbi Marc H. Tanenbaum* (New York: Fordham University Press, 2002), 109–18. Grossman, "Transformation Through Crisis," 52.

124. "Lessons We Can Learn from Judaism," *Eternity*, August 1967, 22.

125. "A Significant Venture," *Christianity Today*, January 21, 1966, 28. For more on Young, see Merkley, *Christian Attitudes towards the State of Israel*, 163–68.

126. Voss and Rausch, "American Christians and Israel," 64.

127. "Our Subtle Anti-Semitism," *Eternity*, August 1967, 23–25.

128. "Have the 'Times of the Gentiles' Been Fulfilled?" *Eternity*, August 1967, 32–34. Alexander Sauerwein found LaSor's response disappointing for casting doubt on God's role in Israel's victory. See his letter to the editor in *Eternity*, November 1967, 6.

129. "Editorials: Prophetic Overtones in the Middle East," *Eternity*, August, 1967, 6.

130. "Shadows of Armageddon," *Christianity Today*, July 21, 1967, 27. An earlier article called the United Nations "a forum of vacillation and deception." "War Sweeps the Bible Lands," *Christianity Today*, June 23, 1967, 20.

131. "Top '67 News Story: Arab-Israeli War," *Moody Monthly*, January 1968, 10.

132. Wilbur M. Smith, *Israeli/Arab Conflict in the Bible* (Glendale, Ca: Regal Books, 1967), 119, 139.

133. If there were any official Washington responses to Bible prophecy, they are rare. Other sources, however, spoke of the dangers of applying Bible prophecy to American-Middle East relations.

134. Bible prophecy promoters made gains politically and with the mainstream media in the post-1970 period. See, for example, Phyllis Bennis and Khaled Mansour, "'Praise God and Pass the Ammunition!': The Changing Nature of Israel's U.S. Backers," *Middle East Report*, no. 208 (Autumn 1998): 16–18, 43; Don Wagner, "For Zion's Sake," *Middle East Report*, no. 223 (Summer 2002): 54–57; Shindler, "Likud and the Christian Dispensationalists," 163; Melani McAlister, "Prophecy, Politics, and the Popular: The Left Behind Series and Christian Fundamentalism's New World Order," The *South Atlantic Quarterly*, 102, no. 4 (Fall 2003), 775; William Martin, "The Christian Right and American Foreign Policy," *Foreign Policy*, no. 114 (Spring 1999), 67; Rammy M. Haija, "The Armageddon Lobby: Dispensationalist Christian Zionism and the Shaping of U.S. Policy Towards Israel-Palestine," *Holy Land Studies* 5, no. 1 (2006), 77; Sara Diamond, *Spiritual Warfare: The Politics of the Christian Right* (Boston: South End Press, 1989), 23; Timothy P. Weber, *Living in the Shadow of the Second Coming: American Premillennialism, 1875–1982* (Grand Rapids, MI: Academie Books, 1983), 4–5; Irvine H. Anderson, *Biblical Interpretation and Middle East Policy: The Promised Land, America, and Israel, 1917–2002* (Gainesville: University Press of Florida, 2005), 43–44.

135. Clyde Wilcox, Sharon Linzey, and Ted G. Jelen, "Reluctant Warriors: Premillennialism and Politics in the Moral Majority," *Journal of the Scientific Study of Religion* 30, no. 3 (September, 1991), 255.

136. Smith, *Before I Forget*, 34.

137. Boyer, *When Time Shall Be No More*, 13–14; Yaakov Ariel, "An Unexpected Alliance: Christian Zionism and its Historical Significance," *Modern Judaism* 26, No. 1 (February, 2006), 82–83.

138. Smith, *Israel-Arab Conflict in the Bible*, 21.

139. Isaason and Thomas, *The Wise Men* and Halberstam, *The Best and the Brightest.* On Israeli leaders, see Merkley, *Christian Attitudes towards the State of Israel*, 15–19. Merkley quotes David Ben-Gurion: "Since I invoke Torah so often, let me state that I don't personally believe in the God it postulates" (17). Also, see Jimmy Carter, *Palestine Peace Not Apartheid* (New York: Simon and Schuster, 2006), 32; Mart, "Eleanor Roosevelt, Liberalism, and Israel," 78; Zameret, "Judaism in Israel," 65.

140. Merkley, *American Presidents, Religion, and Israel*, 55–56.

141. Little, *American Orientalism*, 101. On how the Six-Day War energized American Jewish support for Israel, see Grossman, "Transformation Through Crisis," 27–54. At a June 7 rally in Washington, Morris Abram, president of the American Jewish Committee, declared: "We did not foresee that tiny, encircled Israel would be able to overcome multiple fanatical adversaries equipped with Soviet arms. But the people of the Book have proved the verities of the Book: 'Not by power, not by force, but by thy spirit, sayeth the Lord'" (47).

142. Quoted in Bernard Reich, *Securing the Covenant: United States-Israel Relations After the Cold War* (Westport, CT: Praeger Publishers, 1995), 10.

143. Ben-Gurion declared, "Perhaps even more than others, we need loyal friends." Ben-Gurion, *Israel*, 822.

144. Ben-Gurion, *Israel*, 803.

145. Ben-Gurion, *Israel*, 820.

146. Newell S. Booth, Jr., "Middle Ground in the Middle East?" *Christian Century*, September 20, 1967, 1188–92.

147. Raymond Cox, "Eyewitness: Israel," *Eternity*, July 1967, 6–8.

148. Klinghoffer, *Vietnam, Jews and the Middle East*, 217.

149. Maurice Isserman and Michael Kazin, *America Divided: The Civil War of the 1960s* (New York: Oxford University Press, 2000), 253.

150. New Historian Avi Shlaim did not accept Israel's post-Six-Day War borders because they were not negotiated. See "Interview," 97. From his platform as a former president of the United States, Jimmy Carter holds the same position. See Jimmy Carter, *Palestine: Peace Not Apartheid* (New York: Simon and Schuster, 2006).

151. Those liberal Christians who did not support Israel's right to exist were in the minority. See, the *Christian Century*, August, 30, 1967, 1091.

152. Merkley, *Those That Bless You, I Will Bless*, 185.

FIVE

From Attrition to the Yom Kippur War

The Six-Day War resulted in impressive gains for Israel in the Golan Heights, the West Bank, Gaza Strip, and the Sinai Desert. The war was traumatic for the Arab states. Beyond war casualties, depleted war supplies, destroyed infrastructure, and diminished territory, there was the loss of honor and self-respect. According to Abba Eban, Israel's victory "created a sense of humiliation on the Arab side, which made them almost incapable of negotiating."[1] Shortly after the war, deadly conflict erupted between Israel and the Arabs. The violence between Israel and Egypt was the start of the lesser known War of Attrition—a war with more official status by March 1969 when Nasser declared the June 1967 cease-fire null and void and the Egyptians increased their activities to destroy Israel's line of fortifications along the east side of the Suez Canal.[2] The war persisted until August 1970 and, thus, became Israel's longest war. A little over three years later, Arab forces carried out a surprise attack on Israel during the sacred holiday of Yom Kippur. After the Yom Kippur War there was increasing liberal Protestant criticism of Israel, but conservative Christians continued to marvel at the Israel "miracle."

Soon after the Six-Day War, Arab leaders quickly planned revenge and it was the Syrians who struck first on June 18. With armored personnel vehicles, Syrian troops violated a cease-fire and crossed truce lines to attack Israel's positions on the Golan Heights. More serious were the actions of the Egyptians. It was an especially bitter pill for Egypt that Israel gained so much in the brief war. The Israelis controlled the Sinai up to the Suez Canal and the Abu Rudeis oil field on the Gulf of Suez. Less than two weeks after the Syrian offensive, Egyptian forces began artillery attacks against Israeli patrols exposed along the canal. On a daily basis, Egypt targeted Israel's military and security positions. An Israeli ar-

mored infantry company was successful in driving off an Egyptian ambush, but its leader Major Uriel Menuhin paid with his life when hit by
artillery fire. Over the next two weeks there were major air battles and
the Israeli Air Force shot down four Egyptian MiG-17s and three MiG-
21s.[3]

Acting on behalf of the Arabs, the Soviet Union requested the UN
General Assembly convene a special session in order to pressure Israel to
relinquish its territorial gains. This tactic had little effect on Israeli leaders
who were unwilling to give away their major bargaining chip. For them,
the Arabs' demand that Israel unilaterally and unconditionally withdraw
made no sense. On June 27, Prime Minister Levi Eshkol pointed to Arab
cease-fire violations and declared: "So long as our neighbors will persist
in their policy of belligerence and will make plans for our destruction, we
will not relinquish the areas that are now under our control and that we
deem necessary for our security and self-defense."[4] American policymakers recognized that unless the Arabs considered a comprehensive peace
treaty, there was no practical way the United States could oppose Israel's
position to keep and use the Gaza Strip and the West Bank. As Special
Consultant McGeorge Bundy wrote to President Lyndon Johnson on July
31, "We can't tell the Israelis to give things away to people who won't
even bargain with them."[5]

In late August, Arab leaders met to discuss policy concerning Israeli
occupation of Arab lands. On September 1, the Khartoum Summit Conference presented its united voice "to eliminate the effects of the aggression." The main principles were "no peace with Israel, no recognition of
Israel, no negotiations with it, and insistence on the rights of the Palestinian people in their own country." The Arab leaders also resolved "to
adopt the necessary measures to strengthen military preparations to face
all eventualities."[6] To a mass demonstration in Cairo, President Nasser
formulated three phases of Egyptian military policy: "defensive rehabili-
tation," "offensive defence," and "liberation."[7] Israel saw only Arab
intransigence, but the unwillingness of Arab leaders to recognize the
legitimacy of Israel was no surprise. Having rejected Israel's existence for
two decades, Arab leaders had no desire to explain to the Arab people
reasons for recognizing Israel. If they agreed upon peace negotiations,
Arab leaders might at best regain lost territory. This was not enough. The
main reason for Arabs going to war in the first place was not simply to
regain land; their objective was to destroy Israel. It was unthinkable for
Arab leaders to offer peace in order to regain lost land, but be denied
control of most of Palestine.[8] Egypt continued to routinely attack Israel.
One deadly incident was the sinking of the Israeli destroyer *Eilat*, sailing
in international waters, by Egyptian missiles on October 21, 1967.

On November 22, after much debate and in the hope of finding peace,
the UN Security Council passed Resolution 242. The major point of the
resolution was for Israel to withdraw "from territories of recent conflict."

Unfortunately, the imprecise wording of the document proved to create conflicting interpretations since it failed to make a clear identification of the land under review. Israel was to withdraw from "territories" rather than from "the territories." The distinction was important. Moreover, the resolution failed to clarify whether Israel's withdrawal depended on Arab recognition of the State of Israel.[9] Regardless of where one stood on the issue, it was peculiar that the United Nations, in essence, was telling Israel that territory gained in a war was illegal. Since Israeli policymakers had no plans to withdraw from occupied territory until the Arabs came to the bargaining table, continued stalemate was the order of the day.

Resolution 242 was a key document that implied peace in exchange for territory, but interestingly it gave no specific mention of the "Palestinians." On March 17, 1968, Cairo radio broadcasted that the "real Palestine problem is the existence of Israel in Palestine. As long as a Zionist existence remains even in a tiny part of it—that will mean occupation." It was paramount "to liquidate the Israeli occupation, and there is no difference between the territories lately occupied and those occupied before." But Nasser had to bide his time since Egypt was not militarily ready to "liquidate" Israel. The first step was to keep Israel at a high level of mobilization with a protracted war that taxed its limited manpower. As Mohamed Heikal explained, "If the enemy succeeds in inflicting on us 50,000 casualties in this campaign, we can go on fighting nevertheless, because we have manpower reserves."[10] From this statement one gets a sense of how little some Arab leaders valued human life and how vital the goal was to destroy Israel.

The War of Attrition heated up in September 1968 as a result of an escalation of Egyptian artillery attacks and commando raids. The toll for Israel was twenty-five killed and fifty-two wounded. Believing that significant retaliatory action was its best hope to discourage Egyptian hostility, Israel launched a number of punishing operations. Aircraft missions targeted bridges on the Nile and paratroopers destroyed a large power station at Naj Hamadi, located deep inside Egypt almost 300 miles south of Cairo. These missions appeared to have the desired effect since Egyptian military actions along the Suez Canal lessened for a number of weeks. However, Ezer Weizmann, chief of operations of the Israeli General Staff, questioned the effectiveness of army raids going deep into Egypt with the aim of destroying transformer stations and bridges. He wrote: "A war like this can't be won by commando raids! It won't work! The Israeli army has to be employed in full and overwhelming force, not only to put an end to the War of Attrition—important enough unto itself—but also to check the Egyptian army before it launches more dangerous offensives!"[11]

In early 1969, Egypt returned to a focused military strategy coinciding with a Nasser interview setting the record straight that a military solution came first before any political solution: "The first priority, the absolute priority in this battle, is the military front, for we must realize that the enemy will not withdraw unless we force him to withdraw through fighting."[12] In March, Nasser gave the War of Attrition official status and in a May Day speech he declared Egypt's readiness for destroying the Israeli defensive fortifications built along the canal. After the destruction of this Bar-Lev line, Egypt could "proceed to Sinai to meet the enemy face to face."[13]

In March 1969, Golda Meir replaced Levi Eshkol as prime minister. According to one revisionist historian, Meir was "a fighter" who "exhibited the siege mentality, the notion that Israel had to barricade itself behind an iron wall, the fatalistic belief that Israel was doomed forever to live by the sword."[14] Not categorizing the Palestinians as a separate Arab people requiring their own state, Meir preferred the "Jordan option" in which the Jordanian and Israeli leaders would determine policy concerning the Palestinians.[15]

Fighting was fierce throughout the summer of 1969. In late July, an Israeli aircraft attack on Egyptian forts and Sam-2 missile batteries lasted approximately five hours. One Israeli commando strike on Egyptian positions along the canal resulted in one hundred Egyptian dead and the evacuation of approximately 500,000 civilians living in nearby towns along the canal. What Israel's chief of staff Chaim Bar-Lev termed "escalation for the sake of de-escalation" appeared to garner some success because by late 1969 Egypt sought indirect talks with Israel by way of UN mediators.[16] President Richard Nixon gave Secretary of State William Rogers the task of solving the Egyptian-Israeli conflict. However, the Rogers Plan (announced in June 1970) of having Israel withdraw from previously held Arab land in exchange for recognition did not get off the ground. The Egyptians rejected the plan, as did the Israelis, who saw it as an inferior version of UN Resolution 242.[17] In the Knesset on December 29, Meir declared: "Each of the U.S. proposals concerning boundaries and the return of refugees is a threat to Israel's security. Both, if enforced, would gravely endanger Israel's very existence."[18]

In the early months of 1970, Israel conducted more than twenty bombing missions deep into Egypt. Meir's message to Nasser was clear: "We go into the interior in order to make it well known to him and the people of Egypt that either it's quiet on both sides [of the canal] or there's bombing on both sides. . . . Are we supposed to sit on the Canal and take the shellings?"[19] Nasser's response included a visit to Moscow on January 22, 1970, when he entered an agreement with the Soviets. Setting out to modernize the entire Egyptian air defense system, the Soviets delivered missile units and three squadrons of fighter planes which arrived in early April. A more confident Egypt escalated the war, including one successful raid on an Israeli armored platoon that killed thirteen and captured two. Israel increased the number of sorties across the canal, but it lost a number of aircraft while attacking the Soviet surface-to-air missile emplacements.[20]

On July 31, 1970, Jordan, Egypt, and Israel agreed to a ninety-day cease-fire which went in effect one week later. A key stipulation of the cease-fire stated that neither side could "introduce or construct any new military installations" within fifty kilometers of the cease-fire line. Meir voiced her displeasure that Egypt violated the cease-fire almost immediately, by constructing at least forty-five SAM sites within the canal zone in the first month of the agreement. Also disconcerting for Israeli leaders was that the United States failed to do much in slowing the Soviet-Egyptian buildup.[21]

In late September 1970, Nasser had a fatal heart attack; his death was likely a significant reason the cease-fire remained in force until October 1973.[22] As Egypt's new leader, Anwar Sadat presented Egypt's terms for an Egyptian-Israeli settlement. Once Israel relinquished all territory it captured from Egypt during the Six-Day War, Egypt would "recognize the right of Israel as an independent state" and would "negotiate Israel's right of passage through the Straits of Tiran and the Gulf of Aqaba." Actually, the precondition for Israel's right of passage through the Suez Canal depended "on an agreement between Israel and the Arab countries" that settled the Palestinian refugee problem. Although Sadat's position retreated from the inflexibility of the Khartoum conference of 1967, he clarified that Egypt was unwilling to "enter into normal diplomatic relations with Israel." Recognizing Israel was not yet on the table: "Our people here will crush anyone who would decide this . . . leave it to the coming generations, not me."[23] Egypt and Israel remained at an impasse, but at least the War of Attrition was over. From the end of the Six-Day War to the summer of 1970, Israel lost over 2,600 soldiers. Egyptian losses were appallingly high, with an estimated 10,000 killed in the 1970 spring offensive alone.[24]

Israel continued to face serious issues. Concerning border violence over the years, the UN Security Council resolutions usually worked against Israel since the Soviet Union vetoed condemnation of Arab attacks more often than the United States vetoed condemnation of Israeli attacks.[25] In fact, the UN framework was unable to provide any "purposeful diplomacy" on major Arab-Israeli issues. As Abba Eban explained: "The Soviets vetoed anything the Arabs didn't like, and the Arabs and Communists together had a veto power in the General Assembly."[26] The Soviets also increasingly supplied Egypt with sophisticated weaponry and defensive operations. Another ominous development was Sadat establishing a "tactical alliance" with the Muslim Brotherhood in order to consolidate his power. His release of some Muslim Brotherhood prisoners, his support for Islamic student groups in the universities, and his call for a return to traditional Islamic values represented a clear contrast to Nasser's Arab socialism. As one Muslim Brother noted, "the

Sadat regime is a thousand times better than Nasser's. Nasser would never have allowed us to act as we are now acting, not to carry out our propaganda openly."[27] In Cairo, leaders declared jihad against Israel, and in Amman, Jordan, Muslims discussed "rescuing Jerusalem" from the Israelis.[28] The growth of Islamist factions in Egypt was not good news for Israel.

Another major concern for the Israelis (and some Arab leaders) was mounting Palestinian nationalism. As the Israelis battled the Egyptians along the canal and tangled with the Jordanians and Syrians, there was a rise of terrorist acts by the PLO. The greater visibility of Palestinian leaders voicing nationalism was a growing problem for Israel. The objective for many militants was politicide, a term coined in the late 1960s describing the PLO's desire to destroy Israel.[29]

Palestinian leaders met in Cairo in July 1968, adding to the original PLO covenant of 1964. The Palestinian National Covenant, 1968, was an alarming document for Israel. It clarified the boundaries of Palestine (British mandate boundaries), the Palestinians' legal right to their homeland, and the definition of Palestinian-Arabs as citizens living permanently in Palestine until 1947 and the children born to these Arabs. The word Israel appears in the document only three times. The call was to embrace "armed struggle" and "destroy the Zionist and imperialist presence from Palestine." Article 7 in part stated: "It is a national duty to bring up individual Palestinians in an Arab revolutionary manner."[30]

As long as the Palestinian National Covenant stood, Israel refused to consider negotiating with the PLO which consisted of a number of factions. Led by Yasser Arafat, *Fatah* became the most important group within the PLO. One critical biography of Arafat claims that his "tactics were aimed more at killing the enemy's civilians than at defeating its army."[31] Other groups such as the Popular Front for the Liberation of Palestine and the Democratic Front for the Liberation of Palestine attracted followers wanting social and economic change by revolutionary socialism. Pro-Palestinian interpretations saw this period as one of "Palestinian resistance" to "Israeli repression."[32]

Interestingly, not all Arabs were supportive of the strategy of Palestinian leaders. In September 1970, Palestinian terrorists hijacked and blew up three airplanes at Jordan's capital Amman. King Hussein had enough and Jordanian forces clashed with Palestinian militants, killing about 3,000 and expelling the remaining fighters from Jordan. During Christmas 1970, *Fatah* gave no assurances for the safety of tourists, but the Arab guerrilla organization was temporarily weaker even if the PLO problem did not disappear.[33] The expelled PLO fighters simply resumed their activities from Lebanon. An unfortunate by-product was the birth of Black September, a terrorist group that carried out horrific acts, notably the killing of eleven innocent Israeli athletes at the 1972 Olympic Games in Munich, Germany.

The number of Israel's enemies was growing and some reports from American Christian circles were discouraging. One ten-day tour of the Holy Land by more than sixty American religious editors and writers resulted in less than optimistic predictions for the future. The Israeli Ministry of Tourism painted a picture of Arabs and Israelis "pursuing normalcy," but American Christian commentators wrote of both groups "drifting irreversibly toward another round of war." In fact, several days after E. Russell Chandler and other American journalists returned home, the Israelis and Syrians "waged the heaviest fighting" since 1967. Chandler pointed to religion to explain the roots of the conflict. It was "a land of religious rivalry" obvious to a tourist of Old Jerusalem where pious Jews prayed at the Western Wall, where Muslims flocked to the Mosque of Omar, and where Christians made the "Stations of the Cross along the Via Dolorosa."[34]

Chandler chose no clear favorite in his *Christianity Today* article, but he did write of "the hard line of Israeli policy" of demolishing houses of those guilty of terrorism and deporting political "undesirables," each act intended to discourage subversion. The propaganda war of the number of houses destroyed was another example of a seemingly unbridgeable gap: the Israelis claimed 516 demolished houses and the Arabs claimed 7,500 blown up since the Six-Day War.[35] Beside Chandler's article was another report noting the "great misgivings" of Israelis about the pro-Arab statements of the liberal World Council of Churches (WCC), especially the statement calling for greater study of biblical interpretation so as to "avoid the misuse of the Bible in support of partisan views and to clarify the bearing of faith upon critical political questions." Arnold T. Olson, president of the Evangelical Free Church of America and the National Association of Evangelicals, voiced what the Israelis and others thought of the position of the WCC: The WCC "will now study the Bible to find out what right Israel has to use the scriptures in defending the rebirth of the state."[36]

Whenever there were positive views of Israel in the liberal *Christian Century* the authors were usually Jews. For example, liberal rabbi Balfour Brickner sought to convince readers it was wrong to make an analogy of America's involvement in Vietnam and Israel. Like most American Jews, Balfour saw America's involvement in Vietnam as wrong and its involvement in Israel as correct. But it worried him that there were too many American Jews quiet about the Vietnam War, fearing the Nixon administration might lessen its support for Israel if they voiced their opposition to American involvement in Vietnam.[37]

When Nixon entered the White House in 1969 Christian Zionism was barely on anyone's radar outside of conservative evangelical communities, and the term "Christian Right" had yet to arrive. But the three-year period between the War of Attrition and the Yom Kippur War represented a transformational era for Christians in the United States. Among the whole of the United States, few matched the enthusiasm and support of conservative Christians for Israel. This became all the more obvious with comparisons made with liberal Christian leaders who made greater efforts to delegitimize Israel in various ways.

Typical views from evangelicals and liberal Protestants were poles apart, as a June 1968 issue of *Christianity Today* demonstrated. William Culbertson, president of Moody Bible Institute, drew on numerous Bible verses to substantiate the link between modern Israel and biblical prophecy. His heart went out to the Arab refugees, but Israel was only partly responsible for their misfortune. He also questioned why Arab countries were unwilling to help the refugees. All in all, the existence of the State of Israel was due to "the active support of the world community" and it was reasonable for the Israelis to strive for security. Critical of Israel and Christian Zionists, James L. Kelso, a retired professor at Pittsburgh Seminary, argued that only about two percent of people he encountered understood the basic facts of the creation of modern Israel. He claimed that there were approximately 1 million Arab refugees from the 1948 war and that the Arabs were bitter toward President Truman for approving the military-invasion policy (the same type used against the Communists in Korea) "carried out by the Israelites in Palestine." Citing one missionary, Kelso wrote of the "Israeli war" of 1967 being "perhaps the most serious setback" of Christendom in the past 500 years given the hostility of Muslims toward Christian missionaries.[38]

In his response to Kelso's analysis, Benad Avital of the Embassy of Israel in Washington clarified the "consistent Arab refusal to recognize, accept, and live in peace with the State of Israel."[39] Letters to *Christianity Today* argued that many of Kelso's statements were contrary to the facts. It was difficult to take seriously the claim that Christians applauded Israeli criminality. Harold P. Warren of First Baptist, Oak Park, Michigan encouraged "Christians to speak out on behalf of Israel and be identified as friends of Israel."[40]

Evangelical Douglas Young of the American Institute of Holy Land Studies in Jerusalem was a passionate Christian Zionist who was sensitive to criticism from the pens of liberal clergy. He and others identified A. C. Forrest, editor of the *United Church Observer* (Canada), as one being anti-Zionist and pro-Arab. In an open letter to Forrest, Young wrote: "If war comes to us in the Middle East again, historians will record that your pen, which could have been a contributory to peace, was like a sword of war. . . . [it] will drip with the blood of the wounded and dead of both sides."[41] By the 1960s, the United Church of Canada dropped its earlier evangelical theology and began its decline, losing many church members.[42]

G. Coleman Luck of Moody Bible Institute challenged the pro-Arab position of Elisabeth Elliot, who wrote of her visit to Jerusalem in 1967 after the Six-Day War. Luck acknowledged that both the Arabs and Israelis committed wrongs, but the difference was "that Israel alone, of all nations, has a 'title-deed' from God himself on a portion of this earth." Elliot's questioning whether there was "any ethical basis for the State of Israel" was a moot issue. Luck explained it was essential to remember the Lord promising to bless those who bless Israel.[43] In *Moody Monthly*, Wilbur M. Smith wrote that his count of wars mentioned in the Old Testament was ninety-two, only seven of which did not directly relate to Israel. The largest category of wars was those of the Israelites defending Palestine against invaders. In biblical times, Israel won every war "when she was obeying the laws of God."[44]

In 1971, Smith and fifteen hundred delegates gathered in Jerusalem for a prophecy conference. Other key Americans included prophecy author and educator John Walvoord; Carl Henry, editor of *Christianity Today*; W. A. Criswell of First Baptist Church, Dallas; C. Everett Koop, future surgeon general; pop singer Anita Bryant; and representatives from many evangelical organizations and academic institutions.[45] One Arab Christian in attendance was Mrs. John van der Hoeven, born in Sudan and the wife of the minister in care of Jerusalem's Garden Tomb. She spoke of her childhood education to hate Jews and her later spiritual transformation: "I was born a Greek Orthodox, but I have become a Jew through the blood of Jesus Christ. I must love my brother, the Jew. . . . God has given the land to the seed of Abraham, which is Isaac and not Ishmael (as Moslems declare)." One report on the conference declared that "a future holocaust in the land of Israel (Zech. 12–14) should stir mightily and shake the Church into rethinking the prophetic Scriptures to realize that God has His hand on His people and is shaping them. . . . To miss the import of the prophetic Scriptures is to miss something of the glory of God."[46] While there was significant disagreement among prophecy writers on many points concerning interpretation, those viewing Israel as having "no eschatological import" appeared to be in the minority.[47]

The Israeli government provided the hall for the conference and Mayor Teddy Kollek welcomed the event: "The significance of having such a conference in our city is self-evident. So many of the prophets spoke about Jerusalem; so many prophecies spoke of Jerusalem, its destruction and its rebuilding."[48] In addition to hosting the conference, David Ben-Gurion showed interest in Hal Lindsey's *The Late Great Planet Earth* (1970).[49] In his *Israel: A Personal History* (1971) there were notable references to Bible passages addressing the return of worldwide Jews to their Promised Land. Also in his summation of the legacy of a "Unique Nation," Ben-Gurion used the Book of Isaiah to explain the isolation of ancient Israel (due to its monotheism) and how "the people of Israel did not consider the Golden Age to be in the past but in the future–in the end of days." Although his biblical understanding did not meet the test of conservative Christian Bible scholars, his attempt to include a biblical frame of reference for Israel's future was significant given his predominantly secular-socialist outlook.[50]

A major breakthrough that gave Bible prophecy intense and widespread attention was the publication of Hal Lindsey's *The Late Great Planet Earth*, a "popularization of premillenialism" selling millions of copies.[51] Historian Paul Boyer recognizes "that prophecy belief is far more central in American thought than intellectual and cultural historians have recognized." *The Late Great Planet Earth* eventually earned the title of the best selling nonfiction book of the 1970s. Lindsey was a Texan who had a born-again conversion experience at age twenty-six. With two earlier years of study at the University of Houston, Lindsey entered the conservative Dallas Theological Seminary, known for its teaching of dispensationalism. Lindsey could read the Bible in Hebrew and Greek and after seminary he became an effective Bible prophecy speaker under the auspices of Campus Crusade for Christ, an international organization that sought to share the Gospel message to students at secular universities and colleges. He discovered that Bible prophecy resonated with students, and his lectures on Bible prophecy and American foreign policy were the basis of his best-selling book. Lindsey saw Bible prophecy as a foundation upon which a person's Christian faith could grow, but most of the attention that his book generated was due to its claims concerning global events, particularly the future of Israel.[52]

As for popular magazines, *Moody Monthly* continued its years-long record of offering the most articles on Israel, often presenting inspirational stories and dramatic photographs of historic and present-day Israel. One told the tragic story of the Jewish Zealots at the fortress of Masada, built by Herod the Great between 36 and 30 BC on top of a rocky plateau consisting of sheer high walls of rock. In 70 AD, after the Romans conquered Jerusalem and destroyed the Jewish temple, Jewish Zealots took control of the Masada fortress, surviving on food preserved from the days of King Herod. Huge cisterns from a century earlier supplied the necessary water. Determined to crush this resistance, the Romans built a spectacular rock and timber ramp to access the west side of the seemingly impregnable Masada. In 73 AD, before Roman soldiers breached the fortress, almost 1,000 men, women, and children died as a free people. Men killed their families and drew lots to organize the deaths of everyone to the last man: "Grimly they made their decision."[53]

Louis Goldberg, a faculty member of Moody Bible Institute, authored numerous *Moody Monthly* articles about Israel. He and his wife and two daughters were among the many Americans who visited Israel for the first time in the months following the Six-Day War. Evangelicals read stories and viewed photographs of the Goldbergs' nine-week visit. Goldberg praised Tel Aviv, a sprawling modern city with impressive buildings where only sixty years earlier was "an expanse of sand dunes." For him, the resurgence of the holy language of Hebrew, spoken widely by

the Israeli people, was "a strong testimony to the miracle that had preserved the Jewish people through the centuries and raised up a Jewish
nation."[54]

On top of the Mount of Olives in Jerusalem, the Goldbergs viewed the
Garden of Gethsemane where Jesus prayed the night of Judas's betrayal,
the Church of the Holy Sepulchre situated near the site of Christ's cruci-
fixion, and the Church of the Ascension where some believe Jesus rose to
heaven. The Muslim Dome of the Rock and Eastern Gate "were reminders of the centuries of conflict here between Christian and Muslim."
Travelling northward through "Samaria" to Nazareth where Jesus grew
up, the Goldbergs visited the Church of St. Joseph (site of Joseph's work-
shop), Mary's Well, and the old Synagogue Church on the site where
some believed Jesus worshiped. One visit was to the communally operated farm (kibbutz) at Haon where the incoming nurse was a graduate of
Moody Bible Institute. After traveling to other points of interests in Israel,
Goldberg "sensed a vital strength, imagination and purpose at work to
transform the land of Israel and thereby the whole Middle East."[55]

Goldberg also wrote of specific events of Arab-Israeli conflict. In October 1968, he gave his version "of one of the bloodiest and most heart-
breaking battles of Israel's Way of Liberation in 1948–49." Between Tel
Aviv and Jerusalem at "Heroes' Road," Jewish convoys fought desperately to reach Jews under siege in Jerusalem. Twenty years later, "skeletons"
of destroyed vehicles remained along the road as a powerful statement of
"men whose determination to win had been forged in the fires of Buchen-
wald and Auschwicz." The names of those who perished were on rocks
located near each wreck, and a more impressive reminder of 1948 and
subsequent years was the Monument of Valor inscribed with the following: "To the eternal memory of the fighters and builders. With the 'blood
of their souls' they secured and paved the way to Jerusalem." After the
war in 1948 and subsequent wars, conservative Christians such as the
Goldbergs proudly saw Israel as a land of freedom that ended the centuries of "homelessness and wandering." Conflict with the Arabs remained
a given, but Israel witnessed amazing strides culturally and academical-
ly. Israel had Hebrew University, a top-flight facility with 12,000 students, and several other universities, each one preparing young Israelis to
make contributions in many fields of study and work. Obvious for many
to see were the new and growing cities and also the successful crop-
producing farms on land that once was semi-arid; from 1948 to 1968, land
under cultivation more than doubled from 412,000 acres to over 1,000,000
acres. Goldberg asked: "Is not God at work here in the natural course of
history, and is not this a miracle after 2,000 years of worldwide dispersion?"[56]

Even more impressive was the fact that these gains occurred while
Israel faced the daily reality of hostile borders. Goldberg met Arabs who
opposed any idea of peaceful coexistence. One young Arab told him:

"Some of us feel that our pride has been severely wounded and we want to be revenged." Israel was on "constant alert" as Cairo and Damascus continued to radio broadcast "hate propaganda." With so much attention on Israel's security, young men served in the army for three years, young women for two years, and men did additional military service thirty to sixty days a year. There was a large cost to having the nation's defense forces in constant readiness; the military received 70 percent of all taxes. From Goldberg's observation, Israel's decision not to return conquered territory to the Arabs was understandable because returning land after the 1956 Suez crisis led to a "further breakdown" of Arab-Israeli relations. The situation worsened in the post-Six-Day War period when the Soviets increased their supply of weapons and training to the Egyptians and Iranians.[57]

In 1969 as the intensity of the War of Attrition increased, *Moody Monthly* published other accounts by the Goldbergs, often giving additional details of sites discussed in their earlier reports. One tour began in Jerusalem where they boarded a bus at Jaffa Gate and traveled to Bethlehem, located south approximately six miles down a winding road. On the Bethlehem outskirts they saw a small white-domed building, the traditional tomb of Jacob's wife Rachel. Small in size, Bethlehem has a large open area in the center of the town called Manger Square. At the southeast corner stands the Church of the Nativity, a large stone structure built by Constantine's mother Helena in 336 AD. The entrance consists of two rows of Corinthian pillars and age-old mosaics. Next, there is a staircase winding down to a cave lit by silver and golden lamps. On the floor in Latin reads, "Here Jesus Christ was born of the Virgin Mary."[58]

The Goldbergs wtravelled two hours north to Nazareth and the Sea of Galilee where Jesus encountered a few disciples, quieted a fierce storm, and ministered to many in the area. At the small town of Magdala there is a small white-domed building marking the burial of Mary Magdalene. Up a steep hill from the northern shore of Galilee is the Mount of Beatitudes, where Jesus gave the Sermon on the Mount. Following the road northeast around the lake, a deserted spot is the site of the once bustling town of Capernaum, where Peter lived.[59] Upon returning to Jerusalem, Goldberg described the beauties of the area outside Jerusalem, the Garden of Gethsemane, the Golden Gate, and St. Stephen's Gate of the ancient city. Inside the city, history shouted from the rocks. One could retrace the last steps of Jesus on the Via Dolorosa (the Way of the Cross). Of great importance to prophecy believers is the Chapel of the Ascension near the top of the Mount of Olives. Here the disciples stood and watched Jesus rise to heaven, here the angels announced to the disciples "that He would come again."[60] From these descriptive accounts in the late 1960s, *Moody Monthly* readers received an emotional and vivid picture of the Holy Land, a mixture of the biblical past and modern Israel. For

Americans raised in Christian homes and exposed to Bible stories, Christian Zionist ideas were persuasive.

Both prophecy and politics were front and center in the 1970 *Moody Monthly* interview of Louis Goldberg. In his opinion, the most significant development in the Middle East was the increasing presence of the Soviets as Arabs sought support for their fight against Israel. He believed that the atheism of communist Russia was not a major barrier for many young Arabs less influenced by the Islamic faith. In explaining the attitudes of "Palestinian Arabs," he appeared to see Israel as blameless in 1948 when the Palestinians left their homes: "[D]espite pleas by Israelis, many Arabs fled Palestine before the impending Arab invasion." Although he cautioned against any clear linkage of prophecy to events in 1970, he stated that "we may well be moving toward fulfillment of the conditions set out in Ezekiel 38." Concerning the prophecy of an invasion of Israel by northerners it was significant that Moscow is almost due north of Jerusalem. Goldberg also interpreted that Persia, Libya, and Ethiopia were confederate with the northern power, and that the invasion would take place at a time when Israel enjoyed security and peace. Given the coupling of the Arab-Israeli conflict and Palestinian refugee issue, a solution had to satisfy all parties. But since no resolution was in sight, Christians needed to be aware of the sovereignty and timing of God. At the right moment there would be "some kind of peace," which "may then be the signal for the invasion of the land from the north as prophesied in Ezekiel." In the meantime, as the Soviet Union continued to arm Egypt and other Arab nations it was important for the United States to assist Israel with military arms.[61]

The following year Goldberg wrote that any explanation of Israel's accomplishments that gave "all too little place to God the First Cause, and His revealed Word" fell short. To understand Israel, any reliance on a "humanistic plane of material and efficient causes" were inadequate in an age when many Christians were showing greater interest in the Bible and prophecy.[62] The survival of Israel in the middle of "implacable enemies" was compelling evidence of history "moving in the very directions long indicated by Bible prophecy." He witnessed many indicators pointing to end-time conditions "in the land of a regathered people": more Israeli leaders began to see how the Bible helped build Israeli identity, all of Israel's state schools taught the Bible (between four to six hours weekly), there was a restlessness among agnostics (more than 50 percent of the population) to reevaluate their position on the importance of religion, an increasing number of Israelis read books about Jesus, many religious Jews sensed the start of "the redemption of Israel," and there was greater evidence of Messianic Jews, those Jews "who have declared themselves as Jews in their nationality and for their faithfulness to the state of Israel and as Christians in their religious expression."[63]

When J. Dwight Pentecost returned from a trip to Jerusalem the first question someone asked was whether he saw any signs of the rebuilding of the temple on Mount Moriah. Others inquired because they believed that one reference to a temple in Paul's second letter to the Thessalonians taught that a rebuilt temple must come first before the rapture. Pentecost devoted an article to answering what came first, the rapture or the temple? The rapture itself was clear. Three different passages in the New Testament refer to the event when Christ, without warning, suddenly appears in the clouds of heaven and calls the dead in Christ to rise from their graves. He also catches "up all living saints who are on earth" and unites them with the resurrected saints "into one body of the redeemed" taken to heaven. As for the timing of the building of the temple, it required closer study. Pentecost expected the destruction of Jerusalem by the Arabs and northerners (Russians) in the middle of a seven-year tribulation period following the Rapture. With all buildings (temples included) destroyed, the construction of the temple would take place at the beginning of the second half of the tribulation period. But God would disown this temple because the Antichrist who built it for his headquarters had "repudiated His Son." As Pentecost understood it, prophecy teaching affirmed the "blessed hope" of Christ coming at any time—an event not requiring a rebuilt temple.[64]

To find more political analysis from a Christian perspective of the immediate years before the Yom Kippur War, Americans could turn to *Christianity Today*. One editorial warned of Soviet encroachment in the Middle East and how Soviet military assistance strengthened the Arab world, thus threatening Israel's ability to resist forever: "Nasser has acidly called for the ultimate resolution of the problem by the extermination of Israel, and no one should be naïve enough to suppose that he is incapable of doing just that if and when the option is open to him."[65] The magazine pointed out that American Jews protesting against U.S. involvement in Southeast Asia, and thus inoculating Americans against any military commitments elsewhere, might backfire when Israel needed American assistance. *Christianity Today* was critical of the mainstream media, finding it inconsistent for the *New York Times* to run one editorial opposing intervention in Cambodia and another one favoring intervention in Israel. It appeared that both situations were "the direct result of Communist aggression."[66]

In *Christianity Today*, Lillian Harris Dean reported that among more than four hundred delegates meeting in Beirut in May 1970, for the World Conference of Christians for Palestine was an official spokesman for the PLO who said: "We are simply fighting for our rights and not because of hatred, for we know that hatred would bring us the same diseases afflicting Zionism. We are in the process of building a healthy generation free of hate." Calling this statement "wishful thinking," Dean noted that while this PLO member spoke, Palestinian commandos made deadly raids into northern Israel.[67] A *Christianity Today* editorial recognized that the "displaced Palestinian Arabs" suffered injustice, but the best solution was to grant them "other lands."[68] Clearly, Arab violence was a problem. One "Arab terrorist attack" caused great sadness for Baptist minister Theodore W. Ertle of Grandville, Michigan. He lost his wife Barbara, thirty-one, after a hail of bullets struck a busload of American tourists near Hebron.[69]

The evangelical magazine desired that the Arab-Israeli cease-fire of 1970 was the start of a "permanently peaceful settlement." Unfortunately there was a violation of the cease-fire agreement when Egypt, with the assistance of the Soviets, installed more missiles along the Suez Canal, thereby changing the balance of power. The Israelis expected better results from the American government, which failed to demand that the Egyptians respect the conditions of the cease-fire. The various Palestinian airliner hijackings also made the situation in the Middle East more dangerous. The main problem, however, with any cease-fire agreement was little evidence of integrity on the part of all parties. *Christianity Today* warned of Soviet military assistance to Egypt upsetting "the military balance" and how the United States was slow to supply the Israelis with planes. The West had to take a stand or witness "the dissolution of Israel and the possible genocide of its people."[70]

In early 1971, *Christianity Today* explained its support for Meir's insistence to keep the Golan Heights, Sharm al-Sheikh at the Straits of Tiran, and territory along the Jordan as the best method to maintain Israel's "territorial integrity and viability." Israeli politicians were correct to distrust the Soviet Union, correct to assume the Arabs would strike again, especially since the installation of missile sites at the Suez Canal soon after the last cease-fire, and correct to doubt the trustworthiness of the United States: "Golda Meir and her government have to walk a tightrope keeping the armament supply routes open [with America] and at the same time resisting the demands by the United States that she return *all* territories taken in 1967."[71] Interestingly, *Christianity Today* reported that Meir was one of a number of Israeli dignitaries who watched *His Land*, the film adaptation of Billy Graham's book *His Land* (1969). Production of the movie was by the film division of the Billy Graham Evangelistic Association. After viewing the film, which saw Israel as God's plan, Meir responded: "So many thanks for picturing our land as it is. I've never seen it so beautiful." Likewise, Mayor Kollek spoke highly of the film: "I was deeply moved. . . . I haven't seen a better film about Jerusalem — ever."[72] Graham had good relations with some Israeli leaders, including Meir, who presented him with a Bible inscribed, "To a great teacher in all the important matters to humanity and a true friend of Israel."[73]

In the early 1970s, Israeli politicians continued to face the reality that Israel remained risky for many, even those traveling on tour buses or school buses.[74] There were, however, hopeful signs. In January 1971, Israel looked forward to indirect discussions with Egypt. Serving as the UN special representative, Gunnar Jarring, Swedish ambassador to Moscow, played a key role in this process. The following month Sadat extended the cease-fire and discussed the possibility of opening the Suez Canal to international traffic. The reopening of the canal served the interests of everyone. Egypt's economy needed a boost and the international traffic would stabilize the region and, it was hoped, result in serious peace discussions beneficial to the Israelis.[75]

Proposals submitted by Ambassador Jarring to Egypt and Israel on February 8 centered on Israel withdrawing its forces from "occupied United Arab Republic territory to the former international boundary between Egypt and the British Mandate of Palestine." In return, Egypt would discuss a peace agreement with Israel. Egypt was agreeable to Jarring's proposals, Israel was not. The Israelis saw two significant problems with Jarring's efforts: he avoided the issue of Egypt not negotiating directly with Israel and he underestimated how important it was for Israel not to unilaterally withdraw from the canal zone in exchange for Egyptian promises. It was foolish for Israel to compromise its security with military withdrawal before negotiations began. Sadat's statement to the Palestine National Council at the end of February of realizing "the Arab Will" did not give Israel much confidence.[76] For supporters of Israel, the logic presented by leaders such as Moshe Dayan made better sense: "The Arabs have agreed to sign a peace accord with us not because they have come to terms with the existence of Israel but to induce Israeli withdrawal. We want security, not just peace documents, and would prefer that Israel hold sensible, effective lines for her defense, even if the Arabs refuse to regard them as permanent, rather than return to the 4 June [1967] borders."[77]

In early 1972, Sadat declared that the decision for war was final; the only unknown was the timing of Israel's defeat. The following year, the Soviets' delivery of SCUD surface-to-surface missiles to Egypt put the issue in sharper focus. There were unmistakable signs of war misread by Israeli intelligence officers believing the Arabs were not militarily ready for a serious attack.[78] On early October 6, 1973, the Israelis received confirmation that the Arabs would attack that very day—it was the Day of Atonement (Yom Kippur). When Israeli chief of staff General David Eleazar asked for a "green light" to launch a preemptive air strike, Meir with a heavy heart said no: "We don't know, any of us, what the future will hold, but there is always the possibility that we will need help, and if we strike first, we will get nothing from anyone."[79] That morning Meir informed U.S. ambassador Kenneth Keating that an Arab attack was imminent and that Israel would not strike first. Before the end of the day, 80,000 Egyptian soldiers had overrun Israeli positions along the canal and advanced a few miles into the Sinai.[80] Arab success resulted in heavy losses for Israel. President Nixon later wrote: "It was the one day of the year when Israel was least prepared to defend itself."[81]

The Egyptians and Syrians coordinated their attacks into the Sinai and Golan Heights. The code name for the war was "Operation Badr," named after the site where the Prophet Muhammad scored his first victory over Arab infidels. The Syrians and Egyptians counted heavily on Soviet military support and within days after the war began they received thousands of tanks, 175 aircraft, 100 armored personal carriers, fifty field guns, and a large supply of anti-tank and anti-aircraft weapon systems. It is notable that Cuban crews operated many of the tanks sent.[82]

Washington received precise cables that the war was not going well for the Israelis. Writing for *Christian Century*, Thomas A. Idinopulos first grasped the seriousness of the conflict when he encountered two Israeli soldiers, shouldering machine guns, shouting in Arabic to residents in an apartment two miles south of Jerusalem to keep their lights out and not to travel on the roads. With his wife and two small sons, Idinopulos collected flashlights and water and waited for news of the war. Talking to Arabs he began to understand that Arabs in the West Bank remained resentful of Israel, but they expressed neither a desire to see Jordan go to war with Israel nor "a return of Jordanian rule in the area."[83]

Secretary of State Henry Kissinger realized that Israel's loss of high-performance aircraft in the early days demonstrated Egypt's effective operation of Soviet surface-to-air missiles. The White House also pondered Meir's criticism that Israel's difficult position was due in part to its earlier promise to the United States that it would not take any preemptive action.[84] The Nixon government did, however, rise to the occasion and made plans to counteract Soviet assistance to the Arabs with prompt logistical support. Declaring Defcon 3 (global military alert) also communicated to the Soviets to rethink any plans of aggression against Israel.[85]

Although the Israelis viewed Egypt as the most serious threat, they focused on the Syrian attack due to the proximity of northern Israeli cities to the Golan Heights. On October 8, the Israelis repulsed the Syrian attack and began to reclaim lost ground despite the addition of Iraqi and Jordanian reinforcements for the Syrians. Able to turn their attention to the Sinai, the Israelis began a serious and effective counterattack on the Egyptian line. Fearing Israel might resort to using nuclear weapons, the White House eventually shipped 9,000 tons of matériel including aircraft and tanks. The weapons gave the Israelis a huge psychological boost to push into Egypt without fear of running short of equipment.[86] The Egyptian leaders were in a state of panic, especially when the Israelis entered Egypt at the canal. With the Israelis across the canal, the Soviets were anxious for a cease-fire. The UN Security Council called for one on October 22, effective immediately. Ignoring the resolution, Israel continued its military action into Egypt, only stopping when pressured by the White House. The war was over before Israel could realize a greater military victory.[87] Due to the brevity of the conflict, the Israelis did not use much of the American supplies. However, Sadat attempted to argue that the Egyptian defeat was due to America's involvement in the war. As he stated in his autobiography, he "wasn't prepared to fight the U.S.A."[88] On October 24, two days after UN Security Council Resolution 338, Israel agreed to the UN's cease-fire. Israel's losses were heavy with 2,838 dead and the destruction of 103 aircraft and 840 tanks.[89]

Playing a major role in the crisis due to Nixon's preoccupation with the Watergate crisis, Kissinger had opposed the idea of a preempted military strike by the Israelis. Two months after the war, he told a small group of American Jewish intellectuals that the Israelis "lost most of their aircraft to SAMs, not the Egyptian airforce, and had they preempted they would simply have suffered the same losses four hours earlier."[90] Christian Zionists said little about geopolitical concerns of upsetting the Soviets or world opinion. Trusting God's action in history, John Walvoord in the early stage of the Yom Kippur War declared that "Israel will never be destroyed."[91] As the war progressed, *Christianity Today* predicted an Israeli victory, but the Arabs would not stop from seeking to defeat Israel. The Jewish nation had no peaceful options. If it returned conquered land it risked "extermination," if it kept conquered land it faced "recurring conflict."[92]

Christian Century offered two different perspectives on the crisis. Robert E. Cushman, professor at Duke University divinity school, wrote of a "Zionist 'manifest destiny' for the Holy Land" that compelled the Arab Islamic world to promote a Jihad against Israel. Franklin H. Littell, professor of religion at Temple University, compared Israel—"a unique bastion of respect for the human person and his freedom"—with the Arab world which continued to suffer economic hardship and dictatorial governments. He found the anti-Israel responses of some Christians troubling, particularly the statement of one Protestant board secretary suggesting that "Israel might have to die for the peace of the world." He also wrote of the Soviets moving sophisticated weaponry to the Suez Canal and how the outnumbered Israelis depending upon their air superiority paid a high price because of Russian-made SAM missiles.[93]

Christian Zionists were confident of the outcome, but they were thankful for Nixon's action and they believed that they themselves had a part to play. The First Baptist Church of Dallas placed an advertisement in the *Dallas Morning News* for Christians to write to their politicians and "support Israel <u>NOW</u>." Professor B. Elmo Scogin of the Southeastern Baptist Theological Seminary sent telegrams to Nixon and Kissinger offering his prayers and financial support for the "immediate resupply" of Israel's weapons.[94] As Christian Zionists expected, Israel triumphed against the Syrians. According to evangelical Raymond L. Cox, "As Israeli tanks rumbled into Syria . . . some supposed they would roll all the way to the great river [Euphrates], but God's time had not yet struck. But it will."[95]

The Yom Kippur War differed significantly from the Six-Day War; heavier losses resulted in no long-lasting euphoria.[96] There was the reminder that the Arabs would continue their fight. Professor Gordon D. Young, son of Douglas Young, wrote to his Purdue University colleagues and students that Arab governments believed they could lose many wars, while Israel could not afford to lose one.[97] American leftist and antiwar activist Michael Medved admitted that the 1973 war shook his life "with the force of a philosophical earthquake." In the past, he took Israel's security for granted, but now he recognized "that freedom, security and ultimately survival itself depend on military power."[98] David Ifshin was another American radical who rethought his opposition to American military power after living in Israel during the Yom Kippur War. Much more aware of the devastation caused by Arab states "heavily armed with Soviet weaponry," Ifshin had greater appreciation for the American C5A cargo planes that replenished exhausted Israeli resources.[99]

The war altered the dynamics of Palestinian politics. A growing number of Israelis realized that Palestinian Arabs were no longer going to take a back seat to the Egyptians and Jordanians. The PLO became the "legitimate representative of the Palestinian people."[100] As the national consciousness of the Palestinians grew, the Israelis would need to be open to friends wherever they find them; clearly, they had had few friends on the international scene. In late December 1973, Kissinger concluded: "Politically, Israel faced the critical opposition of the Soviet Union, Europe, Japan, and all the Moslem states. The U.S. was the only friend at the end of the war. It is an extraordinarily precarious position, because any issue brought to the UN would have a guaranteed overwhelming vote against Israel."[101]

One price paid by the Americans was costlier gas. On October 17, 1973, the Organization of Arab Petrol Exporting Countries promised cuts to oil production every month "until such time as total evacuation of Israeli forces from all Arab territory occupied during the June 1967 war is completed, and the legitimate rights of the Palestinian people are restored."[102] Some members were especially aggressive and wanted stiffer conditions. For example, two months into the embargo, Saddam Hussein, president of Iraq's Revolutionary Council, argued that the "true and successful way to use oil as a weapon against America and the Zionist enemy is to nationalize American oil interests of any country standing by the enemy." Libya's Muammar al-Gaddafi took it one step further, threatening to "hit America" by shutting off all oil to Europe: "We shall ruin your [European] industries as well as your trade with the Arab world."[103] Moderate views prevailed and the Arabs lifted their embargo in March 1974 even though the Israeli forces had not withdrawn from their territorial gains.

The long lines at gas stations resulted in ordinary Americans taking a greater interest in the Middle East. Interestingly, as American Jews drew closer to Israel after the Yom Kippur War other Americans did the reverse, obvious to many including Henry Kissinger who stated there was "a noticeable turn against all-out support for Israel."[104] Although Kissinger was not referring specifically to church communities, there were clear signs of liberal Christian leaders becoming more critical of Israel. A persistent sticking point was Israel's possession of the West Bank.[105] Much of this criticism was a result of liberal Christian focus on the plight of Palestinian refugees and censure of so-called western imperialism—a message expressed loudly by the secular Left. In late 1973, Catholic intellectual Michael Novak pointed to ominous signs of anti-Semitism when he asked: "Is the final destination of the left, after so many romantic but attractive moments, anti-Semitism?"[106] Adopting some Marxist themes, various liberal Christian leaders drifted further away from the largest group of Americans who continued to stand strong for Israel—evangelical Christians who showed no ambiguity on what they viewed was the proper relationship between the United States and Israel.

In the wake of the Yom Kippur War, some conservative Christian journalists noted the eventual somber mood in Israel. Of course, the Israelis were joyful to defeat their Arab enemies, but such joy was fleeting. *Moody Monthly* explained: First, the Arabs stopped regarding Israel "as almost invincible." Second, the death of more than 2,600 men was a heavy burden for the Israeli people. Third, there was considerable anger toward the military intelligence officials for allowing the Arabs to invade by surprise. Fourth, the notion of the Suez Canal representing a strong defense line was a false one. Fifth, the rise of defense costs and inflation spelled economic hardship. Sixth, there was the realization that Israel would likely have to return land to its enemies in any bargain for peace, a decision that would weaken Israel's security. Finally, it appeared that Israel's friends were fewer and its foes were greater in number. But *Moody Monthly* saw opportunity in the somber climate of the Israeli people. Unchanged was the prophetic view of Israel's special place in God's plan of history: "Perhaps the very sense of need which now faces these people will help to trigger true spiritual revival in that land." Whereas Israeli bumper stickers after the 1967 war read, "Hats off to the Israel Defense Forces," some now read, "Israel, trust in the Lord."[107]

While Israelis stood stronger than ever before, Palestinian leaders became more active in building Palestinian identity and nationalism. In the immediate years after the Yom Kippur War, many Israelis cited terrorism as their main security concern.[108] On public television, Americans watched the seven-part series *Arabs and Israelis* co-produced by an Israeli and an Egyptian. The goal was "a balanced view," but it seemed problematic for some that there was no reference to the UN resolution of 1947 establishing both a Jewish and Palestinian state. Other important omissions meant that uninformed viewers "may come away with a distorted, anti-Israel slant, compounded of a dangerous mixture of ignorance and understandable pity for the Palestinians."[109]

Although the suffering of the Palestinian refugees was obvious to anyone, Christian Zionists believed that Israeli leaders made reasonable and serious efforts at peace. In their eyes, Israel did not create the ongoing Palestinian refugee problem nor was Israeli refugee policy unreasonable given the goal of security for all Israeli citizens. Moreover, the accusation coming from leftist circles that the Yom Kippur War was Israel's fault was illogical. American evangelicals continued to see God working in history. Their coverage of Israel remained supportive, presenting the timeless themes of Christian Zionism.

NOTES

1. Avi Shlaim, "Interview With Abba Eban, 11 March 1976," *Israel Studies* 8, no. 1 (Spring 2003), 159.
2. Ritchie Ovendale, *The Origins of the Arab-Israeli Wars* (London: Longman, 1984), 187.
3. Herzog, *The Arab-Israeli Wars*, 210–11.
4. Quoted in Sicker, *Israel's Quest for Security*, 113.
5. *FRUS*, 1964–1968, Volume XIX, Arab-Israeli Crisis and War, 1967, Document 399, Page 739. history.stategov/historicaldocuments/frus1964-68v19/d399 (accessed June 13, 2014).
6. See Appendix of Documents in Hahn, *Crisis and Crossfire*, 148–49.
7. Herzog, *The Arab-Israeli Wars*, 212.
8. Sicker, *Israel's Quest for Security*, 114–15.
9. Hahn, *Crisis and Crossfire*, 150.
10. Quoted in Sicker, *Israel's Quest for Security*, 118. Given Israel's small population, Heikal added: "And if we succeed in inflicting 10,000 casualties, he will indisputably find himself compelled to stop fighting, because he has no manpower resources at his disposal."
11. Quoted in Rabinovich and Reinharz, eds., *Israel In the Middle East*, 225.
12. Sicker, *Israel's Quest for Security*, 119.
13. Sicker, *Israel's Quest for Security*, 119. For a concise and helpful description of the Bar-Lev line, see Dayan, *Moshe Dayan*, 447–48
14. Shlaim, *The Iron Wall*, 285, 323.
15. Reich, "Israeli National Security Policy," 9.
16. Sicker, *Israel's Quest for Security*, 120.
17. Merkley, *American Presidents, Religion, and Israel*, 65.
18. Quoted in Sicker, *Israel's Quest for Security*, 121. Also, see Spiegel, *The Other Arab-Israeli Conflict*, 186–87.
19. Quoted in Sicker, *Israel's Quest for Security*, 122.
20. Sicker, *Israel's Quest for Security*, 122.
21. Sicker, *Israel's Quest for Security*, 124–25.
22. Herzog, *The Arab-Israeli Wars*, 238.
23. Sicker, *Israel's Quest for Security*, 125–26.
24. Sicker, *Israel's Quest for Security*, 122.
25. Peretz, "The United States, the Arabs, and Israel," 120–21.
26. Quoted in Shlaim, "Interview With Abba Eban, 11 March 1976," 161.
27. Paul Chamberlain, "A World Restored: Religion, Counterrevolution, and the Search for Order in the Middle East," *Diplomatic History* 32, no. 3 (June 2008), 458–62.

28. "Turkish Eyes on Jerusalem," *Christianity Today*, November 22, 1968, 45.

29. There was considerable division among leaders on what was the best approach for "the liberation of *all* of Palestine." See Safran, *Israel*, 267.

30. For an except, see Hahn, *Crisis and Crossfire*, 152–54.

31. Barry Rubin and Judity Colp Rubin, *Yasir Arafat: A Political Biography* (Oxford: Oxford University Press, 2005), 38.

32. Cattan, *Palestine, the Arabs and Israel*, ix.

33. In fact, the mayor of Bethlehem saw no reason to have a strong Israeli security presence during the Christmas season. "Bethlehem Bids for Normalcy," *Christianity Today*, January 1, 1971, 40.

34. E. Russel Chandler, "Crucial Issues in the Mideast," *Christianity Today*, February 27, 1970, 14.

35. Chandler, "Crucial Issues in the Mideast," 15.

36. "Bible Misuse," *Christianity Today*, February 27, 1970, 35.

37. Balfour Brickner, "Vietnam and the Jewish Community, *Christian Century*, April 29, 1970, 531–34. Brickner found it unfortunate that the majority of American Jews accepted "the logic that a moratorium on American Jewish criticism of our government's conduct of the Vietnam war is good for Israel."

38. "Perspectives on Arab-Israeli Tensions," *Christianity Today*, June 7, 1968, 6–9.

39. "Israel's Answer," *Christianity Today*, September 29, 1967, 18.

40. "In the Wake of War," *Christianity Today*, August 18, 1967, 24.

41. "United Church Observer: No Trees for Forrest," *Christianity Today*, May 22, 1970, 37.

42. Kevin Flatt, *After Evangelicalism: The Sixties and the United Church of Canada* (Montreal and Kingston: McGill-Queen's University Press), 2013.

43. "With Mixed Emotions," *Christianity Today*, September 26, 1969, 25.

44. *Moody Monthly*, June 1968, 73.

45. Boyer, *When Time Shall Be No More*, 188.

46. Louis Goldberg, "Four Days at Jerusalem," *Moody Monthly*, September 1971, 28–29.

47. See Boyer, *When Time Shall Be No More*, 191.

48. "Who Is This Man?" *Moody Monthly*, June 1971, 17. On the government's support of the conference, see Boyer, *When Time Shall Be No More*, 204.

49. At Ben-Gurion's home (now a museum), the book is on his desk. See Goldman, *Zeal for Zion*, 293.

50. Ben-Gurion, *Israel*, 833–34, 840.

51. Boyer, *When Time Shall Be No More*, ix, 3, 5.

52. Weber, *On the Road to Armageddon*, 188–90.

53. Louis Goldberg, "Message From Masada," *Moody Monthly*, July–August 1968, 9, 16.

54. Louis Goldberg, "The Goldbergs Discover Israel I," *Moody Monthly*, September 1968, 9.

55. Goldberg, "The Goldbergs Discover Israel I," 42–45.

56. Louis Goldberg, "Israel–The Twenty Year Miracle," *Moody Monthly*, October, 1968, 69–72.

57. "The Goldbergs Discover Israel: IV. Dimensions of the Future," *Moody Monthly*, December 1968, 67–68.

58. Louis Goldberg, "Where the Bible Happened," *Moody Monthly*, April 1969, 29, 39. An additional report can be found in the May issue.

59. Goldberg, "Where the Bible Happened," 39, 41.

60. Goldberg, "Where the Bible Happened," 78–79.

61. "What Will Happen in the Mid-East?" *Moody Monthly*, November 1970, 19–21, 57–59.

62. *Moody Monthly*, April 1971, 43.

63. Louis Goldberg, "Religious Thought in Israel," *Moody Monthly*, October 1971, 21–23.

64. J. Dwight Pentecost, "Which Comes First the Rapture or the Temple? *Moody Monthly*, October 1971, 30–31, 67–69.

65. "Cambodia and Israel," *Christianity Today*, May 22, 1970, 21–22.

66. "Cambodia and Israel," *Christianity Today*, May 22, 1970, 21.

67. "Beirut Conference: Zionist Racism?" *Christianity Today*, June 5, 1970, 46.

68. "An Arab-Israeli Détente?" *Christianity Today*, August 21, 1970, 31.

69. "The Middle East: A Stern Test," *Christianity Today*, March 13, 1970, 32.

70. "Storm Signals in the Near East," *Christianity Today*, January 7, 1972, 26.

71. "Pressures on Israel, *Christianity Today*, April 9, 1971, 30–31.

72. "This Land Is 'His Land,'" *Christianity Today*, May 8, 1970, 38–39.

73. Martin, *A Prophet with Honor*, 265.

74. Arnold T. Olson, "Israel: Birthplace of Peace," *Action* 29, no. 4 (Winter 1970), 12.

75. Sicker, *Israel's Quest for Security*, 126.

76. Sicker, *Israel's Quest for Security*, 127–29.

77. Quoted in Sicker, *Israel's Quest for Security*, 130.

78. Henry Kissinger explained: "Every Israeli (and American) analysis before October 1973 agreed that Egypt and Syria lacked the military capability to regain their territory by force of arms; hence there would be no war. The Arab armies must lose; hence they would not attack." Henry Kissinger, *Years of Upheaval* (Boston: Little, Brown and Company, 1982), 459.

79. Meir, *My Life*, 426–27.

80. Schoenbaum, *The United States and the State of Israel*, 199.

81. Richard Nixon, *RN: The Memoirs of Richard Nixon* (New York: Grosset and Dunlap, 1978), 921.

82. Kober, "Great-Power Involvement and Israeli Battlefield Success in the Arab-Israeli Wars, 1948–1982," 34. Further evidence of Soviet influence is Sadat's acknowledgment that the Arabs wanted the war in the spring, but the Soviets asked for a postponement until after June.

83. "The Middle East War and the West Bank," *Christian Century*, November 28, 1973, 1164–65.

84. Kissinger, *Years of Upheaval*, 476–77.

85. Kober, "Great-Power Involvement and Israeli Battlefield Success in the Arab-Israeli Wars, 1948–1982," 43, 45.

86. Kober, "Great-Power Involvement and Israeli Battlefield Success in the Arab-Israeli Wars, 1948–1982," 45–46.

87. Sicker, *Israel's Quest for Security*, 135–37.

88. Anwar el-Sadat, *Anwar el-Sadat: In Search of Identity* (New York: Harper and Row, Publishers, 1978), 290.

89. Shlaim, *The Iron Wall*, 321. Shlaim claims that the more balanced outcome between Israel and the Arab states "promoted a more realistic attitude on both sides and established a more promising basis for bargaining and compromise."

90. "Kissinger and the American Jewish Leadership after the 1973 War," 199.

91. "Talk of the End," *Christianity Today*, October 26, 1973, 59.

92. "Middle East: The War Seeds Sprout," *Christianity Today*, October 26, 1973, 106.

93. "The Mideast Crisis: Two Views," *Christian Century*, November 7, 1973, 1093–95. Littell was president of Christians Concerned for Israel.

94. Banki, *Christian Responses to the Yom Kippur War*, 42, 44.

95. Raymond L. Cox, "Journey to Carchemish," *The Sunday School Times and Gospel Herald*, August 1, 1974, 15.

96. Shindler, *A History of Modern Israel*, 144.

97. Banki, *Christian Responses to the Yom Kippur War*, 101.

98. Peter Collier and David Horowitz, eds., *Second Thoughts: Former Radicals Look Back at the Sixties* (Lanham, MD: Madison Books, 1989), 20–21.

99. Collier and Horowitz, eds., *Second Thoughts*, 87.

100. Shindler, *A History of Modern Israel*, 153.

101. "Kissinger and the American Jewish Leadership after the 1973 War," 211.

102. Quoted in Rüdiger Graf, "Making Use of the 'Oil Weapon': Western Industrialized Countries and Arab Petropolitics in 1973–1974," *Diplomatic History* 36, no. 1 (January 2012), 185.

103. Quoted in Graf, "Making Use of the 'Oil Weapon,' 195.

104. "Kissinger and the American Jewish Leadership after the 1973 War," *Israel Studies* 7, no. 1 (Spring 2002), 196.

105. Sizer, *Christian Zionism*, 84.

106. Banki, *Christian Responses to the Yom Kippur War*, 26–27.

107. "Somber Mood in Israel," *Moody Monthly*, June 1974, 21.

108. Gloria H. Falk, "Israeli Public Opinion on Peace Issues," in *Israeli National Security Policy: Political Actors and Perspectives,* eds. Bernard Reich and Gershon R. Kieval (New York: Greenwood Press, 1988), 191.

109. Peter Sourian, "Television," *The Nation*, April 19, 1975, 477–78.

SIX
Israel's Best Friend

The extent of American media attention on Israel is remarkable. Often the negative coverage is guilty of applying a double standard, obvious when critics hold the Israelis to a higher standard of morality than they do Arabs in conflict with Israel.[1] The Jewish state could use more friends on the international scene. What is surprising is that a group rarely receiving praise, or even acknowledgment, from American Jews was among the most consistent champions of Israel. While many others were quick to condemn Israel as it made difficult and unpopular decisions in its fight for survival in a hostile region, conservative Christians were trustworthy supporters, routinely voicing uplifting reports of the Jewish state. In recent years, there were American scholars and Israeli officials suggesting that America's Christian Zionists were Israel's truest friends.[2] The friendship was unconditional due to the key biblical text of Christian Zionism: "I will bless those who bless you [Abraham and his descendents], and I will curse him who curses you" (Genesis 12:3).[3]

The conservative Christian support for Israel in the years 1948 to 1975 was a story hidden from many Israelis. With some exceptions, this was likewise the case in the United States with Jews, journalists, commentators, and politicians.[4] Conservative Christians only received greater attention when the Christian Right emerged in the post-1975 period. Most Israelis and American Jews lacked a clear understanding of conservative Christianity and its distinctiveness compared to other expressions of Christianity. But this did not stop American conservative Christians, who were outside the cultural and political circles of power, from standing strong with Israel in its conflicts with Arabs. Typically marginalized by cultural and political elites, they became best friends to a people maligned in history and criticized by vocal twentieth-century activists and politicians.[5]

139

History clearly demonstrates American Jews favoring the political left. American Jewish support for Israel was in part due to its social democratic style of government.[6] As Jewish intellectual Norman Podhoretz writes, the vast majority of Jews were liberal. It is puzzling for Jews that conservative evangelicals support them with such enthusiasm. Even when American Jews failed to find clear evidence of anti-Semitism in evangelical circles, they simply assumed that it existed among evangelicals.[7] When there was a Jewish awareness of conservative Christian support for Israel, many Israelis and American Jews continued to view evangelical Christians with suspicion. In a recent poll asking American Jews to give a "thermometer rating" on how they felt about evangelicals—zero degrees representing very cold to one hundred representing very warm—the average rating for evangelicals was 24 degrees. Over one third of Jews gave evangelicals a 0 rating.[8] The story was similar in Israel; many Israelis distrusted or did not like Bible-believing Christians. There was the problem of evangelicals supporting conservative views on domestic social issues and the issue of Christian evangelism, both seen as a threat to Jewish freedom and identity. According to Menahem Benhayim of Eilat, Israel, the Israeli Ministry of Religious Affairs was well aware of evangelicals' strong support for Israel, but most Israelis and the Israeli media continued to see evangelicals as "anti-Semitic Christians."[9] Confronting anti-Semitism, evangelicals made significant efforts to explain that Gentiles (the Romans) rather than the Jews killed Jesus.[10]

In recent years, critics of evangelical support for Israel claim that behind the actions of evangelicalism there is a hidden agenda in which the Jews are more or less pawns in a theological end-of-the-world scenario. Many liberal detractors in the United States, notably within the American Jewish community, and in Israel, held that it was unhealthy for the Israelis to have such "friends." Other Jews were more appreciative of evangelical support as Israelis faced constant threats. Remarkably, Jewish neoconservative writers such as Irving Podhoretz speak more favorably of evangelicals than do liberal Protestants. What neoconservatives and evangelicals shared was a greater appreciation of achieving national security by way of a strong military.

Podhoretz devotes considerable attention to why liberal Jewish intellectuals in America fear conservative Christians. He argues that most Jews believed that these Christians were eager "to tear down the wall of separation between church and state" and thus turn Jews into second-class citizens.[11] Intellectuals were unaware or did not believe those conservative Christians who attempted to reassure Jews that they opposed a so-called Christian theocracy. American Jews and conservative evangelicals were mostly opposite each other at the ballot box for the presidency. With the exception of the South, where right-wing Democrat politicians were a force for many years, conservative evangelicals typically voted Republican. Podhoretz explains that the Jews looked to the Democratic

Party as the closest American counterpart of the European Left that had been more supportive of Jewish emancipation than conservative political forces.[12] In 1968, Hubert Humphrey's Jewish support was 81 percent to Richard Nixon's 17 percent. Yitzhak Rabin, Israel's ambassador to the United States, favored Nixon in 1972 and there were signs that George McGovern's attitude toward Israel was "tepid," but Nixon could only muster 35 percent to McGovern's 65 percent of the Jewish vote. In other presidential elections, Democrats Harry Truman, Adlai Stevenson, John F. Kennedy, and Lyndon Johnson all received between 60 and 90 percent of the Jewish vote.[13]

Although conservative Christians gave their votes to the Republican Party and they remained isolated from Jewish circles, they proved year after year, in evangelical magazines and other in-house publications, their support for Israel. They wrote enthusiastically on biblical prophecy and the Middle East, often portraying Arabs as inferior, violent, and culturally backward as did most Washington policymakers. Some cultural historians exploring religious discourse know that there is more to the story that needs unpacking.[14]

In its discussion of Christian-Jewish relations and the issue of evangelical activity in Israel, *Christianity Today* pointed out that there were some Jewish leaders who sensed the "genuine sympathy for and interest among evangelical Protestants in the destiny of the Jew."[15] Christian Zionists understood that there were Israeli politicians who stretched the truth, practiced deception, allowed corruption, and made other major errors of judgment that cost lives. But in the big picture, conservative Christians did not expect or look for perfection. They were champions of Israel and they soldiered on even if their love for the Jews was mostly a one-sided affair.

In the early stage liberal Protestants defended Israel on humanitarian and pragmatic grounds, but their defense lacked the staying power of conservative Christians.[16] A small number of Christian anti-Zionists made it their mission to expose the problems of Israel. These critics usually failed to discuss the legitimacy of UN and superpower decisions that led to Israel's rebirth in 1948. Historian Paul Merkley claims that Christian anti-Zionists prefer a counter-history version that questions the legality of Israel's existence: "Did Israel *really* come into existence by decision of the nations, they ask?" They continue the discussion of whether the Jews should have a home: "Anti Zionists live in the same counterfactual world as do the Muslims, who speculate about the *right* of Israel to exist and who refuse to permit its name to appear on maps while demanding that it be liquidated."[17] To explain the thinking of Protestants critical of Israel, Merkley points to theology: "Christian Zionism is anathema in liberal theology because it takes with unqualified seriousness and literalness the historical process that in fact has brought Israel back to Israel."[18]

Critics of Christian Zionism who argue that dispensationalist theology was a destructive force appear to misjudge the influence of dispensationalism on those defending Israel; even in fundamentalist publications most Christian Zionists gave no mention of dispensationalist teaching. Stating that God favored the Jews did not mean an admission of accepting dispensationalism. Some opponents claimed that Christian Zionism was racist. In his article on dispensationalism, Michael Stallard dismisses this claim. He clarifies that dispensationalists teach that the Jews are a *"chosen* race not a *superior* race." That God sees the Jews as special does not mean they are superior over other groups.[19]

For Stallard, "the debate over the ethical treatment of Arabs in Palestine by Israelis supported by the United States . . . involves primarily an interpretation of *history* and not theology." Dispensationalists expect that the teachings of Jesus are universally applicable to Arabs and Jews. History reveals that only one group expresses the extermination of the other. The murder of Jewish athletes at the 1972 Munich Olympic Games, the rise of airline hijacking by Palestinians, and the general rise of terrorism acts in Israel spoke volumes. What was the will of other Arab nations, especially those rich in oil, in assisting the Palestinian people with money and land? It is important to note, Stallard declares, that Israel provides citizenship and voting rights to hundreds of thousands of Muslims and Christian Arabs and permits Arabs to hold seats in the Knesset. Of course, there are abuses on both sides; no one should ignore the shortcomings of Israel and its powerful military. Any genuine oppression of Palestinians by Israel demanded attention and correction.[20]

Critics who claimed Christian Zionists were warmongers was another issue Stallard tackled. Given their literal interpretation of the Bible, dispensationalists read of the prediction of war and thus, they expected war. However, *"expecting* war and wanting war are two different things." There was reluctance among many dispensationalists to promote peace activism, but this was in part due to the poor track record of Arab nations honoring truces with Israel. Sadly, "the anti-Zionist actions of many Arabs speak louder than any peace treaty proposals." According to Stallard, "dispensationalists would rise up and rejoice" if Arabs agreed to live in peace with Israel. Dispensationalist theology states that "war is not a necessary pre-condition for the rapture of the Church to take place." The existence of Israel and the rise of the Antichrist, who would sign a peace treaty, were the only biblical prerequisites necessary for the tribulation to occur. A better scenario for dispensationalists was "seeking the security of Israel and not happily pursuing war."[21]

The evangelical press coverage was sensitive to the precariousness of Israel's national security with a couple of exceptions. For example, *Eternity* in 1955 recognized that without a treaty of peace Israel and Egypt were still at war with "bloody fighting and real casualties." But the evangelical magazine was critical of sensational American journalism that made the conflict worse than was the case. According to *Eternity*, the Israelis took life in stride and the event causing the most excitement was news of an oil gusher promising to lift the economy. The editor down-played the seriousness of Egypt purchasing weapons from Czechoslova-kia.[22] Less optimistic, many other conservative Christians maintained two points concerning peace: First, since men were sinners, the balance of power was the key to peace. Second, no peace could endure.[23] This con-servative Christian realism struck a chord with Americans frustrated with the rise of crime in the United States and what they believed was a loss of personal security.[24] Many Americans could appreciate the impor-tance of law and order for Israelis.

In a 1957 letter to *Christianity Today*, Elizabeth G. Chapman used histo-ry to explain why Christians supported the Jews rather than the Arabs: First, the Jews had ruled Palestine for more than a thousand years. Sec-ond, Arab immigration to Palestine increased only after the Jews brought prosperity to a land misused by the Arabs. Third, the Jews contributed magnificent support ("manpower, applied science and money") to the allies during World War II.[25] The socialist components of Israeli society such as the *kibbutzim* (communal living centers) did not stop conservative Christians from pointing to the material progress of democratic capital-ism in Israel.

Of course, various conservative Christians also expressed concern for the Palestinian refugees, stating that it was important for Israel to respect human rights. Conservative Protestant churches offering educational and other services to the Palestinians included the Assemblies of God, the Christian and Missionary Alliance, and the Southern Baptists. Holding to a Christian Zionist interpretation of the Land of Israel "did not necessi-tate the banishment of Arabs from the land."[26]

A difficulty that these Christian groups faced was that Muslims saw western culture as imperialistic, including Christianity, which they viewed as a western religion. Christian missions were difficult in Islamic countries. Saudi Arabia disallowed any Christian activity. Evangelicals encountered major hurdles when Muslims prevented other Muslims from accepting Christ as Savior.[27] In 1958, Frank E. Keay reported in *Christianity Today* that Muslims interpreted the preaching of the gospel "as an attempt to bring them under the domination of 'Western imperial-ism.'" To many Muslims, a Christian missionary equipped with a station wagon and other modern appliances representing western wealth was "an agent of imperialism." Christians confronted the issue of their doc-trine of the trinity clashing with "Islam's uncompromising attitude to the unity of God." And believing that the Prophet Muhammad received "God's last word to man," Muslims rejected any teaching in the Bible contrary to the Quran.[28] Farid Salamen, an Arab refugee from Palestine writing from Beirut, declared: "It is shameful for people as responsible as clergymen to be enslaved by misguided Zionist propaganda."[29]

Although in the early period of Israel's history there was no clear evidence of liberal Protestants pushing a "western imperialism" argument, some became very passionate about the poor economic state of Arab refugees. This was a noble position to take. However, liberals presenting a humanitarian argument rarely noted that since the War of Independence even neighboring Arabs viewed Palestinian refugees as a security threat and that Arab leaders had a dreadful record of taking care of their poor compared to the treatment of Arabs who benefited from Israeli social programs.[30] Christian Zionists found Israel's economic development impressive especially since Israeli leaders had faced major problems including the accommodation of millions of Jewish immigrants and the maintenance of a first-class military and national security system.[31]

One defender of Israel's Arab refugee policy was Christian Zionist G. Douglas Young. In 1961, he questioned the inflated number of Arab refugees and pointed out that almost all other refugees worldwide "had been resettled in the lands that received them." How neighboring Arab nations acted went against standard procedure. Their refusal to resettle refugees from Palestine demonstrated their preference to "use" the refugees for propaganda purposes. Moreover, there was a double standard when commentators said little or nothing about the hundreds of thousands of virtually penniless Jews who Israel welcomed from Arab nations which had confiscated Jewish property and belongings.[32] Other Christian Zionists who wrote that it was a privilege to spend time with Arabs, some of whom were "very wonderful," observed that there was a significant amount of distrust between various Arab groups.[33]

Pro-Israel comments from Christian circles were helpful to Israeli officials who welcomed positive messages originating from the West. It was Christian Zionists who did not forget that Egypt, Syria, and Lebanon opposed citizenship to hundreds of thousands of Palestinian refugees residing in their respective countries.[34] Israel's Ministry of Religious Affairs and other Ministry departments were aware of the important role American Christians played in promoting Israel throughout the United States. These government agencies collected data on major Protestant denominations, especially how each denomination viewed Israel's military and political goals.[35] While mainline Protestants fractured on issues such as the Palestinian refugees and American politicians courting Jewish votes, conservative Christians united behind Israel.[36] This was significant in that the links between Israel and the United States were important for Israel's national security.[37]

In the 1960s, an increasing number of American liberal Christian writers wrote forcefully in defense of the Arabs. The gains by Israel were "patent acts of expansionism," comparable to "the most violent, ruthless (and successful) aggression since Hitler's blitzkrieg." And importantly, there needed to be rejection of the biblical literalism "behind political Zionism." The writers were not Arabs or communists; they appeared to represent mainstream liberal Protestantism unable "to see the over-whelming moral justice of Israel's cause and . . . stand up for it with courage." To stay true to the Arab cause and, thus, limit Muslim hostility to Christians living among them, the anti-Zionist Christian community had to maintain that Palestinians "are barred from their land. . . . For once it acknowledged and confirmed theologically the unqualified right of Israel to live, it would be confronted not only with an ideological crisis but also with the moral necessity of casting its lot publicly with Israel, in opposition to unceasing Arab exterminationism."[38]

Some Christian anti-Zionists looked to secular intellectuals for guid-ance. One of the more trenchant critics of Israel was Edward Said. Many diplomatic historians found his scholarship of the Middle East troubling, but his words had weight in some leftist circles.[39] Other notable anti-Israel writing came from Noam Chomsky, a Jewish scholar who present-ed some of the more strident anti-Zionist material of the post-1967 peri-od.[40] Chomsky wrote of the "monstrous historical injustice" that Pales-tinian Arabs suffered. The answer was "an international left with a strong base in the United States" that encouraged "Israel to break free of West-ern influence." Once free, Israel could support "anticolonial forces" in the Middle East and thus realize a socialist society in the region. But an obstacle was that American militarists exploited "the threat to Israel" and the important role of American power protecting Israel.[41]

Other Jews traveled a different road than Chomsky. Most Jews re-mained opposed to the Vietnam War, but some declared that the Six-Day War was a "just war." American Jews became more nuanced with the term "anti-imperialism." They concluded that it was wrong for Arabs to argue that Israel was imperialistic. Who were the real imperialists? Arab "obsession" to see Israel destroyed was unjust and it strengthened the power of Arab "feudal kings." American Jews pondered about the "fra-ternal greetings from Ho Chi Minh to Nasser" and the rhetoric of those desiring to destroy the small, progressive State of Israel. American litera-ture published by black militants "pushed radical Jews into Israeli arms." One black leftist newsletter included an anti-Semitic cartoon of a Jewish hand (labeled with a dollar sign and a Star of David) with a rope prepar-ing to strangle Gamal Abdel Nasser and Muhammad Ali.[42] Martin Peretz wrote: "Slowly it began to dawn on some elements of the Left that cyni-cism was amply distributed around the globe, and around the political spectrum." A number of Jewish intellectuals began to lament and criticize leftist opposition to Israel. Nathan Glazer, who later defended the funda-mentalism of Christian Zionist Jerry Falwell, demanded that Jewish intel-lectuals be less naïve about the designs of American radicals.[43]

Methodist clergyman and vice president of Christians Concerned for Israel, A. Roy Eckardt, was not optimistic that genuine reconciliation could ever happen between Arabs and Israelis. For Eckardt, the norma-tive Arab position as declared by President Anwar Sadat spoke volumes:

"The Zionist conquest which oppresses us will not come to an end by the return of the conquered territories. *This is a new war of the Crusades, which will continue in our generation and in coming generations.*" Eckardt argued that few American scholars and pundits understood the degree of Arab hatred of Israel, and, instead, believed in the fantasy that this "withdrawal" or that "concession" by Israel would set the course for compromise and peace. The Arabs would never be satisfied: "Israel could 'withdraw' to a half-acre settlement along the Mediterranean sands, and she would remain as 'guilty' as she is now. . . . Any temporary atrophy within the cancer that is Israel would only be preparation for a future metastasis." If American politicians did not accept this, there would be one failed attempt after another to negotiate peace. Simply put, the "honest broker" schemes in American foreign policy were inane when applied to Israel: "'Evenhandedness' respecting two opponents, the first of whom condemns the second's claim to life, is not true evenhandedness, but a tacit alliance with the first party." Eckardt prayed he was wrong, but when all was said and done reconciliation was an illusion.[44] In *Eternity* magazine, Bernard Ramm was another who wrote of the great distance between Arab and Jew: "The American evangelical Christian cannot understand what the Arab thinks, what he says and what he does until he understands how complete and profound is this Arab hatred of Zionism." Even for decades, the Arab would suffer "economic loss if by so doing he strikes at Zionism."[45]

The conclusions of American Christians who stood with Israel shared much with the thinking of key Israeli leaders. In his book *David's Sling* (1970), Shimon Peres wrote of Israel's challenge to survive the "totality of Arab hostility" demonstrated in economic blockages, military attacks, and terrorism against Israel since its establishment. Even when Israel scored military victories there was no sense of closure of war. Peres argued that the Arabs were emotional in word and argument: "Arab argument, instead of being fashioned with the ingredients of cogent and sober reasoning, tends to fit the mould of propaganda and incitement." Nasser himself fell victim to the early and wildly false propaganda of Arab victory in the Six-Day War. Hours passed before an Egyptian military leader had enough courage to tell him that the Israelis had destroyed Egypt's Air Force early on June 5.[46]

As Peres explained, the Arabs would always have far greater population numbers, territorial size, and army strength. In the early 1970s, the Jewish population was 2.5 million versus 80 million Arabs and Arab territory was 300 times larger than Israel. "No compromise" could satisfy the Arabs because they believed "in their historic capacity of the long pull." The Arabs were especially militaristic. Without a free press, independent political parties, and freely elected parliaments, they lacked a system of checks and balances or institutions to rein in military aggressiveness.[47]

Faced with the constant threat of attack, Israel developed a system allowing society to quickly convert into a defensive army without hampering the country's productivity. And Israeli soldiers had the best weapons money could buy. It is no surprise that national defense was costly. In the early 1970s, Israel's defense budget exceeded 24 percent of the national revenue.[48] When visiting Israel in 1973, Governor Jimmy Carter learned of Israel's need to be strong as its enemies tested it every day, a fact that did not stop his drift to anti-Zionism years later.[49]

Various episodes such as when Denis Michael Rohan, an Australian Christian, set fire to a Muslim mosque in August 1969 demonstrated the "tragic, latent hostility between the Muslim-Arab world and the Jew."[50] There was less than $100,000 in damage, but the incident caused more anti-Israel furor throughout the Arab world than the Six-Day War. Those who did not underestimate the influence of Islam understood the Muslim protests. As Reuben Gross, a lawyer and Orthodox Jew, explained, "It is the eschatological implication of Israel and a unified Jerusalem that has shaken them."[51] The act represented insanity to secular observers, but a number of conservative evangelicals understood the deeper theological meaning of Rohan's plan, even if they sided with the well-known Bible prophecy teachers who claimed that the rebuilding of the temple was not a necessary event to occur before the second coming of Christ. When the Jordanians lost control of Jerusalem, the "ancient dream" of rebuilding the Jewish temple "assumed realistic outlines." On why a Christian foreigner took the first step, Gross declared: "Eschatological stirrings are touching Christians more than we Jews. . . . The Gentile thinks simple and straight. You need childlike simplicity to grasp it. . . . We Jews have absorbed so much of the poisons of exile, we have refused to take our own history seriously."[52]

Nonetheless, the yearning for Zion remained strong for many Jews. Russian Jews spoke of how the experiences of Jews were inseparable from the land. One elderly Russian arrived in Israel determined to live in Jerusalem before she died. While in a Tel Aviv hospital as a permanent invalid she insisted on a transfer to a Jerusalem hospital, well aware of the medical risk of death from the move. Such stories illustrated the longing for the Promised Land—"a yearning not easily set aside by what happens politically in peace or in war."[53] New arrivals to Israel in the early 1970s faced the seriousness of terrorism derived from Islam rather than Arab nationalism. In Egypt, Nasser fought under the banner of Arab nationalism whereas Sadat advanced the link between Islamic assertiveness and military action.[54] There was Muslim assurance that they would eventually defeat the Jews because their theology insisted on Islamic triumph over all other faiths: "If the Arabs do not eventually defeat Israel in combat, Muhammad lied, the Koran is in error, and Allah is not the true God."[55]

The greater role Islam played in Arab political and military decisions clarified to Christian Zionists that their support of Israel needed to stay firm. Many Americans intimate or only having a general awareness of Old Testament teachings did believe that something special was unfolding in the Middle East, even if most had no clear understanding of the details and political nuances of Cold War politics that was the primary focus of Washington policymakers. A growing number of evangelicals and fundamentalists wrote books on biblical prophecy, with a large number of Americans buying and reading about the biblical restoration of Israel. Some of the literature presented a blunt message as was the case with Wilbur Smith's *Israeli/Arab Conflict and the Bible* that included a chapter entitled "The 'Perpetual Hatred' of the Arabs." He traced the Arab hatred of Israel "century after century" to the birth of Ishmael recorded in Genesis 16. Stating his hope of not sounding "sensational," Smith argued that Nasser's threats to destroy Israel in the prewar period were "almost word for word" with Psalm 83 that speaks of the destruction of Israel by its enemies.[56] But those who spoke and wrote most passionately on Christian Zionism lacked the will, direction, or organization to have their voice heard and discussed seriously by elite beltway policymakers. This only began to change in the seventies. Although Christian Zionism would not gain the political power that some of its critics claimed, the media paid more attention to Christian conservatives standing with Israel.[57]

Conservative Christians learned valuable lessons from the Cold War. They were consistent supporters of national security by way of extensive military strength and preparedness, but others saw American foreign policy as too aggressive. These critics believed that the government played on public fears of global communism in order to justify excessive military activities and costs. Evangelicals disagreed on the basis that atheistic communism stifled the freedoms of citizens ruled by communist leaders. Freedom of speech and freedom of worship were essential if evangelicals abroad were to carry out the Great Commission.

Disagreeing with those who held that accommodation and concession with Arab leaders was the correct path for Israel's security, an informal network of conservative Christians saw strong military action as necessary and they wanted the United States government to provide Israel with whatever economic and military support it required to prevent its destruction. With Israel looking for any international support it could find, various Israeli leaders became more welcoming of American conservative Christians, an outcome rife with irony.

Some of Christian Zionists' fiercest opponents were mainstream Protestant leaders who witnessed the growth and vitality of conservative evangelical and pentecostal churches as mainline churches experienced declining church membership. In the 1970s, more Americans became aware of the significant number of evangelicals in society. Most liberals, particularly within the American Jewish community, found evangelical support of Israel worrisome, especially when such support was often more passionate than what emerged from American Jews themselves.[58] The angriest critics were usually liberal Protestants. According to Ian McPhee of Chicago, Illinois, the political entity of Israel was "cut off from the root of blessing and an enemy of the gospel," and, thus, proper American support was prayer rather than parade. Any "public political bally-hoo" supporting Israel "represented not only a sadly misdirected emphasis but also a very real threat to missions in Arab countries, and especially Arab Christians in those countries."[59] Others suspicious of evangelicals were the Washington policymakers who, maintaining geopolitical goals and secular thinking, pursued "rational, tangible, or political goals." They sought economic and political stability in the Middle East, particularly by giving the appearance that the United States favored neither the Jews nor the Arabs.[60]

Various Israelis were distrustful of evangelical activity in Israel. Evangelicals in Israel did experience some limitations to their religious freedoms. When a group of Christians sought to start a Christian kibbutz, they received approval from the Israeli government but only on the condition that there was no missionary activity. This condition was too steep for American and Swiss Christians interested in the project and they pulled up roots, leaving a group of Dutch and German Christians to keep the settlement in operation.[61]

In an article entitled "'Christians, Go Home,'" *Christianity Today* wrote of the uncertain future of Christian missionary efforts in Israel. Concerned about Christian evangelism in Israel, religious affairs minister Zerah Warhaftig was one who targeted groups such as Jews for Jesus. A countermeasure discussed was to prevent immigrant status to Christian "Jews" by using "a Christian-excluding application of the Law of Return"—the law allowing only Jews the right to settle in Israel. Some American Christians responded by registering their "conversion" to Judaism in the United States before immigrating to Israel. Jewish Orthodox opponents sought to have these conversions rescinded, but such opposition was troubling for Shlomo Hizak, director of the Mount of Olives International Bible Center: "A Jew can be a criminal Jew, an atheist Jew, a Communist Jew, and still be accepted. Why don't the people accept a Jew who believes in the Messiah?" The strong reaction of religious Jews to evangelistic activity was their abhorrence to the idea of actively searching for converts, something "never practiced by Jews."[62]

In 1972, evangelist Louis Kaplan of Phoenix, Arizona sent sixteen young people to Israel for missionary activity. Despite the opposition of Rabbi Meir Kahane's Jewish Defense League, the group distributed thousands of Bibles and evangelical literature. When someone left a note threatening to burn down their youth center, they simply moved to another site and continued their work of bringing others to Christ. Having visited Israel six times, Kaplan declared: "I want to emphasize that our ministry has never been hindered by the Israeli government."[63] Carl F. H. Henry discussed other cases of "radical orthodox rabbinical elements" seeking to end the religious liberty of evangelicals and messianic Jews, but neither Jackov Shapiro, the Israeli minister of justice nor Prime Minister Meir supported legislation against Christians. In his defense of missionary work, Shapiro explained that "whoever wants to rule Jerusalem, the seat of three religions, will have to put up with such activity."[64]

In 1973, *Christianity Today* reported that over 13,000 Israelis signed a petition for outlawing missionary activity in Israel.[65] The highest Jewish religious council rejected an appeal of a Tel Aviv man who wanted to have AD dates on his father's gravestone. The Rabbinate argued that the Christian-Gregorian dating, based on Jesus' birth, was improper, but it lost when the Supreme Court of Israel ruled for the use of the Gregorian calendar.[66] Near Bethlehem, unknown vandals destroyed the head of an almost completed fifteen-foot sculpture of Christ that an Arab-Christian artist worked on for a year.[67] The Israeli government deported Pentecostal missionary Arnold Butler of San Jose, California. The alleged reason for deportation was his inability to support his family and for disrupting the peace. On Yom Kippur, Butler upset Israelis when he handed out New Testaments at the Wailing Wall.[68]

Such conflicts between Christian Zionists and Israelis had no impact on Christian Zionist love for Israel. Southern Baptist missionaries in Israel went on record stating their opposition to anti-Semitism which they called a "'sin against Christ' and a denial of Jesus' teaching."[69] There were hopeful signs, like when Israel's press chief informed a group of touring evangelical editors that young Israelis represented the first generation in 1,900 years of Jewish history "holding practically no prejudice toward Jesus of Nazareth."[70] Christian Zionists such as Ginny Guttendorf of Pittsburgh, Pennsylvania, clarified that American evangelicals needed to meet with Jewish leaders and reassure them of evangelical support "without coercion of conversion."[71]

Rather than discussing evangelical issues in Israel, the American liberal Protestant press typically wrote about how the Israeli government dealt with Arabs. The *Christian Century* warned Israel about using totalitarian methods "against Arabs who live in Israel." Although the magazine claimed to appreciate Israel's desire for law and order, it argued that "shortsighted military decisions to curb demonstrations and harass leaders can only provide further reason for students and older PLO-oriented Arabs to resist Israeli occupation."[72] Editor James M. Wall acknowledged that the Arabs did a poor job handling the refugee camps, but he demanded Israel "improve its treatment of the people under its military occupation."[73] This was a noble desire, but many like Wall wrote little about the serious security issues facing ordinary Israelis. It was obvious that militant Arabs used the West Bank as a base for terrorist activities against Israel and yet Wall appeared to think that Israeli accommodation to Arab demands was the correct approach. After visiting Israel in late 1973, he addressed the topic of Israel in two reports. He admitted that there were Arabs who benefited from the "new-found prosperity" created by the Jews, but he suggested Israel's security strategy was what one expected more "from a military dictatorship than from a democracy."[74]

Discussing a college protest at Bir Zeit College, the only college in the West Bank, Wall asked: "How long can a state function as an occupying military power and not lose its soul?"[75] He commented on the Israeli government temporarily closing Bir Zeit College because of its alleged subversive activities and he acknowledged Israel's argument: "To the Israeli looking for security, a West Bank Arab seeking autonomy becomes a terrorist. And the world knows from the incidents in Munich, Rome and elsewhere, Arab terrorists can be cruel and deadly." However, Wall questioned whether Bir Zeit was a site of terrorism, suggesting that the Israeli government deported individuals without evidence of wrongdoing. Overall, the matter was straightforward for Wall—it was time for Israel to relinquish its occupation of the West Bank.[76]

In his response to Wall's reports, Hertzel Fishman, Israel's minister of education, wrote of Wall's attempt to be even-handed, something Fishman rarely saw in other *Christian Century* editorials. But Wall was wrong on a number of key issues, according to Fishman. The idea that the main reason for the creation of the State of Israel was the Holocaust ignored the historic quest for a Jewish homeland clearly expressed in Jewish religious literature, folkways, and customs. Also, often forgotten was that "many years" before the Holocaust the Jews built hundreds of settlements in Palestine on land purchased from Arabs. Wall's understanding of Israeli "expansionism" failed to point out that apartment buildings constructed "on the road to Ramallah" were within the legal boundaries of Jerusalem. Fishman took issue with the "supermoralists" who expected Israel to recognize the PLO, led by "extremists" unwilling to promote a genuine peace settlement with Israel. Finally, it was important to note that the entire Israeli cabinet, including its left-wing component, agreed that the deportation of political activists to Jordan was the correct decision and not the "capricious action on the part of a 'military dictatorship.'"[77] It is notable that Israeli officials saw no need to correct the analysis of conservative American Christians.

The *Christian Century* does deserve credit for publishing articles written by Jews and Christians more sympathetic to the difficulties Israel encountered. The director of the B'nai B'rith Foundation in Israel, Rabbi Jack J. Cohen, presented a dark view of the forces opposed to Israel: "There is no doubt that a Holocaust could now be in the making. Holocaust is on the minds of people here." As Episcopal priest Malcolm Boyd pointed out, there were times of calmness, but in 1974 Israelis were "never far removed from reminders of war as harbingers of fear, tension and intermittent despair."[78]

With the rise of terrorism, there was no shortage of conservative Christians supportive of Israel year in and year out. The Reverend Jesse Jackson's criticism of Israel received much attention, but there were evangelical black pastors such as the Reverend Charles Mims, pastor of Los Angeles' 1,500 member-Tabernacle of Faith Baptist, representative of millions of African Americans who saw Israel as part of God's plan.[79] This group was mostly liberal in a socioeconomic sense, but their theology was conservative.

Representing the broader evangelical community, *Christianity Today* marveled over Israel's first twenty-five years and the preservation of "a national continuity for so many centuries." Of course, the "reborn" Israel made mistakes in its military actions, but the burden of its security concerns was heavier than what most countries faced.[80] American conservative Christian visitors to Israel gave uplifting reports of Israel. It was an honor for fundamentalist W. A. Criswell of the Dallas, Texas, First Baptist Church to participate in raising money for reforestation in Israel. After he planted a tree in the Baptist Forest near Nazareth, he justified the efforts of his church by stating that "our Lord loves this land."[81]

In the *Sunday School Times and Gospel Herald*, Raymond Cox wrote insightful articles on Israel in the context of visiting Americans. An Arab guide named Mahmoud Khamis explained that the Arabs were "not happy about being ruled by the Israelis," but many West Bank Arabs secretly admitted that life was better than was the case under King Hussein's regime. The Israelis taught Arab farmers how to increase the productivity of their crops: "In fact, the yield already is six to eight times larger in this area than it was under the Jordanian administration." When Khamis could not answer why the Jewish enemy assisted the Arabs to better their conditions, another answered that the Jews preferred Arab peace and prosperity. Simply put, 'We'd rather have them throw bundles of wheat than grenades!'"[82] In another article, Cox pointed out that the Jordanians never allowed Jews to enter the Arab territory of Jerusalem after the War of Independence.[83]

Cox noted that Ramleh was the only new town founded by the Arabs during their "thirteen-hundred-year occupation."[84] He judged Hebron to be one of the top two inhospitable towns "for visitors in the Holy Land." There was a mood of sullenness and Arabs were reticent to do commerce with Christian "infidels." One ironic exception was an "urchin" who badgered him "to buy—of all things—a postcard picturing Moshe Dayan, Israel's military genius and the Jew the average Arab hates most!"[85] Arab life in the Gaza Strip was grim: "Much damage from the Six-Day War was conspicuous. Empty buildings, closed businesses, and interrupted construction abounded." Adversely affecting economic development was the norm of violence. Having just passed through a city intersection in

Gaza, Cox experienced a close call when terrorists hurled a bomb at "an army truck just behind me." The refugee problem in Gaza was a mess, but a comparison to Israel's treatment of Jewish refugees was instructive: "Forgotten by most people is the fact that many Jews were uprooted from Arab countries even as Arabs fled Israel."[86] The problem did not go away and distressing were the reports of the murder of Jews in Muslim countries; in early 1974, fewer than one hundred Jews lived in Baghdad.[87]

The economic situation in other parts of the Middle East was also dismal. Even though sections of Damascus, Syria "look reasonably modern, most inhabitants survive in squalid surroundings."[88] It appeared to Cox that a sense of fatalism burdened the Arab world: "To this day rural Arabs couldn't care less that westerners suppose their way of life to be backward. They welcome their way as 'Allah's will' and have no desire to change."[89] In one visit to the Knesset, Cox saw how serious a task it was for legislators to prepare for the "Arab military menace beyond the borders." The Knesset could do its best to "bring lasting solutions to problems threatening Israel's peace, security, and economy," but only Jesus was the answer to "secure Israel's future ultimately."[90] As he clarified, "He must come in glory to establish His millennial reign!"[91]

Although the number was likely very small, there were Arab Christians who saw "the re-establishment of Israel as a sign of the end times and the imminent coming of Christ." The circumstances of so many Jews gathering in the Middle East "must mean something."[92] Included in Carl F. H. Henry's edited book *Prophecy in the Making* (1971) is an article by Fouad Sakhnini. Speaking as an Arab Christian, Sakhnini wrote: "We as Christian Arabs who believe in prophecy would love to see peace with justice, recognizing the right of the Jews as well as the Arabs. We are neither pro-Arab nor pro-Israeli. We are pro-right, pro-truth and pro-Christ."[93] Other evangelicals believed that Christian Arabs needed "evangelization" because most who professed to be Christians based "their affiliations on ancestry rather than on the personal experience of Christ's saving grace."[94]

Conservative evangelical writers recognized the significance of most Arabs rejecting the idea of co-existence with Israel. The rising profile of Palestinian leader Yasser Arafat alerted Christians to new thinking concerning Middle East. With a UN vote of 105 to 4, Arafat got his invitation to address the UN General Assembly in 1974. The pistol-packing leader of the PLO declared that Israel had to decrease its land to the pre-1967 borders, negotiate the rebirth of Arab Palestine, and agree to the internationalization of Old Jerusalem. "I had come," Arafat explained, "bearing an olive branch, and a freedom fighter's gun. Do not let the olive branch fall from my hand." His speech lasted eighty minutes and the applause he received signified the many hardened hearts of nations opposing Israel and the general "UN stampede to the Arab side." But Clare Boothe Luce believed that European members had no great enthusiasm for Arafat or fervent compassion for the "homeless" Palestinians. Instead, oil was a major reason why Europe deserted Israel. Luce acknowledged the religious fervor of the Arabs: "from the beginning their war on Israel has been seen as a holy war, or jihad," but her suggestion that Israel return to pre-1967 borders went against what conservative Christians believed.[95]

A producer of two Christian documentary films on Israel, Mal Couch drew on his understanding of the Bible for why evangelicals "must stand behind the nation of Israel." The State of Israel's brief history, particularly the Six-Day War, demonstrated "an open miracle of God." Although Israeli politicians made mistakes in words and actions, it was vital for evangelicals to heed God's promise to the Jews and the lessons of history. Simply put, if the Jews "are beloved to God, they had better be beloved to us." Those who mistreated the Jews would eventually pay. Pointing to the worst of European anti-Semitism and England's turning its back on the Jews, Couch saw the destruction of the world wars on Europe and the oil crisis in Great Britain in late 1973 as two examples of God's judgment. The British compromised their initial support for Jewish political gains in order to secure Arab oil, but America needed to resist the temptation "to desert Israel because of the oil pinch—at a time when she needs us most."[96]

Citing a *Washington Post* article, *Christianity Today* was thankful that the Russians had emasculated the UN Assembly ages ago given that the United Nations gave Arafat a "resounding ovation" following his threat to destroy Israel. The UN Assembly had the power to incite murder, but not the ability "to conduct the crime itself." *Christianity Today* wished for peace, but prophecy told of "no permanent peace apart from the coming of the Prince of Peace."[97] On November 10, 1975, UN General Assembly Resolution 3379 stated that Zionism was racist, a significant development for a number of commentators.[98] In January, 1975, a *Moody Monthly* editorial saw the signs of the international climate changing as fewer countries took a stand for Israel. Citing Old Testament prophecy, the editorial highlighted the issue of nations gathering against Israel: "No one can predict how many events must follow between where we are today and the final confrontation, but the movement toward a more isolated Jewish state seems all too plain at present."[99] Bible-believing Christians following biblical prophecy had no illusions of peace dreamed in the minds of the UN or American politicians desiring to solve the unsolvable.

It is instructive to note the Christian Zionism of one specific American Baptist fundamentalist who visited Israel in the 1970s and later secured his place as a staunch supporter of Israel. Jerry Falwell's first trip to Israel resulted in "a greater commitment to God's land and people." As a "Bible-believing Christian," he held that the rebirth of Israel was a fulfillment of Bible prophecy. With Genesis 12:3 in mind, America needed to support Israel financially and militarily without hesitation on the basis "that God deals with all nations in relation to how these nations deal with

Israel."[100] Central to his explanation for the problems that Israelis faced from others was "that as God's chosen people they are the object of Satan's hatred." An effective antidote to poisonous anti-Semitism was "the concern and activities of Bible-believing Christians who love and respect the Jewish people and stand fully for Israel's just cause."[101] However, his attraction to Israel was not solely theological. In a humanitarian sense, all groups "have a Divine right to a land and a national purpose." Politically, Israel represented democracy and freedom and the only reliable friend of the United States in the region. Militarily, a strong independent Israel represented America's defense line in a region that did not allow permanent American bases, an important fact given oil resources and the threat of Soviet incursion.[102]

A nationally known Baptist pastor and fundamentalist leader, Falwell was rarely critical of major decisions by the Israeli government. Acting responsibly, Israel's wars have "been fought out of necessity. The one thing that one must not lose sight of when referring to the Arab-Israeli conflict is that the Arabs have indicated time and again that, given the chance, they are determined to destroy the Jews . . . and not the other way around." Falwell fully supported the Israeli bombing of the Iraqi nuclear reactor at Osirak on June 7, 1981.[103]

As for Israel's relationship with Palestinian leaders, Falwell saw no benefits in Israel attempting to bargain with Arafat and the PLO: "There is no way to sit down at a negotiating table with murderers. That is exactly what Mr. Arafat and the PLO are all about; they are terrorists and murderers. There is no way to negotiate with heartless destroyers of men, women, and children such as the PLO."[104] Arabs in general were unable to understand the Judeo-Christian tradition of Israel and the United States. Falwell saw little hope in sharing "a common destiny with nations that aggressively seek to control other peoples and follow doctrines that foster territorial aggrandizement in the name of religion."[105] As dictatorships, Arab nations could quickly change their leaders and policies, thus the longevity of any agreement between an Arab state and Israel was suspect.[106]

From Falwell's reading of the Bible, Israel included the area promised to Abraham, an area greater than the political boundaries of modern Israel. Given Israel was about the size of New Jersey, it was unrealistic for it to relinquish land to Palestinians. Judea and Samaria (the West Bank) belonged to Israel because it "is the heartland of the Jewish Biblical and historical patrimony and, as such, the eternal possession of the Jewish people." But Falwell understood the political realities that Israel faced, and, thus, he showed some flexibility on political and diplomatic decisions: "If Israel desires to give up part of her land to her neighbors, that is her business, but I do not favor that approach."[107]

Falwell saw nothing wrong with Palestinians living in Israel as a minority; Jews had lived as a minority in Arab lands for centuries. When

Israel became a nation it absorbed hundreds of thousands of Jewish refugees from Arab states and Falwell argued that Egypt, Jordan, Lebanon,
Syria, and others were wrong to bar Palestinians from gaining citizenship
in their respective countries, especially when the Arab nations were responsible for causing the Arab-Israeli wars and for displacing their own
people: "The Arab refugee problem was a creation of the Arab nations
and continues to this day largely as a result of Arab policy." There was
significant evidence of inter-Arab struggles, but there was one thing that
all Arab Muslims shared—"hatred for Israel." Actually, Muslim leaders
opposed any group in the Middle East not following Islam.[108]

Falwell linked liberal Protestants' increasing criticism of Israel to the
greater commitment of National Council of Churches leadership to
"Marxist-Leninist philosophy." In particular, liberation theologians within the NCC saw the PLO as a champion of freedom. Proof of this development for Falwell included an expose on the NCC by the CBS television
news program *60 Minutes*. He did take heart that liberal churches of the
NCC were "diminishing in numbers and finances" while churches holding to evangelical theology showed dynamic growth.[109]

Skeptical over the sincerity of Falwell's beliefs, American Jewish leaders often incorrectly reported on his position on Israel. However, it is
noteworthy that Falwell received the Vladimir Jabotinsky medal from
Israel's Prime Minister Menachem Begin in 1980. Despite the fact that
Christian Israelis lacked some freedom to publicly proclaim Christ and
evangelize others, Falwell's support for Israel was rock-solid. He believed "that the best friends Israel has in the world today are among
Evangelical and Fundamentalist Christians."[110]

The intellectual left generally found religion to be unimportant in explaining America's commitment to Israel. In an April 1975 article in the
Nation, two historians wrote that America's link to the State of Israel "was
a direct result of the Nazi policy of extermination and of nothing else."
These historians also wanted the United States to remove tactical nuclear
weapons from Europe, a move which they believed would induce the
Soviets from Israel's Arab enemies.[111] Certainly, this solution for lower-
ing the tension in the Middle East made no sense to conservative Christians. They were aware of the socialist and secular aspects of Israeli
government and society. However, they also recognized that the influence of communism was minimal: "[A]s the state of Israel has shown,
there are few who have not learned what communism really means."[112]
Democratic capitalism offered a more productive future. In the post-Six-
Day War period, Israeli control of Gaza and the West Bank resulted in
dramatic economic improvement. From 1967 to 1987, the per capita in-
come increased 300 percent in the West Bank and rose from $80 to $1,706
in the Gaza Strip.[113] Some liberal Protestant leaders admitted that Arabs
prospered in the post-1967 period in contrast to the poor economic devel-

opment of territory ruled by the Jordanians in the previous two decades.[114]

Christian Zionists understood that Christ's teachings were applicable to both the Arabs and Jews; any genuine oppression of the Arabs deserved criticism.[115] Charles C. Ryrie, theology professor at Dallas Theological Seminary, recognized that Israel was not blameless: "And while the efforts of a political state may ultimately be used by God in the mysterious accomplishing of his purpose, his use of the wrath of men does not excuse that wrath or make right the wrongs that the state may commit."[116] In his interpretation of the Bible, John H. Moyer of Ellwood City, Pennsylvania, saw God's favoring of the Jews, but he cautioned Christian Zionists not to be arrogant with this fact.[117] However, Christians Zionists were suspicious of ideas of accommodation and reconciliation. The *National Review* noted that in liberal circles there was a call for Israel to take "the path of reconciliation."[118] Christians were to be faithful to Abraham's promises to the Jewish people even if the Israelis themselves were quite secular. Evidence of the secularization of Israel was that 80 percent of the population was secular in orientation and only 6 percent of the 220 *kibbutzim* were "avowedly religious in character."[119]

When Yitzhak Rabin became prime minister of Israel in June 1974 his focus was on two issues: national security and good relations with the United States.[120] Certainly, Israel could count on conservative Christians. Desiring that America "take a stand for Israel," Carolyn Bruckner of Miami, Florida, argued that "Christians should support Israel in every way possible." She recognized and opposed any careless killing during Israeli retaliation operations, but this was no reason for Christians to be silent about their support for Israel.[121] America needed to be vigilant. In a 1975 letter to *Moody Monthly*, Dave Wells of Huntington, West Virginia, challenged any claim that the Israel had a military superiority over its foes. His numbers of military manpower had Israel with 260,000 compared to the 400,000 of Egypt, Syria, and Jordan. The Israelis also had 1,200 fewer tanks and 200 fewer aircraft.[122]

There was no genuine peace between Israel and surrounding Arab states in the years 1948 to 1975 and increasing worldwide criticism of Israel was a given despite some signs of moderation from Israelis. For example, conservative Israeli politicians such as Menachem Begin, by the mid-1970s, were no longer considering Israeli acquisition of land east of the Jordan River as had been the case in the earlier period.[123] New historians such as Avi Shlaim wanted America to pressure the Israeli government to be more accommodating to Arab demands.[124]

Conservative Christians were off the radar of most Washington policymakers, but they provided ample supportive literature of Israel that was neither blind nor uncritical as some critics charged. Given their understanding of Original Sin, evangelicals understood that no party was innocent in war since military power was subject to abuse. Still, Christian

Zionists appreciated Israel's fight for survival in a hostile region and routinely defended the Jewish state, a state deserving praise for its economic and political developments. There was something admirable about a Christian Zionist position that rejected the zero-sum idea "that for Israel to stand someone else has to fall." [125] It was natural for Bible-believing Christians to see the Jews as a people returning to their ancestral homeland. G. Douglas Young wrote of the "joys, privileges and freedom in Israel," the land "where at long last once again, Jewish energy, creativity and 'follow-through' are making the wastes a garden, the desert to blossom, the crooked places straight." [126]

There were Christian Zionists who lamented the poor state of Arab and Palestinian life, but their biblical understanding clarified to them who was to receive the land. This position and the linkage of American Christians and conservative Israelis were worrisome for anti-Zionist Christians, who rarely looked beyond the emotional story and humanitarian crisis of Palestinian refugees. [127] Without any specific evidence, critics such as James L. Kelso argued that numerous American Christians applauded Israeli "crimes" and the "murder" of Arabs. Did he really think a sincere Christian could applaud "murder"? It is more accurate to say that Christian Zionists marveled at Israel's military victories and creation of wealth, while at the same being aware that no one was sinless.

Another common theme among some anti-Zionist Christians was that dispensationalism virtually alone explained Christian Zionism. Supposedly the motivation of Christian Zionists was the goal to usher in the second coming. Any serious examination of those Christians standing strong with Israel tells another story: only a minority held to premillenial dispensationalism. [128] Yes, many Christian Zionist writers were dispensationalists. However, few wrote explicitly about dispensationalism and any evidence of Christian Zionists desiring to hasten Armageddon is rare, if nonexistent, in the literature, including in the memoirs of leading dispensationalists. [129]

Scholars estimate that the number of dispensationalists is in the range of 2.5 percent of American adults. There were Christian Zionists who accepted the inerrancy of the Bible without embracing dispensationalism. Many who accepted one tenet of dispensationalism had no idea of other tenets. As for the majority of evangelicals who represented the largest group within Christian Zionism, they simply believed what the Bible promised for the Jews. [130] Moreover, there were numerous American Christians outside of evangelical circles who voiced their concern and support for Israel. [131]

But how did Israelis respond to those who were more explicit with prophecy teaching? In his study of American Christian Zionism, Stephen Spector makes an important point on how many Israeli officials viewed the Christian end-times scenario as unthreatening. Their responses were similar to the story Israeli writer Amos Oz heard from his grandmother in the mid-twentieth century: "Christians believe that the Messiah was here once and he will certainly return one day. The Jews maintain that he is yet to come. . . . If the Messiah comes, saying, 'Hello, it's nice to see you again,' the Jews will have to concede. If, on the other hand, the Messiah comes, saying, 'How do you do, it is very nice meeting you,' the entire Christian world will have to apologize to the Jews."[132] All in all, those who viewed Christian Zionism as embracing a loveless theological plot and who stereotyped Christian Zionists as uncaring of real Jewish people misread the motivation of Bible-believing Christians.

Ben-Gurion wrote: "In days of old the Prophets of Israel required their nation to be a unique people and a light unto the Gentiles. To this day this prophecy lives in the hearts of the best of the Jewish people and it is this that guides them."[133] Arguably the 1970s was the crucial decade for the emergence of a steadfast pro-Israel position, within the Christian Right, which baffled or worried liberals. The various ways conservative Christians voiced their support for Israel and the myriad ways friends and foes responded were important components of a new dynamic in American political life. The consistent position of many evangelicals suggests that evangelicalism became Israel's best friend, at least on the issue of financial and military support, a development that met much resistance among liberal Protestant leaders. For a number of Christian Zionists, enemies of Israel appeared to be also enemies of western civilization.[134]

American Christian Zionists were unapologetic about their support for Israel in its first twenty-five years. William Hull in an earlier period and many other Christian Zionists later presented numerous examples of Israel's economic creativity and industry.[135] In a 1975 letter to the *Jerusalem Post*, G. Douglas Young declared: "I have been accused of being a Zionist—a Christian Zionist—by some of my coreligionists in Israel and in the administered areas. I would like to take this means of thanking them for this compliment."[136] Beyond the praise found in Christian Zionist literature, countless Americans coast to coast heard church sermons that told of God's promises to Israel. Even a superficial appraisal of the economic and political status of the Muslim world revealed major differences from the Israeli experience. But there was much more to the story. The economic and military success of Israel gave many Christians proof that God was active in history.

There was the understanding among Christian Zionists that God loved his chosen people and that the roots of Christian faith and gift of eternal life came through the Jews. In addition, Christian Zionists became Israel's best friends because receiving God's blessings was a good thing. In a nutshell, proof of the fulfillment of biblical prophecies and God's love for the Jews and Christian Zionists' acceptance of God's promise to Abraham (Genesis 12:3) was enough for many Christians to make their stand for Israel.

NOTES

1. For an excellent article on the issue of a double standard, see Charles Krauthammer, *Things That Matter: Three Decades of Passions, Pastimes and Politics* (New York: Crown Forum 2013), 251–57.

2. John J. Mearsheimer and Stephen M. Walt, *The Israel Lobby and U.S. Foreign Policy*, (New York: Farrar, Straus, and Giroux, 2007), 133. Yaakov S. Ariel writes: "Following the Six-Day War, evangelical involvement with Jews and Israel intensified. Dozens of pro-Israel evangelical groups organized in the United States, and evangelicals have been counted among Israel's most loyal supporters in America." See Yaakov S. Ariel, *Evangelizing the Chosen People: Missions to the Jews, 1888–2000* (Chapel Hill: University of North Carolina Press, 2000), 198.

3. Merkley, *American Presidents, Religion, and Israel*, 78.

4. As late as the mid-1970s, evangelicalism was "a subject rarely covered . . . in even the best university educations." Michael Novak, *Writing from Left to Right: My Journey from Liberal to Conservative* (New York: Image 2013), 167.

5. Going an extra step, Timothy Weber is very specific. "[D]ispensationalist evangelicals became Israel's best friends in the last part of the twentieth century." See Weber, *On the Road to Armageddon*, 9. The theme of suffering was powerful. Even the so-called Messianic Jews, those who accepted Christ as Savior, took courage in that others before them "suffered for God as they have sought to be a presence witness, among their people and among all people." See Louis Goldberg, "The Messianic Jew," *Christianity Today*, February 1, 1974, 11.

6. Schoenbaum, *The United States and the State of Israel*, 80. Also see Zeitz, "'If I am not for myself . . .'", 285–86.

7. For example, although David Danzig of the American Jewish Committee, in 1962, could not find "outright anti-Semitism" in the secular and religious components of the Radical Right, he "simply took it for granted that such a movement must necessarily represent a danger to Jews." See Podhoretz, *Why Are Jews Liberals?* 157–58.

8. Spector, *Evangelicals and Israel*, viii.

9. "The Israeli Issue," *Moody Monthly*, October 1974, 6.

10. For example, see "The Gentiles," *Christianity Today*, January 15, 1965, 47. One Bible verse cited by Jacob Gartenhaus of the International Board of Jewish Missions, Inc. is Luke 18: 31–34.

11. Podhoretz, *Why Are Jews Liberals?* 166, 186

12. Podhoretz, *Why Are Jews Liberals?* 142

13. Podhoretz, *Why Are Jews Liberals?* 130, 135–37, 139–41, 169–70.

14. See Andrew Preston, "Bridging the Gap between the Sacred and the Secular in the History of American Foreign Relations," *Diplomatic History* 30, no. 5 (2006): 783–812. He states that "religion has consistently been one of the dominant forces in shaping American culture, politics, economics, and national identity" (786). Also, on religion and U.S. foreign relations, see Eric R. Crouse, "New Evangelicalism, *Christianity Today*, and U.S. Foreign Policy, 1956–1965," *Canadian Evangelical Review*, no. 30–31 (Fall 2005–Spring 2006): 38–54; Leo Ribuffo, "Religion and American Foreign Policy: The Story of a Complex Relationship," *The National Interest* 52 (Summer 1998): 36–51; and Frederick Marks, "Religiosity and Success in American Foreign Policy," *The Society for Historian of American Foreign Relations* (Newsletter) 30, no. 3 (September 1999): 9–22.

15. "On Christian-Jewish Understanding," *Christianity Today*, November 10, 1961, 33.

16. On liberal Christians' support of Israel, see Carenen, *The Fervent Embrace*.

17. Merkley, *Those That Bless You, I Will Bless*, 233–34.

18. Merkley, *Those That Bless You, I Will Bless*, 238.

19. Stallard, "Is Dispensationalism Hurting American Political Policies in the Middle East?" 464.

20. Stallard, "Is Dispensationalism Hurting American Political Policies in the Middle East?" 467–70.

21. Stallard, "Is Dispensationalism Hurting American Political Policies in the Middle East?" 472–74.

22. "A Survey of 1955," *Eternity*, January 1956, 8.

23. For example, William K. Harrison, "Reminiscences and a Prophecy," *Christianity Today*, March 4, 1957, 13.

24. See Michael W. Flamm, "The Politics of 'Law and Order,'" in *The Conservative Sixties*, eds. David Farber and Jeff Roche (New York: Peter Lang, 2003), 142–52.

25. "Jordan's Stormy Banks," *Christianity Today*, January 7, 1957, 26.

26. Ariel, "An Unexpected Alliance," 80–81.

27. This was even the case in America. See "Moslem Activity in U.S. 'Matter for Prayer,'" *Moody Monthly*, August 1956, 7.

28. Frank E. Keay, "The Challenge of Islam," *Christianity Today*, December 22, 1958, 10–12. For more on the difficulty of Christian missions in the Middle East, see L. LaVerne Donaldson, "The Gospel in the Arab World," *Moody Monthly*, November 1959, 57–59.

29. *Christianity Today*, November 25, 1957, 26.

30. Schoenbaum, *The United States and the State of Israel*, 71. Banki, *Christian Responses to the Yom Kippur War*, 27.

31. Merkley, *Those That Bless You, I Will Bless*, 211. Nadav Safran writes of the "signs of vitality and affluence everywhere" in the early 1970s (although he also notes that Israel was not free of economic problems). See Safran, *Israel*, 107–109.

32. "Christian, Jew and Arab," *Christianity Today*, October 27, 1961, 16.

33. "Portents in the Middle East," *Moody Monthly*, May 1960, 11.

34. Merkley, *Those That Bless You, I Will Bless*, 209.

35. Carenen, *The Fervent Embrace*, 62.

36. Carenen, *The Fervent Embrace*, 63.

37. Reich, "Themes in the History of the State of Israel," 1478.

38. A. Roy and Alice L. Eckardt, "Again, Silence in the Churches," *Christian Century*, August 2, 1967, 992–95. The blitzkrieg statement was by H. P. Van Dusen, past president of Union Theological Seminary. See "Casting Lots for Jerusalem," *Christianity Today*, August 18, 1967, 29.

39. For Said's impact on foreign policy historians, see Andrew J. Rotter, "Saidism without Said: Orientalism and U.S. Diplomatic History," *American Historical Review* 105, no. 4 (October 2000): 1205-217. The intellectual left, on rare occasion, acknowledged the creativity and productivity of the Israelis. For example, see Alice Marquis, "Israel Teaches California," The *Nation*, April 5, 1975, 403-404.

40. A very hard-hitting critique of Chomsky is the interview of writer Benjamin Kerstein. See Michael J. Totten, "Noam Chomsky: The Last Totalitarian," *World Affairs Journal*, http://www.worldaffairsjournal.org/print/56007 (accessed November 6, 2013).

41. Chomsky, *Peace in the Middle East?* 55, 56, 80, 95–96, 102. But Chomsky claimed that Israel could not yet be described as "a tool of Western imperialism." However, "as a prediction it may well be so" (95).

42. Klinghoffer, *Vietnam, Jews and the Middle East*, 166–67. See the June/July SNCC (Student Nonviolent Coordinating Committee) *Newsletter*.

43. Klinghoffer, *Vietnam, Jews and the Middle East*, 167, 206. On Glazer's defending fundamentalism, see Eric R. Crouse, *The Cross and Reaganomics: Conservative Christians Defending Ronald Reagan* (Lanham, MD: Lexington Books, 2013), 4.

44. A. Roy Eckardt, "The Fantasy of Reconciliation in the Middle East," *Christian Century*, October 13, 1971, 1198–202. For a dated but helpful analysis of American foreign policy and Israel, see Douglas Little, "Gideon's Band: America and the Middle East since 1945," in *America in the World: The Historiography of American Foreign Relations since 1941*, ed. Michael J. Hogan (Cambridge: Cambridge University Press, 1995), 473–77.

45. "Behind the Turmoil and Terror in the Mideast," *Eternity*, September 1967, 33.

46. Peres, *David's Sling*, 9, 11–12.

47. Peres, *David's Sling*, 10–11, 13.

48. Peres, *David's Sling*, 114.

49. Carter, *Palestine Peace Not Apartheid*, 27. Carter's book generated ample criticism from Zionists.

50. E. Russel Chandler, "Crucial Issues in the Mideast," *Christianity Today*, February 27, 1970, 14.

51. "Eschatological Stirrings: Madman at the Mosque," *Christianity Today*, February 27, 1970, 35.

52. "Eschatological Stirrings: Madman at the Mosque," 35.

53. "Zion and the New Israelis: Life at the Cliff Beach Hotel," *Christian Century*, April 17, 1974, 426.

54. Fawaz A. Gerges, "Islam and Muslims in the Mind of America," *Annals of the American Academy of Political and Social Science* 558, Islam: Enduring Myths and Changing Realities (July 2003), 75–76.

55. Christian Zionist John Hagee quoted in Spector, *Evangelicals and Israel*, 88.

56. Smith, *Israel/Arab Conflict in the Bible*, 80–83. In his memoirs, Smith discussed the "vicious animosity of the Arabs toward the Jews." Smith, *Before I Forget*, 262.

57. For more about Christian Zionist political influence in recent years see Mearsheimer and Walt, *The Israel Lobby and U.S. Foreign Policy*, 132–39.

58. Podhoretz, *Why Are Jews Liberals?* 3.

59. *Moody Monthly*, July–August 1974, 4.

60. Gideon Rose, "Neoclassical Realism and Theories of Foreign Policy," *World Politics* 51, no. 1 (1998), 148. Lazarowitz, "Different Approaches to a Regional Search for Balance," 25–54; Hahn, *Caught in the Middle East*, 1.

61. "Christian Kibbutz: Blossoming Like a Rose?" *Christianity Today*, April 24, 1970, 37.

62. "'Christians, Go Home,'" *Christianity Today*, March 16, 1972, 38–39.

63. "Hot and Humorous," *Christianity Today*, July 6, 1973, 51.

64. "Religious Pressure in Israel," *Christianity Today*, May 11, 1973, 32–33.

65. *Christianity Today*, May 25, 1973, 60.

66. "A.D.," *Christianity Today*, June 22, 1973, 39.

67. "World Scene," *Christianity Today*, July 20, 1973, 49.

68. "Personalia," *Christianity Today*, February 16, 1973, 57.

69. "World Scene," *Christianity Today*, Sept. 15, 1972, 62.

70. *Christianity Today*, January 19, 1973, 52.

71. *Moody Monthly*, (July–August 1974), 4.

72. "Civil Rights and Freedom in Embattled Israel," *Christian Century*, December 4, 1974, 1142.

73. "Facing Reality at Bir Zeit College," *Christian Century*, February 27, 1974, 222. "Hanna Nasir and the Israelis," *Christian Century*, August 6–13, 1975, 701.

74. "Report From Israel: What Price Security?" *Christian Century*, December 26, 1973, 1267–68.

75. "Security on Palestine's West Bank," *Christian Century*, January 2–9, 1974, 4.

76. "Facing Reality at Bir Zeit College," 222–23.

77. "Security and Israel's Future," *Christian Century*, February 6, 1974, 155–56.

78. Malcolm Boyd, "Conversations in Jerusalem: Will There Be Another Holocaust?" *Christian Century*, December 11, 1974, 1173, 1175.

79. Voss and Rausch, "American Christians and Israel," 71–73.

80. "The State of Israel at Twenty-Five," *Christianity Today*, May 11, 1973, 27.

81. "On Criswell's Brow," *Christianity Today*, August 6, 1971, 36.

82. Raymond L. Cox, "Jack and Betty Visit Philip's Fountain," *The Sunday School Times and Gospel Herald*, July 15, 1973, 16. In his letter to the *National Review*, Lawrence Mosher of the *The National Observer* wrote that the Arabs' main focus was economic development and, thus, they were ready "to get out from under the Israeli issue." See "Israel and Arabs," *The National Review*, March 14, 1975, 252.

83. Raymond L. Cox, "Jack and Betty Visit King David's Tomb," *The Sunday School Times and Gospel Herald*, July 15, 1974, 14.

84. Raymond L. Cox, "Jack and Betty Visit a Bedouin Tent," *The Sunday School Times and Gospel Herald*, June 15, 1974, 15.

85. Raymond L. Cox, "Road to Hebron," *The Sunday School Times and Gospel Herald*, September 1, 1973, 17.

86. Raymond L. Cox, "Journey to Gaza" *The Sunday School Times and Gospel Herald*, February 1, 1974, 16–17.

87. "Zion and the New Israelis: Life at the Cliff Beach Hotel," *Christian Century*, April 17, 1974, 426.

88. Raymond L. Cox, "Pearl of the Desert," *The Sunday School Times and Gospel Herald*, October 1, 1974, 15.

89. Raymond L. Cox, "Three Routes to Sodom," *The Sunday School Times and Gospel Herald*, May 1, 1974, 14.

90. Raymond L. Cox, "Past, Present, Future," *The Sunday School Times and Gospel Herald*, August 1, 1973, 16–17.

91. Raymond L. Cox, "Where the King is Coming!" *The Sunday School Times and Gospel Herald*, March 1, 1974, 15.

92. "Arab Refugees Dread White Christmas," *Christianity Today*, December 20, 1968, 33.

93. Fouad Sakhnini, "The Gospel and Arab Thinking," in *Prophecy in the Making*, ed. Carl F. H. Henry (Carol Stream, IL: Creation House, 1971), 139–40.

94. Raymond L. Cox, "The Three-Day-a-Year City!," *The Sunday School Times and Gospel Herald*, December 1, 1973, 17. One scholar sympathetic to the Palestinian cause notes that the memberships of evangelical churches have done well in Jerusalem, but the historic Eastern-rite churches experienced decline from 1967 to 1998. These included Greek Orthodox (4000 reduced to 3500), Armenian Orthodox (2000 to 1500), and Syrian Orthodox (300 to 250). Michael Dumper identifies one trend of some of the Eastern-rite churches: an increase of the "Palestinianization of clergy" which encouraged a "Palestinian theology of liberation." Michael Dumper, "The Christian Churches of Jerusalem in the Post-Oslo Period," *Journal of Palestine Studies* 31, no. 2 (Winter 2002), 55, 64n1.

95. Clare Boothe Luce, "Ultimatum to the UN," *National Review*, January 31, 1975, 97. Also, "Let's Not Let Israel Down," *Moody Monthly*, June 1974, 30, 83–84.

96. Mal Couch, "Let's Not Let Israel Down," *Moody Monthly*, June 1974, 30.

97. "Israel This Christmas: Keeping Watch," *Christianity Today*, December 1974, 18.

98. Rudin, *Israel for Christians*, 10. An American rabbi, Rudin wrote his book to provide Christians with "a balanced and accurate picture of modern Israel" (ix).

99. "A Colder World for Israel?" *Moody Monthly*, January 1975, 21.

100. Simon, *Jerry Falwell and the Jews*, 61, 64, 98.

101. Simon, *Jerry Falwell and the Jews*, 92, 96.

102. Simon, *Jerry Falwell and the Jews*, 63, 65–67.

103. Simon, *Jerry Falwell and the Jews*, 65.

104. Simon, *Jerry Falwell and the Jews*, 69.

105. Simon, *Jerry Falwell and the Jews*, 72. Falwell stated that it was America's destiny "to support and enhance freedom for individuals and nations and to bring the principles of justice and morality into the human arena."

106. Simon, *Jerry Falwell and the Jews*, 84.

107. Simon, *Jerry Falwell and the Jews*, 63, 76, 83.

108. Simon, *Jerry Falwell and the Jews*, 75, 77, 82, 98.

109. Simon, *Jerry Falwell and the Jews*, 89–90.

110. Simon, *Jerry Falwell and the Jews*, 59–60, 68, 88.

111. Judith M. Hughes and H. Stuart Hughes, "A Clear and Present Commitment," *The Nation*, April 26, 1975, 486.

112. H. L. Ellison, "Judaism: Religion of the Jews," *Christianity Today*, December 21, 1959, 8.

113. George Gilder, *The Israel Test* (Minneapolis, MN: Richard Vigilante Books, 2009), 49–50.

114. "Facing Reality at Bir Zeit College," 222.

115. Stallard, "Is Dispensationalism Hurting American Political Policies in the Middle East?" 470.

116. Quoted in Weber, *On the Road to Armageddon*, 185.

117. "The Israeli Issue," *Moody Monthly*, October 1974, 6.

118. Discussed in "Israel as an Issue," *National Review*, March 28, 1975, 323.

119. Chandler, "Crucial Issues in the Mideast," 14.

120. Shlaim, *The Iron Wall*, 325.

121. "Bravo, Israel," *Moody Monthly*, September 1974, 4.

122. "Keeping Israel Up," *Moody Monthly*, March 1975, 6.

123. Nadav G. Shelef, "From 'Banks of the Jordan' to the 'Whole Land of Israel:' Ideological Change in Revisionist Zionism," *Israel Studies* 9, no. 1 (Spring 2004): 125–48. In 1948, Menachem Begin declared: "The Wall of the Old City is not the border of Jerusalem; the Jordan is not the border of our country and the sea is not the border of our nation" (130).

124. "Interview," 105.

125. Merkley, *Those That Bless You, I Will Bless*, 236.

126. Voss and Rausch, "American Christians and Israel," 64–65.

127. Donald Wagner, "Evangelicals and Israel: Theological Roots of a Political Alliance," *Christian Century*, 4 November 1998, 1021–22.

128. Stephen Spector's study of American Christian Zionism of recent years presents ample evidence of the wider parameters of Christian Zionism. See Spector, *Evangelicals and Israel*.

129. For example, Smith, *Before I Forget* or Walvoord, *Blessed Hope*. Walvoord explained that "[prophetic] Teaching should be adjusted to fit newspaper headlines" (80). What was the focus for his final years? It was simply "to go out teaching His Word" (137).

130. Spector, *Evangelicals and Israel*, 188. Shalom Goldman writes: "The majority of evangelicals do not subscribe to dispensationalism; nevertheless they are moved to support Israel, for they see its establishment as the fulfillment of the biblical promise." See Goldman, *Zeal for Zion*, 37.

131. See Banki, *Christian Responses to the Yom Kippur War*.

132. Quoted in Spector, *Evangelicals and Israel*, 159.

133. Ben-Gurion, *Israel*, 846.

134. Merkley, *Those That Bless You, I Will Bless*, 237.

135. In *The Fall and Rise of Israel*, William Hull devoted a chapter to Israeli economic success. See the "Overcomers," 355–60.

136. Quoted in Voss and Rausch, "American Christians and Israel," 80n35.

Bibliography

GOVERNMENT DOCUMENTS

United Nations, General Assembly, United Nations Palestine Commission
U.S. Department of State, *Papers Relating to the Foreign Relations of the United States* (*FRUS*)

MAGAZINES AND NEWSPAPERS

American Holiness Journal
Atlantic Monthly
Christian Century
Christianity Today
Commentary
Cornerstone
Eternity
HIS: Student Magazine of the Inter-Varsity Christian Fellowship
The King's Business
Middle East Report
Moody Monthly
The Nation
National Geographic
National Review
New York Times
Sunday School Times
Sunday School Times and Gospel Herald
World Affairs Journal

MEMOIRS

Abuelaish, Izzeldin. *I Shall Not Hate: A Gaza Doctor's Journey.* Toronto: Random House Canada, 2010.
Begin, Menachem. *The Revolt*, Rev. ed. New York: Dell Publishing Co., Inc., 1978.
Ben-Gurion, David. *Israel: A Personal History.* New York: Funk & Wagnalls, Inc., 1971.
———. *Israel: Years of Challenge.* New York: Holt, Rinehart and Winston, 1963.
Dayan, Moshe. *Moshe Dayan: The Story of My Life.* New York: William Morrow and Company, Inc., 1976.
Eban, Abba. *Personal Witness: Israel Through My Eyes.* New York: G. P. Putnam's Sons, 1992.
el-Sadat, Anwar. *Anwar el-Sadat: In Search of Identity.* New York: Harper & Row, Publishers, 1978.
Glubb, John Bagot. *A Soldier with the Arabs.* London: Hodder and Stoughton, 1957.

Hull, William. *The Fall and Rise of Israel: The Story of the Jewish People During the time of their Dispersal and Regathering.* Grand Rapids, MI: Zondervan Publishing Company, 1954.

Kissinger, Henry. *Years of Upheaval.* Boston: Little, Brown and Company, 1982.

Levin, Harry. *Jerusalem Embattled: A Diary of the City under Siege, March 25th, 1948 to July 18th, 1948.* London: Victor Gollancz Ltd, 1950.

Meir, Golda. *My Life.* New York: G. P. Putnam's Sons, 1975.

Nixon, Richard. *RN: The Memoirs of Richard Nixon.* New York: Grosset & Dunlap, 1978.

Novak, Michael. *Writing from Left to Right: My Journey from Liberal to Conservative.* New York: Image, 2013.

Peres, Shimon. *David's Sling.* New York: Random House, 1970.

Sharon, Ariel. *Warrior: The Autobiography of Ariel Sharon.* New York: Simon and Schuster, 1989.

Smith, Wilbur M. *Before I Forget.* Chicago: Moody Press, 1971.

Truman, Harry S. *Memoirs by Harry S. Truman, Volume Two: Years of Trial and Hope.* Garden City, NY: Doubleday & Company, Inc., 1956.

Walvoord, John F. *Blessed Hope: The Autobiography of John F. Walvoord.* Chattanooga, TN: AMG Publishers, 2001.

BOOKS AND JOURNALS

Abrahamian, Ervand. "The US Media, Huntington and September 11." *Third World Quarterly* 24, no. 3 (June 2003): 529–44.

Acemoglu, Daron and James A. Robinson. *Why Nations Fail: The Origins of Power, Prosperity, and Power.* New York: Crown Business, 2012.

Adwan, Sami et al., eds. *Side by Side: Parallel Histories of Israel-Palestine.* New York: Prime, 2012.

Alteras, Isaac. *Eisenhower and Israel: U.S.-Israeli Relations, 1953–1960.* Gainesville: University Press of Florida, 1993.

Anderson, Irvine H. *Biblical Interpretation and Middle East Policy: The Promised Land, America, and Israel, 1917–2002.* Gainesville: University Press of Florida, 2005.

Ariel, Yaakov S. *Evangelizing the Chosen People: Missions to the Jews, 1888–2000.* Chapel Hill: University of North Carolina Press, 2000.

———. "An Unexpected Alliance: Christian Zionism and Its Historical Significance." *Modern Judaism* 26, no. 1 (2006): 74–100.

Ateek, Naim. "Introduction: Challenging Christian Zionism." In Naim Ateek et al., eds. *Challenging Christian Zionism: Theology, Politics and the Israel-Palestine Conflict.* London: Melisende, 2005.

Banki, Judith Hershcopf. *Christian Responses to the Yom Kippur War.* New York: The American Jewish Committee, 1974.

Banki, Judith H. and Eugene J. Fisher, eds. *A Prophet for Our Time: An Anthology of the Writings of Rabbi Marc H. Tanenbaum.* New York: Fordham University Press, 2002.

Bar-Siman-Tov, Yaacov. "The Limits of Economic Sanctions: The American-Israeli Case of 1953." *Journal of Contemporary History* 23, no. 3 (July 1988): 425–43.

———. "The United States and Israel since 1948: A 'Special Relationship'?" *Diplomatic History* 22, no. 2 (1998): 231–62.

Bar-Yosef, Eitan. "Christian Zionism and Victorian Culture." *Israel Studies* 8, no. 2 (Summer 2003): 18–44.

Bergman, Elihu. "Unexpected Recognition: Some Observations on the Failure of a Last-Gasp Campaign in the U.S. State Department to Abort a Jewish State." *Modern Judaism* 19, no. 2 (1999): 133–71.

Bialer, Uri. "Top Hat, Tuxedo and Cannons: Israeli Foreign Policy From 1948 to 1956 as a Field of Study." *Israel Studies* 7, no. 1 (Spring 2002): 1–80.

Bickerson, Ian J. and Carla L. Klausner. *A History of the Arab-Israeli Conflict*, sixth ed. New York: Prentice Hall, 2010.

Bloomfield, Arthur E. *Before the Last Battle Armageddon*. Minneapolis, MN: Bethany Fellowship, Inc., 1971.

Boyer, Paul. *When Time Shall Be No More: Prophecy Belief in Modern American Culture* Cambridge, MA: Harvard University Press, 1992.

Brands, H. W. *Into the Labyrinth: The United States and Middle East, 1945–1993*. New York: McGraw Hill, 1994.

Bunch, Clea Lutz. "Strike at Samu: Jordan, Israel, the United States, and the Origins of the Six-Day War." *Diplomatic History* 32, no. 1 (January 2008): 55–76.

Burns, E. L. M. *Between Arab and Israeli*. Toronto: Clarke, Irwin & Company Limited, 1962.

Carenen, Caitlin. *The Fervent Embrace: Liberal Protestants, Evangelicals, and Israel*. New York: New York University Press, 2012.

Carpenter, Joel A. *Revive Us Again: The Reawakening of American Fundamentalism*. New York: Oxford University Press, 1997.

Carter, Jimmy. *Palestine: Peace Not Apartheid*. New York: Simon & Schuster, 2006.

Catton, Henry. *Palestine, the Arabs and Israel: The Search for Justice*. London: Longman Group Limited, 1969.

Chamberlain, Paul. "A World Restored: Religion, Counterrevolution, and the Search for Order in the Middle East." *Diplomatic History* 32, no. 3 (June 2008): 441–69.

Chernus, Ira. "Operation Candor: Fear, Faith, and Flexibility." *Diplomatic History* 29, no. 5 (November, 2005): 779–809.

Chomsky, Noam. *Peace in the Middle East? Reflections on Justice and Nationhood*. New York: Vintage Books, 1974.

Christison, Kathleen. "Bound by a Frame of Reference, Part II: U.S. Policy and the Palestinians, 1948–88." *Journal of Palestine Studies* 27, no. 3 (1998): 20–34.

Clark, Victoria. *Allies for Armageddon: The Rise of Christian Zionism*. New Haven, CT: Yale University Press, 2007.

Cohen, Michael J. "Truman and Palestine, 1945–1948: Revisionism, Politics and Diplomacy," *Modern Judaism* 2, no. 1 (February 1982): 1–22.

Collier, Peter and David Horowitz, eds. *Second Thoughts: Former Radicals Look Back at the Sixties*. Lanham, MD: Madison Books, 1989.

Costigliola, Frank and Thomas G. Paterson. "Defining and Doing the History of the United States Foreign Relations: A Primer." In *Explaining the History of American Foreign Relations*, 2nd ed., edited by Michael J. Hogan and Tomas G. Paterson. Cambridge: Cambridge University Press, 2004.

Crouse, Eric R. *The Cross and Reaganomics: Conservative Christians Defending Ronald Reagan*. Lanham, MD: Lexington Books, 2013.

———. "New Evangelicalism, *Christianity Today*, and U.S. Foreign Policy, 1956–1965," *Canadian Evangelical Review*, no. 30–31 (Fall 2005–Spring 2006): 38–54.

DeHaan, M. R. *The Jew and Palestine in Prophecy*. Grand Rapids, MI: Zondervan Publishing House, 1950.

Dershowitz, Alan. *The Case for Israel*. Hoboken, NJ: John Wiley & Sons, 2003.

Diamond, Sara. *Spiritual Warfare: The Politics of the Christian Right*. Boston: South End Press, 1989.

Dumper, Michael. "The Christian Churches of Jerusalem in the Post-Oslo Period." *Journal of Palestine Studies* 31, no. 2 (Winter 2002): 51–65.

Erb, Paul. *Bible Prophecy: Questions and Answers*. Scottdale, PA: Herald Press, 1978.

"Evangelicals and Israel." *Center Conversations*, no. 25 (November, 2003): 1–25.

Evensen, Bruce J. "A Story of 'Ineptness': The Truman Administration's Struggle to Shape Conventional Wisdom on Palestine at the Beginning of the Cold War." *Diplomatic History* 15, no. 3 (July 1991): 339–59.

Falk, Gloria H. "Israeli Public Opinion on Peace Issues." In *Israeli National Security Policy: Political Actors and Perspectives*, edited by Bernard Reich and Gershon R. Kieval. New York: Greenwood Press, 1988.

Fea, John. "An Analysis of the Treatment of American Fundamentalism in United States History Survey Texts." *The History Teacher* 28, no. 2 (1995): 205–16.

Finkelstein, Norman. "Myths, Old and New," *Journal of Palestine Studies* 21, no. 1 (Autumn 1991): 66–89.

Flamm, Michael W. "The Politics of 'Law and Order.'" In *The Conservative Sixties,* edited by David Farber and Jeff Roche. New York: Peter Lang, 2003.

Flapan, Simha, *The Birth of Israel: Myths and Realities.* New York: Pantheon Books, 1987.

Flatt, Kevin. *After Evangelicalism: the Sixties and the United Church of Canada* (Montreal: McGill-Queen's University Press, 2013.

Gazit, Shlomo. "Israel and the Palestinians: Fifty Years of Wars and Turning Points." *Annals of the American Academy of Political and Social Science* 555, (1998): 82–96.

Gerges, Fawaz A. "The 1967 Arab-Israeli War: U.S. Actions and Arab Perceptions." In *The Middle East and the United States: A Historical and Political Reassessment,* 2nd ed., edited by David W. Lesch. Boulder, CO: Westview Press, 1999.

———. "Islam and Muslims in the Mind of America," *Annals of the American Academy of Political and Social Science* 558, Islam: Enduring Myths and Changing Realities (July 2003): 73–89.

Gilder, George. *The Israel Test.* Richard Vigilante Books, 2009.

Ginor, Isabella and Gideon Remez. "The Spymaster, the Communist, and Foxbats over Dimona: the USSR's Motive for Instigating the Six-Day War," *Israel Studies* 11, no. 2 (Summer 2006): 88–130.

Goldman, Shalom L. "Review Essay: Christians and Zionism." *American Jewish History* 93, no. 2 (2005): 246–60.

———. *Zeal for Zion: Christians, Jews, & the Idea of The Promised Land.* Chapel Hill: University of North Carolina Press, 2010.

Graf, Rüdiger. "Making Use of the 'Oil Weapon': Western Industrialized Countries and Arab Petropolitics in 1973–1974," *Diplomatic History* 36, no. 1 (January 2012): 185–208.

Graham, Billy. *World Aflame* (Montreal: Pocket Books, 1966).

Griessman, B. Eugene. "Philo-Semitism and Protestant Fundamentalism: The Unlikely Zionists." *Phylon* 37, no. 3 (1976): 197–211.

Grossman, Lawrence. "Transformation Through Crisis: The American Jewish Committee and the Six-Day War," *American Jewish History* 86, no. 1 (1998): 27–54.

Hahn, Peter L. *Caught in the Middle East: U.S. Policy toward the Arab-Israeli Conflict, 1945–1961.* Chapel Hill: University of North Carolina Press, 2004.

———. *Crisis and Crossfire: The United States and the Middle East Since 1945.* Washington, DC: Potomac Books, 2005.

———. "The View from Jerusalem: Revelations about U.S. Diplomacy from the Archives of Israel." *Diplomatic History* 22, no. 4 (1998): 509–32.

Haija, Rammy M. "The Armageddon Lobby: Dispensationalist Christian Zionism and the Shaping of U.S. Policy Towards Israel-Palestine." *Holy Land Studies* 5, no. 1 (2006): 75–95.

Halberstam, David. *The Best and Brightest.* New York: Fawcett Crest, 1972.

Harding, Susan. "Imagining the Last Days: The Politics of Apocalyptic Language." *Bulletin of the American Academy of Arts and Sciences* 48, no. 3 (1994): 14–44.

Haron, Miriam. "Britain and Israel, 1948–1950," *Modern Judaism* 3, no. 2 (May, 1983): 217–23.

Herzog, Chaim. *The Arab-Israeli Wars: War and Peace in the Middle East.* New York: Random House, 1982.

Hogan, Michael J. and Thomas G. Patterson. "Introduction." In *Explaining the History of American Foreign Relations,* 2nd ed., edited by Michael J. Hogan and Thomas G. Patterson. Cambridge: Cambridge University Press, 2004.

Inbar, Efraim. *Israel's National Security: Issues and Challenges Since the Yom Kippur War.* New York: Routledge 2008.

"Interview: Israeli New Historian Avi Shlaim." *Middle East Policy* XVI, no. 3 (Fall 2009): 96–105.

Isaacson, Walter and Evan Thomas. *The Wise Men: Six Friends and the World They Made.* New York: Touchstone, 1988.

Isserman, Maurice and Michael Kazin. *America Divided: The Civil War of the 1960s.* New York: Oxford University Press, 2000.

Jacobs, Matthew F. "The Perils and Promise of Islam: The United States and the Muslim Middle East in the Early Cold War." *Diplomatic History* 30, no. 4 (2006): 705–39.

Kaplan, Robert D. *The Arabists: The Romance of an American Elite.* New York: Simon and Schuster, 1995.

Karsh, Efriam. "Rewriting Israel's History." *The Middle East Quarterly* (June 1996): 19–29.

Katz, Emily Alice. "It's the Real World After All: The American-Israel Pavilion—Jordan Pavilion Controversy at the New York World's Fair, 1964–1965." *American Jewish History* 91, no. 1 (March 2003): 129–55.

"Kissinger and the American Jewish Leadership after the 1973 War." *Israel Studies* 7, no. (Spring 2002): 195–217.

Klinghoffer, Judith. A. *Vietnam, Jews and the Middle East: Unintended Consequences.* New York: St. Martin's Press, Inc., 1999.

Kober, Avi. "Great-Power Involvement and Israeli Battlefield Success in the Arab-Israeli Wars, 1948–1982." *Journal of Cold War Studies* 8, no. 1 (Winter 2006): 20–48.

Kochavi, Arieh J. "British Assumptions of American Jewry's Political Strength, 1945–1947." *Modern Judaism* 15, no. 2 (1995): 161–82.

Krauthammer, Charles. *Things That Matter: Three Decades of Passions, Pastimes and Politics.* New York: Crown Forum 2013.

Lazarowitz, Arlene. "Different Approaches to a Regional Search for Balance: The Johnson Administration, the State Department, and the Middle East, 1964–1967." *Diplomatic History* 32, no. 1 (January 2008): 25–54.

Levey, Zach. "Israel's Quest for a Security Guarantee from the United States, 1954–1956." *British Journal of Middle Eastern Studies*, Vol. 22, No. 1–2 (1995): 43–63.

Levité, Ariel E. and Emily B. Landau, "Arab Perceptions of Israel's Nuclear Posture, 1960–1967." *Israel Studies* 1, no. 1 (Spring 1996): 34–59.

Lewis, Bernard. *The Middle East and the West.* Bloomington: Indiana University Press, 1964.

Lindsay, D. Michael. "Ties The Bind and Divisions That Persist: Evangelical Faith and the Political Spectrum." *American Quarterly* 59, no. 3 (2007): 883–908.

Lindsay, Hal. *The Late Great Planet Earth.* Grand Rapids, Mich.: Zondervan, 1998.

Little, Douglas. *American Orientalism: The United States and the Middle East since 1945.* Chapel Hill: University of North Carolina 2002.

———. "Gideon's Band: America and the Middle East since 1945." In *America in the World: The Historiography of American Foreign Relations since 1941*, edited by Michael J. Hogan. Cambridge: Cambridge University Press, 1995.

———. "The Making of a Special Relationship: The United States and Israel, 1957–68." *International Journal of Middle East Studies* 25, no. 4 (1993): 563–85.

Litvak, Meir and Esther Webman. "Perceptions of the Holocaust in Palestinian Public Discourse." *Israel Studies* 8, no. 3 (2003): 123–40.

Malachy, Yona. *American Fundamentalism and Israel: The Relation of Fundamentalist Churches to Zionism and the State of Israel.* Jerusalem: The Hebrew University of Jerusalem, Institute of Contemporary Jewry, 1978.

Maoz, Zeev. "The Mixed Blessing of Israel's Nuclear Policy." *International Security* 28, no. 2 (Fall 2003): 44–77.

Marks, Frederick. "Religiosity and Success in American Foreign Policy." *The Society for Historian of American Foreign Relations* (Newsletter) 30, no. 3 (September 1999): 9–22.

Marsden, George. *Fundamentalism and American Culture: The Shaping of Twentieth-Century Evangelicalism, 1870–1925.* New York: Oxford University Press, 1980.

———. *Understanding Fundamentalism and Evangelicalism.* Grand Rapids, MI: William B. Eerdmans, 1991.

Mart, Michelle. "Eleanor Roosevelt, Liberalism, and Israel." *Shofar* 24, no. 3 (Spring 2006): 58–89.

————. *Eye on Israel: How America Came to View Israel as an Ally*. Albany: State University of New York Press, 2006.

Martin, Walter R. *The Kingdom of the Cults*. Minneapolis, MN: Bethany Fellowship, Inc. Publishers, 1965.

Martin, William. "The Christian Right and American Foreign Policy." *Foreign Policy*, no. 114 (Spring 1999): 66–80.

————. *A Prophet with Honor: The Billy Graham Story*. New York: William Morrow and Company, Inc., 1991.

McAlister, Melani. "Prophecy, Politics, and the Popular: The Left Behind Series and Christian Fundamentalism's New World Order." The *South Atlantic Quarterly* 102, no. 4 (Fall 2003): 773–98.

Mearsheimer, John and Stephen M. Walt. *The Israel Lobby and U.S. Foreign Policy*. New York: Farrar, Straus, and Giroux, 2007.

Merkley, Paul Charles. *American Presidents, Religion, and Israel: The Heirs of Cyrus*. Westport, CT: Praeger, 2004.

————. *Christian Attitudes towards the State of Israel*. Montreal: McGill-Queen's University Press, 2001.

————. *Those That Bless You, I Will Bless: Christian Zionism in Historical Perspective*. Brantford, ON: Mantua Books, 2011.

Morris, Benny. *1948: A History of the First Arab-Israeli War*. New Haven, CT: Yale University Press, 2008.

————, ed. *Making Israel*. Ann Arbor, MI: University of Michigan Press, 2007.

Nash, George H. "Forgotten Godfathers: Premature Jewish Conservatives and the Rise of *National Review*." *American Jewish History* 87, no. 2–3 (1999): 123–57.

Neff, Donald. "Jerusalem in U.S. Policy." *Journal of Palestine Studies* 23, no. 1 (Autumn 1993): 20–45.

————. *Warriors at Suez: Eisenhower Takes America into the Middle East*. New York: Linden Press, 1981.

Noll, Mark et al., eds. *Evangelicalism: Comparative Studies of Popular Protestantism in North America, the British Isles, and Beyond 1700–1900*. New York: Oxford University Press, 1994.

Oren, Michael B. *Power, Faith, and Fantasy: America in the Middle East: 1776 to the Present* New York: W.W. Norton and Co. Inc., 2007.

————. *Six Days of War: June 1967 and the Making of the Modern Middle East*. New York: Presido Press, 2003.

Ottolenghi, Michael. "Harry Truman's Recognition of Israel." *The Historical Journal* 47, no. 4 (December 2004): 963–88.

Ovendale, Ritchie. *The Origins of the Arab-Israeli Wars*. London: Longman, 1984.

Ozacky-Lazar, Sarah and Mustafa Kabha. "The *Haganah* by Arab and Palestinian Historiography and Media." *Israel Studies* 7, no. 3 (Fall 2002): 45–60.

Pappe, Ilan. *A History of Modern Palestine*. Cambridge: Cambridge University Press, 2004.

Peretz, Don. "The United States, the Arabs, and Israel: Peace Efforts of Kennedy, Johnson, and Nixon." *Annals of the American Academy of Political and Social Science* 401 (1972): 116–25.

Perko, F. Michael. "Contemporary American Christian Attitudes to Israel Based on the Scriptures." *Israel Studies* 8, no. 2 (2003): 1–16.

————. "Toward a 'Sound and Lasting Basis': Relations between the Holy See, The Zionist Movement, and Israel, 1896–1996." *Israel Studies* 2, no. 1 (1997): 1–21.

Peters, Joan. *From Time Immemorial: The Origins of the Arab-Jewish Conflict over Palestine*. New York: Harper & Row, Publishers, 1984.

Pipes, Daniel. "Breaking All the Rules: American Debate over the Middle East." *International Security* 9, no. 2 (1984): 124–50.

————."[Christian Zionism:] Israel's Best Weapon?" *New York Post*, July 15, 2003. http://www.danielpipes.org/pf.php?id=1148 (accessed September 8, 2007).

Podeh, Elie. "The Desire to Belong Syndrome," *Israeli Studies* 4, no. 2 (Fall 1999): 121–49.

———. "History and Memory in the Israeli Educational System: The Portrayal of the Arab-Israeli Conflict in History Textbooks (1948–2000)." *History and Memory* 12, no. 1 (2000): 65–100.

Podhoretz, Norman. *Why Are Jews Liberals?* New York: Doubleday, 2009.

Preston, Andrew. "Bridging the Gap between the Sacred and the Secular in the History of American Foreign Relations." *Diplomatic History* 30, no. 5 (2006): 783–812.

Rabinovich, Itamar and Jehuda Reinharz, eds. *Israel in the Middle East: Documents and Readings on Society, Politics, and Foreign Relations, 1948–Present.* New York: Oxford University Press, 1984.

Radosh, Allis and Ronald. *A Safe Haven: Harry S. Truman and the Founding of Israel.* New York: Harper Perennial, 2009.

Rausch, David A. *Communities in Conflict: Evangelicals and Jews.* Philadelphia, PA: Trinity Press International, 1991.

———. "Our Hope: An American Fundamentalist Journal and the Holocaust, 1937–1945." In *Fundamentalism and Evangelicalism*, edited by Martin E. Marty. New York: K.G. Saur, 1993.

Reich, Bernard. "Israeli National Security Policy: Issues and Actors." In *Israeli National Security Policy: Political Actors and Perspectives*, edited by Bernard Reich and Gershon R. Kieval. New York: Greenwood Press, 1988.

———. *Securing the Covenant: United States-Israel Relations After the Cold War.* Westport, CT: Praeger Publishers, 1995.

———. "Themes in the History of the State of Israel." *American Historical Review* 96, no. 5 (1991): 1466–78.

Ribuffo, Leo. "Religion and American Foreign Policy: The Story of a Complex Relationship." *The National Interest* 52 (Summer 1998): 36–51.

Rose, Gideon. "Neoclassical Realism and Theories of Foreign Policy." *World Politics* 51, no. 1 (1998): 144–72.

Ross, Robert W. *So It Was True: The American Protestant Press and the Nazi Persecution of the Jews.* Eugene, OR: Wipf and Stock Publishers, 1998.

Rotter, Andrew J. "Saidism without Said: Orientalism and U.S. Diplomatic History." *American Historical Review* 105, no. 4 (October 2000): 1205–17.

Rubin, Barry and Judity Colp Rubin. *Yasir Arafat: A Political Biography.* Oxford: Oxford University Press, 2005.

Rudin, A. James. *Israel for Christians: Understanding Modern Israel.* Philadephia: Fortress Press, 1983.

Ryrie, Charles Caldwell. *Dispensationalism Today.* Chicago: Moody Press, 1965.

Safran, Nadav. *Israel: The Embattled Ally.* Cambridge, Mass.: Harvard University Press, 1981.

Said, Edward W. *Orientalism*, 25th anniversary ed. New York: Vintage Books, 2004.

Sakhnini, Fouad. "The Gospel and Arab Thinking." in Carl F. H. Henry, ed. *Prophecy in the Making.* Carol Stream, IL: Creation House, 1971.

Sandeen, Ernest R. *The Roots of Fundamentalism: British and American Millenarianism 1800–1930.* Chicago: University of Chicago Press, 1970.

Schlesinger, Jr. Arthur M. *A Thousand Days: John F. Kennedy in the White House.* New York: Fawcett Premier, 1971.

Schoenbaum, David. *The United States and the State of Israel.* New York: Oxford University Press, 1993.

Shalom, Zaki. "Kennedy, Ben-Gurion and the Dimona Project, 1962–1963." *Israel Studies* 1, no. 1 (Spring 1996): 3–33.

Shelef, Nadav G. "From 'Banks of the Jordan' to the 'Whole Land of Israel:' Ideological Change in Revisionist Zionism." *Israel Studies* 9, no. 1 (Spring 2004): 125–48.

Shemesh, Moshe. "The IDF Raid on Samu': The Turning-Point in Jordan's Relations with Israel and the West Bank Palestinians." *Israel Studies* 7, no. 1 (Spring 2002): 139–67.

———. "The Palestinian Society in the Wake of the 1948 War: From Social Fragmentation to Consolidation." *Israel Studies* 9, no. 1 (2004): 86–100.

———. "Prelude to the Six-Day War: The Arab-Israeli Struggle Over Water Resources." *Israel Studies* 9, no. 3 (Fall 2004): 1–45.

Shindler, Colin. *A History of Modern Israel*. Cambridge: Cambridge University Press, 2008.

———. "Likud and the Christian Dispensationalists: A Symbiotic Relationship." *Israel Studies* 5, no. 1 (2000): 153–182.

Shlaim, Avi. "Interview With Abba Eban, 11 March 1976." *Israel Studies* 8, no. 1 (Spring 2003): 153–77.

———. *The Iron Wall: Israel and the Arab World*. London: The Penguin Press, 2000.

Sicker, Martin. *Israel's Quest for Security*. New York: Praeger, 1989.

Sizer, Stephen. *Christian Zionism: Road-map to Armageddon*. Leicester, UK: Inter-Varsity Press, 2004.

Slater, Jerome. "Lost Opportunities for Peace in the Arab-Israeli Conflict: Israel and Syria, 1948–2001." *International Security* 27, no. 1 (Summer 2002): 79–106.

Smith, Wilbur M. *Egypt and Israel: Coming Together?* Wheaton, IL: Tyndale House Publishers, Inc., 1957.

———. *Israeli/Arab Conflict in the Bible*. Glendale, CA: Regal Books, 1967.

———. *World Crises and the Prophetic Scriptures*. Chicago: Moody Press, 1951.

Spector, Stephen. *Evangelicals and Israel: The Story of American Christian Zionism*. Oxford: Oxford University Press, 2009.

Spiegel, Steven L. *The Other Arab-Israeli Conflict: Making America's Middle East Policy, from Truman to Reagan*. Chicago: University of Chicago Press, 1985.

Stallard, Michael, "Is Dispensationalism Hurting American Political Policies in the Middle East?" In *Dispensationalism Tomorrow and Beyond: A Theological Collection in Honor of Charles C. Ryrie*, edited by Christopher Cone. Fort Worth, TX: Tyndale Seminary Press, 2008.

Stein, Leslie. *The Making of Modern Israel 1948–1967*. Cambridge: Polity Press, 2009.

Stevens, Georgiana G. ed. *The United States and the Middle East*. Englewood Cliffs, NJ: Prentice-Hall, Inc., 1964.

Stockton, Ronald R. "Christian Zionism: Prophecy and Public Opinion." *Middle East Journal* 41, no. 2 (Spring 1987): 234–53.

Tal, David. "Israel's Road to the 1956 War." *International Journal of Middle East Studies* 28, no. 1 (February 1996): 59–81.

———. "Symbol Not Substance? Israel's Campaign to Acquire Hawk Missiles, 1960–1962." *The International History Review* 22, no. 2 (June 2000): 304–17.

Voss, Carl Hermann, and David A. Rausch. "American Christians and Israel, 1948–1988." *American Jewish Archives* 40 (April 1988): 41–81.

Walvoord, John F. "The Abrahamic Covenant and Premillennialism." *Bibliotheca Sacra* 109, no. 435 (July–September 1952): 217–25.

———. "Amillennialism as a Method of Interpretation." *Bibliotheca Sacra* 107, no. 425 (January–March 1950): 42–50.

———. "Amillennialism as a System of Theology." *Bibliotheca Sacra* 107, no. 426 (April–June 1950): 154–67.

———. "Amillennial Eschatology." *Bibliotheca Sacra* 108, no. 429 (January–March 1951): 7–14.

———. "Amillennialism from Augustine to Modern Times." *Bibliotheca Sacra* 106, no. 424 (October–December 1949): 420–31.

———. "Amillennialism in the Ancient Church." *Bibliotheca Sacra* 106, no. 423 (July–September 1949): 291–302.

———. "The Millennial Issue in Modern Theology." *Bibliotheca Sacra* 106, no. 421 (January–March 1949): 34–47.

———. *The Nations in Prophecy*. Grand Rapids, MI: Zondervan Publishing House, 1967.

———. "Premillennialism and the Tribulation." *Bibliotheca Sacra* 113, no. 451 (July 1956): 193–99.

———. "Postmillennialism." *Bibliotheca Sacra* 106, no. 422 (April–June 1949): 149–68.

———. "The Times of the Gentiles." *Bibliotheca Sacra* 125, no. 497 (January 1968): 3–9.

———. "Will Israel Build a Temple in Jerusalem?" *Bibliotheca Sacra* 125, no. 498 (April 1968): 99–106.

Watt, David Harrington. "The Private Hopes of American Fundamentalists and Evangelical, 1925–1975." *Religion and American Culture* 1, no. 2 (Summer 1991): 155–75.

Weber, Timothy P. *Living in the Shadow of the Second Coming: American Premillennialism, 1875–1982*. Grand Rapids, MI: Academie Books, 1983.

———. *On the Road to Armageddon: How Evangelicals Became Israel's Best Friend*. Grand Rapids, MI: Baker Academic, 2004.

Whiting, Arthur B. "The Rapture of the Church." *Bibliotheca Sacra* 102, no. 408 (July–September 1945): 490–99.

Wilcox, Clyde, Sharon Linzey, and Ted G. Jelen. "Reluctant Warriors: Premillennialism and Politics in the Moral Majority." *Journal of the Scientific Study of Religion* 30, no. 3 (September, 1991): 245–58.

Wilson, Evan M. *Decision on Palestine: How the U.S. Came to Recognize Israel*. Stanford, CA: Hoover Institutional Press, 1979.

Winston, Diane. "Back to the Future: Religion, Politics, and the Media." *American Quarterly* 59, no. 3 (2007): 969–89.

Woodberry, Robert D. and Christian S. Smith. "Fundamentalism et al: Conservative Protestants in America." *Annual Review of Sociology* 24 (1998), 25–27.

Wuest, Kenneth S. "The Rapture—Precisely When?" *Bibliotheca Sacra* 114, no. 453 (January 1957): 60–69.

Yaqub, Salim. *Containing Arab Nationalism: The Eisenhower Doctrine and the Middle East*. Chapel Hill: University of North Carolina Press, 2004.

———. "Imperious Doctrines: U.S.-Arab Relations from Dwight D. Eisenhower to George W. Bush." *Diplomatic History* 26, no. 4 (Fall 2002): 571–92.

Zameret, Zvi. "Judaism in Israel: Ben-Gurion's Private Beliefs and Public Policy." *Israel Studies* 4, no. 2 (Fall 1999): 64–89.

Zeidan, David. "A Comparative Study of Selected Themes in Christian and Islamic Fundamentalist Discourses." *British Journal of Middle Eastern Studies* 30, no. 1 (2003): 43–80.

Zeitz, Joshua Michael. "'If I am not for myself . . .': The American Jewish Establishment in the Aftermath of the Six Day War." *American Jewish History* 88, no. 2 (June 2000): 253–86.

Index

Abdullah, King of Transjordan, 27, 30, 36n54, 63; and Jihad, 41; uncaring of Palestinians, 42

Abraham, 55, 77, 105, 139, 157

Abram, Morris, 103–104, 114n141

Abuelaish, Izzeldin, vii, 98

Acheson, Dean, 71

AJC. *See* American Jewish Committee

ALA. *See* Arab Liberation Army

Alexandria, 63

Algeria, 88–89

Allis, Oswald T., 76

Altalena, 45

Altern, Arich, 66

American Association for Jewish Evangelism, 78, 96

American Board of Missions to the Jews, 95

American Christian Palestine Committee, 52

American Holiness Journal, 53, 54, 65, 78

American Institute of Holy Land Studies, 104, 122

American Jewish Committee (AJC), 103–104

American University of Beirut, 30, 32

amillennialism, 89

Amman, 45, 120

Anglo-American Committee of Inquiry, 24

anti-Semitism, 8, 23, 34, 103, 140, 150, 154

Apostle Paul, 4

Appleman, Hyman J., 78

Arab "feudalistic economy", 76

Arab Higher Committee, 27

"Arab-Israeli conflict" (terminology), 1, 13n6

Arab League, 39, 69, 88

Arab League Propaganda Office, 76

Arab Legion, 4–5, 31, 40–42, 45, 47, 50, 64; and Jihad, 41; control of the West Bank, 47

Arab Liberation Army (ALA), 26, 27, 45; and Jihad, 27

Arafat, Yasser, 10, 120, 153–155

Armageddon, 9, 54, 84n121, 102, 105, 158

Armerding, Carl, 65

Ashkenazim Jews, 20, 51

Assemblies of God, 91, 143

Aswan Dam project, 72

Atiyah, Edward, 76

Auschwitz, 98, 125

Austin, Warren, 32

Avital, Benad, 122

Azar, Shmuel, 63

Baehr, Karl, 52

Baghdad, 153

Baker, Dwight L., 91

Balfour, Arthur James, 20

Balfour Declaration, 20–21, 24, 59n113

Bar-Lev, Chaim, 118

Barnhouse, Donald Grey, 24, 79

Bat Gallim , 63

Bauman, Louis, 23, 54

Baumann, Walter, 66

Begin, Menachem, 29, 156, 157, 164n123

Bell, L. Nelson, 101

Ben-Gurion, David, 19, 25, 27, 31, 49, 50, 64, 69, 107, 159; and Adolf Eichmann, 93; and *Altalena* espisode, 45; and American Association for Jewish Evangelism, 96; and American pressure, 62; apologized for Deir Yassin, 30; and Britain, 70; and his cabinet, 61; and Declaration of Independence, 32, 34;

About the Author

Eric R. Crouse is professor of history at Tyndale University College, Toronto, where he teaches modern American history.

CPSIA information can be obtained at www.ICGtesting.com
Printed in the USA
BVOW07*0111241014

371966BV00002B/2/P